NAMING WHAT WE KNOW

NAMING WHAT WE KNOW

Threshold Concepts of Writing Studies

Edited by
LINDA ADLER-KASSNER
ELIZABETH WARDLE

UTAH STATE UNIVERSITY PRESS
Logan

© 2015 by the University Press of Colorado

Published by Utah State University Press
An imprint of University Press of Colorado
5589 Arapahoe Avenue, Suite 206C
Boulder, Colorado 80303

 The University Press of Colorado is a proud member of
The Association of American University Presses.

The University Press of Colorado is a cooperative publishing enterprise supported,
in part, by Adams State University, Colorado State University, Fort Lewis College,
Metropolitan State University of Denver, Regis University, University of Colorado,
University of Northern Colorado, Utah State University, and Western State Colorado
University.

∞ The paper used in this publication meets the minimum requirements of the American
National Standard for Information Sciences – Permanence of Paper for Printed Library
Materials. ANSI Z39.48-1992

ISBN: 978-0-87421-989-0 (paper)
ISBN: 978-0-87421-990-6 (ebook)

Library of Congress Cataloging-in-Publication Data

Naming what we know : threshold concepts of writing studies / Edited by Linda Adler-
Kassner, Elizabeth Wardle.
    pages cm
    ISBN 978-0-87421-989-0 (paperback) — ISBN 978-0-87421-990-6 (ebook)
1. English language—Rhetoric—Study and teaching. 2. Creative writing—Study and
teaching. 3. Academic writing—Study and teaching. I. Adler-Kassner, Linda, editor. II.
Wardle, Elizabeth A., editor.
    PE1404.N35 2015
    808'.042071—dc 3
                                    2014036571

CONTENTS

PREFACE

Ray Land

⁕

During the first half of my professional career in education, my time was occupied almost entirely with the teaching of writing and encouraging students to appreciate and critique all kinds of written works. As I moved at a later stage into educational and pedagogical research, the critical roles of language and of writing in the processes of student learning and understanding remained for me paramount. In our work in the field of threshold concepts and troublesome knowledge, my colleague Erik Meyer and I noted from the outset how the conceptual transformations and shifts in subjectivity students experienced in the various disciplines we investigated were invariably and inextricably accompanied by changes in their own use of discourse. More than that, we observed how an encounter with unfamiliar discourse, or different uses or forms of language, often was the trigger that provoked a state of liminality and subsequent transformation in their understanding of a particular phenomenon. Such linguistic encounters might be experienced as troublesome, alien, counterintuitive, or perhaps exhilarating, but this engaging struggle with meaning through talk and subsequent written expression seems to serve as a crucible in which new understanding is forged. We are reminded of T. S. Eliot's (1974) "intolerable wrestle with words and meanings." Intolerable, perhaps, at times, but always invaluable. As a more unlikely source of insight, Karl Albrecht, the billionaire German founder of one of the world's largest supermarket chains, once wisely observed, "Change your language, and you change your thoughts."

We have long known of course, from the research of great scholars such as Vygotsky (1978) and Bakhtin (1988), of the pivotal roles language and writing play in the formation of new understandings and conceptual mastery, and of the crucial importance of the social contexts in which language and written composition are both experienced and produced. Such work has powerfully informed the now-extensive body of work that has been produced in relation to threshold concepts (Flanagan 2014). What this work has lacked and needed until now, however, has been scholarly enquiry that directly addresses the learning thresholds inherent within writing studies itself. It is therefore a great pleasure and privilege to welcome this timely addition to the thresholds literature under the skillful editorship of Linda Adler-Kassner and Elizabeth Wardle.

What is distinctive about the need to inquire further into the study of writing—and this distinction emerges self-evidently from this volume—is that such study operates across two important dimensions. Like other academic subjects, it has developed over the last half century to take its place within the academy as a field of study in its own right with established programs operating in colleges and universities across the world. The reach of this discipline goes much further, however, in that the practices and understandings of this particular discipline, composed knowledge, infuse and are intrinsic to successful performance in all other disciplines. So it is not surprising that in a collection of studies such as this, we will discover discipline-specific threshold concepts as well as more generic learning thresholds and practices portable to other knowledge domains. Everyone has writing needs throughout their development and career. Acquisition of literacy in early years might well be viewed as the mother of all learning thresholds in that failure to negotiate this portal is in many respects tantamount to a future of social dysfunction and exclusion. As we progress through our academic and professional work, the writing tasks and demands that confront us, in increasingly intense and frequently high-stakes contexts we have not previously encountered or experienced, require new understandings and challenging transformations.

The range of themes, issues, and thought-provoking questions that arise from the chapters that follow is admirable. In part 1, we find ourselves immersed in debates and explorations regarding writing as conception, as technology, and as mediating artifact. We consider writing as both action and activity and analyze the contextual and situated nature of writing. We explore addressivity, the realms of writing as cognition as well as its relation to subjectivity. The threshold nature of various tools, processes, and strategies of writing is assessed, while throughout we are reminded that we can never step outside of culture and that writing never offers an ideology-free zone. In part 2, the camera lens pulls back to bring into view how threshold concepts usefully facilitate not only our students' learning but also faculty development and outreach. We consider the role of threshold concepts in writing across the curriculum, in writing and rhetoric undergraduate majors, as well as in writing within other disciplines and professional programs. The compelling nature of these discussions lies in their precise focus and specificity, their grounded nature, whether we are talking about first-year composition, rhetoric and composition doctoral education, or the particular challenges of working within student learning outcomes frameworks. As the English poet William Blake (1904) reminded us:

> Labour well the Minute Particulars: . . .
> He who would do good to another must do it in Minute Particulars . . .
> For Art and Science cannot exist but in minutely organized Particulars.

The editors refer to this collection as "final-for-now" definitions of some of what our field knows. They are right to emphasis the contingent and changing nature of knowledge in writing practices and to eschew any attempt at an essentialist classification. These analyses can only ever be provisional stabilities. Their observation that "what we see as most important will continue to evolve" and that they "cannot represent the full set of threshold concepts for our field" resonates closely with David Perkins's (2010) earlier view that threshold concepts work better when "more exploratory and eclectic than categorical and taxonomic" (xliv). The fecundity of threshold concepts, he argued, derived from "the evolutionary proclivity of the idea toward adventurous and fruitful mutation." We have argued elsewhere (Meyer and Land 2005) that an objectivist position would contradict our initial characterizing of threshold concepts as discursive in nature, subject to the endless play of signification that language implies. This would, furthermore, disregard the inevitable variation in the forms learners' understandings might take. Such matters notwithstanding, the threshold concepts offered for consideration by the varied studies in this analysis are an important representation of the conceptual and ontological shifts students must undertake to achieve capability in writing. These are, in effect, what we have termed the *jewels in the curriculum*, the concepts identified by Adler-Kassner and Wardle as "critical for anyone who wants to write more effectively, whatever their discipline or profession."

I once heard the distinguished Hungarian scholar Ference Marton, founder of phenomenography and variation theory, observe, "The one single thing that would improve the quality of teaching and learning in higher education would be if academics in different disciplines took time to meet together and discuss what they should be teaching in their subject, and how they should be teaching it" (Marton 2009). Such an approach has been practiced in this volume, a method characterized by the editors as "modified crowd sourcing," whereby a group comprising some of the most gifted instructors, researchers, and writers in this field today have been asked to name what they know. This is a contested discussion in which stakeholders from outside the academy have no hesitation in laying claim to knowing. There is pressing need for studies based on scholarship, drawn from the expertise of the community of practice. The writers in this collection can name what they know with authority, and, demonstrably, they know a great deal.

This wide-ranging collection simultaneously fills an important gap in the threshold concepts literature and opens up a significant and rich new avenue of research. The chapters that follow offer fresh perspectives and insights that will engage diverse readers and stimulate new policy, practice, and writing scholarship. Selecting this book for your resource library is an excellent step.

Prepare to be engaged.

References

Bakhtin, M. M. 1988. *The Dialogic Imagination*, edited by Michael Holquist. Translated by Caryl Emerson and Michael Holquist. Austin: University of Texas Press.

Blake, William. 1904. In *The Prophetic Books of William Blake: Jerusalem*, edited by Eric Robert Dalyrimple Maclagan and Archibald George Blomefield Russell. London: A. H. Bullen.

Eliot, T. S. 1974. "Four Quartets." In *Collected Poems 1909–1962*. London: Faber.

Flanagan, Mick. 2014. *Threshold Concepts: Undergraduate Teaching, Postgraduate Training and Professional Development: A Short Introduction and Bibliography*. London: University College London. http://www.ee.ucl.ac.uk/~mflanaga/thresholds.html.

Marton, Ference. 2009. Paper presented at the EARLI Conference, Amsterdam, Netherlands, August 25.

Meyer, Jan H. F., and Ray Land. 2005. "Threshold Concepts and Troublesome Knowledge: Epistemological Considerations and a Conceptual Framework for Teaching and Learning." *Higher Education* 49 (3): 373–88. http://dx.doi.org/10.1007/s10734-004-6779-5.

Perkins, David. 2010. Foreword to *Threshold Concepts and Transformational Learning*, edited by Jan H. F Meyer, Ray Land, and Caroline Baillie. Rotterdam, Amsterdam: Sense.

Vygotsky, L. S. 1978. *Mind and Society: The Development of Higher Mental Processes*. Cambridge, MA: Harvard University Press.

ACKNOWLEDGMENTS

The seeds of this book were planted at the Elon University Research Seminar on Critical Transitions: Writing and the Question of Transfer. We thank Elon University and the seminar facilitators—Jessie Moore, Chris M. Anson, and Randy Bass—as well as our fellow seminar participants. For one blissful week during the summers of 2011, 2012, and 2013 we were privileged to be part of "transfer camp" (as we called it). The time, space, and brilliant interlocutors in the seminar are present throughout this book.

We also thank the participants in the threshold concepts wiki and the contributors to this collection. One Tuesday morning in January 2012, we e-mailed forty-five colleagues to ask if they would participate in an experiment that seemed a little crazy. We had our first response within ten minutes, the first of many enthusiastic yeses, which made us think that this might come to something after all. We are grateful to the scholar/teachers who participated in this project, as well as to all of those who provided feedback during the process of its development. This book, we believe, is a testament to the generosity and spirit of collaboration and collegiality that are hallmarks of our field.

Thanks also to the many colleagues and professionals who provided feedback on the threshold concepts included here, as well as on others that have been developed in the many workshops we have conducted and conferences at which we've presented (individually and together).

Finally, thanks to some individuals: Adam Salazar for taking on the detail-oriented work of organizing and copyediting early drafts of the manuscript; Nkosi Shanga for his ongoing support and his ability to spot and take lovely photos, like the one of St. George's Castle in Lisbon that graces the front cover of this book; and to Scott Kassner and Nora Kassner for all that they do.

Introduction

COMING TO TERMS
Composition/Rhetoric, Threshold Concepts, and a Disciplinary Core

Kathleen Blake Yancey

From the modern beginnings of the field of rhetoric and composition, we in the field have shared a self-evident claim about the primary focus of rhetoric and composition: that it has at its center the practice of writing and its teaching. At the same time, this observation, as straightforward as it may seem, begs more than one question. What do we mean by writing? Is it practice, or practices? Is what we are talking about writing, or composing, or both? What concepts can or do we draw upon to theorize writing practices? What of any of this do we share with students, when, and how? Historically, questions such as these, typically using the classroom as the site where they are worked out, have defined the field. In the first issue of *College Composition and Communication*, for example, John Gerber (1950, 12) spoke to this point exactly:

> Someone has estimated that there are at least nine thousand of us teaching in college courses in composition and communication. Faced with many of the same problems, concerned certainly with the same general objectives, we have for the most part gone our separate ways, experimenting here and improvising there. Occasionally we have heard that a new kind of course is working well at Upper A. M. or that a new staff training program has been found successful at Lower T. C. But we rarely get the facts. We have had no systematic way of exchanging views and information quickly. Certainly we have had no means of developing a coordinated research program.

Some fifty-five years later, Richard Fulkerson, delivering in 2005 a third iteration of analysis in a career-long search to trace the field's coherence—he published his first analysis in 1979, the second in 1990—speaks to the situation of the field in the early twenty-first century, and from a Gerberian perspective, it's both good news and bad. On the one hand, we have what Gerber longed for, the scholarship and multiple venues permitting "*a systematic way of exchanging views and information*

DOI: 10.7330/9780874219906.c000a

quickly." On other hand, that very scholarship allows Fulkerson to make a claim not unlike Gerber's: we are not coherent, do not have a core set of beliefs or values.

> Within the scholarship, we currently have three alternative axiologies (theories of value): the newest one, the social or social-construction view, which values critical cultural analysis; an expressive one; and a multifaceted rhetorical one. I maintain that the three axiologies drive the three major approaches to the teaching of composition[:] (1) critical/cultural studies [CCS], (2) expressivism, and (3) procedural rhetoric. (Fulkerson 2005, 655)

What we do have despite our differences, according to Fulkerson, is our teaching of writing process and a commitment to writing pedagogy, even if, as Fulkerson claims, our commitment is really plural; it takes different forms. What seems to be missing, since the beginning of the field and even in this late age of print, is any consensus in the field on what we might call the *content of composition*: the questions, kinds of evidence, and materials that define disciplines and would thus define us as well.[1] Fulkerson's theory is that, at least in the case of CCS, its focus on texts allows for a kind of content that faculty find inherently satisfying and that, in the specific instance of CCS, scholars and teachers in rhetoric and composition value given their backgrounds and their commitments to social justice.

> Both the lit-based course and the cultural studies course reflect, I suspect, content envy on the part of writing teachers. Most of us (still) have been trained in textual analysis: we like classes built around texts to analyze. (And I am certainly not immune to that envy. I *enjoy* leading discussions of complex nonfiction that challenges students to think hard about basic beliefs.) (Fulkerson 2005, 663)

This, then, is the field-specific scene for *Naming What We Know*, which proceeds along very different lines and makes a very different kind of argument than the field has seen previously. As coeditors Linda Adler-Kassner and Elizabeth Wardle explain in the next chapter of this volume, the project has two parts: (1) identifying threshold concepts, in this case thirty-seven of them, providing a core for the field in terms of what we know; and (2) outlining how they can be helpful in various writing-focused and writing-related contexts. To develop the thirty-seven threshold concepts, Adler-Kassner and Wardle invited many scholars to "[look] at the research and theory to determine what they could agree we collectively know" (4). In addition, drawing on these concepts, a subset of these scholars share with us how we might use the concepts in our pedagogical projects and in our extra-classroom work with students and colleagues.

Invitations to contribute to this project, then, provided an occasion to think about the field in the company of colleagues, about what it is we have learned over the last half century, and about what it is we think we now know—about writing and composing, about the features and practices of writing we take as axiomatic, and about the terms that locate and define writing. Put another way, Adler-Kassner and Wardle's invitation functioned as an exigence, an opportunity to uncover and interrogate assumptions; in that sense, identifying the threshold concepts presented here was a collective philosophical exercise involving exploration as much as consolidation of what we know. Moreover, that there *are* such concepts, features, and practices is evidenced by the conceptual map presented in the first part of *Naming*. At the same time, our work, the work of rhetoric and composition located in rhetoric writ large, has historically included a practical component; threshold concepts are helpful in this sphere as well, as we see in the second half of the book, where contributors recount the various ways—in retrospect, in the current moment, and in a future time—that threshold concepts help us engage as teacher-scholars, whether we are teaching first-year composition students, designing a new major, engaging with doctoral students, or working with our colleagues in general education or writing across the curriculum.[2]

***

What do threshold concepts offer composition studies? At first glance, they may seem like a kind of canon, a list of the defining key terms of the discipline, with an explicit emphasis on definition and the implication of dogma. At a second glance, and according to all the writers in part 2 of *Naming*, they seem much more contingent—presented here not as canonical statement, but rather as articulation of shared beliefs providing multiple ways of helping us name what we know and how we can use what we know in the service of writing. That use value, as described in the chapters, takes various forms. In one version, threshold concepts function as boundary objects, allowing us to toggle between the beliefs of the discipline and those of individual institutions; in another version, they function as a heuristic or portal for planning; in yet another version, they seem a set of propositions that can be put into dialogue with threshold concepts from a subdiscipline or from a different discipline for a richly layered map of a given phenomenon. Each of the chapters within shows us how such versions might work.

Heidi Estrem opens the first set of chapters in part 2, "Using Threshold Concepts in Program and Curriculum Design," with her chapter outlining the role threshold concepts have played in general education reform efforts at Boise State University. Writing outcomes, she observes (as do others like Elizabeth Wardle and Blake Scott), are too targeted to the end point, too keyed to a linear trajectory of learning, too decontextualized, and over time too standardized.

> Generalized, outcomes-based depictions of student learning about writing hold two immediate challenges: (1) they locate evidence of writing at the *end* of key experiences—certainly one valuable place to begin understanding learning, but not the only place; and (2) they often depict writing as only a skill (albeit an "intellectual" or at least "practical" one) (AAC&U 2013). While outcomes-based depictions hold a certain kind of currency and explanatory power in educational reform efforts and will likely continue to do so, a threshold concepts approach provides a differently meaningful framework for intervening in commonplace understandings about writing. Threshold concepts offer a mechanism for faculty to articulate the content of their courses, identify student learning throughout the course experience, and create shared values for writing in a way that a focus on end products—on outcomes—cannot. (89)

Focusing on upper-level communication in the disciplines (CID) courses, Estrem demonstrates how an approach to writing in the disciplines shaped by the idea of threshold concepts changes the game, in part through highlighting the idea underlying the threshold concepts that writing is a discipline with the discipline hosting the CID and *its* threshold concepts, in part by creating a common framework for the institution locating the CIDs both vertically and horizontally:

> Within our new learning outcomes framework, the communication-in-the-disciplines (CID) courses are both discipline specific (housed in departments, taught by departmental faculty) *and* explicitly linked to the Writing Undergraduate Learning Outcome. In these courses, then, writing is taught not as an isolated skill but as disciplinary practice, an embodiment of "how people 'think' within a discipline" (Meyer and Land 2003, 1). The CID courses are thus a particularly rich site for considering (1) what the threshold concepts for writing *at the introduction to the discipline* might be; (2) how they illuminate or complicate the Writing University Learning Outcome; and (3) how their depiction might begin to foster particular kinds of identification and alliance, both vertically along the Writing Undergraduate Learning Outcome trajectory (how might threshold concepts for writing connect from English 101 and 102, UF 200, CID, and Finishing Foundations?) *and* horizontally, among faculty who teach communication-in-the-disciplines courses across campus (how might these courses with substantially different content and focus foster student writing development in appropriate ways?). (96)

In the second chapter in part 1, Doug Downs and Liane Robertson take up the role of threshold concepts in first-year composition (FYC), which, given the field's recent attention to transfer, seems a timely question. Even without that salience, however, the role threshold concepts might play in FYC is a good question since, by definition, writers *are* nascent members of the field, at least to the extent that they are informed practitioners. What can threshold concepts help us understand about what it means to be informed? Downs and Robertson write in retrospect since they have not used threshold concepts to design curriculum, but they agree that FYC should focus on two aspects of threshold concepts: "To say that FYC will focus on threshold concepts, then, is to say that it will, in part, focus on misconceptions and work toward richer conceptualizations of writing" (105). For purposes of transfer, four areas or categories in FYC are crucial:

> Our experiences have suggested that four areas present particular challenges when we attempt to address FYC's twin missions (addressing misconceptions and teaching for transfer): writing as human interaction (rhetoric); textuality; epistemology (ways of knowing and the nature of knowledge); and writing process. Students' misconceptions about writing most often relate to one of these categories. (107)

The goal of this approach isn't only a change in writing practices or a greater understanding of writing, but, much as Yancey, Robertson and Taczak (2014) argue in *Writing across Contexts: Transfer, Composition, and Sites of Writing*, that students develop their own theory of writing. As Downs and Robertson explain:

> Every writer has a set of knowledges and beliefs about writing, some explicit and some tacit, that make up their personal theory of writing. The conceptions that make up this personal theory are developed through education, experience, observation, and cultural narratives of writing; few writers will ever explicitly articulate their theory, but they will live by it. By *theory*, we mean a systematic narrative of lived experience and observed phenomena that both accounts for (makes sense of) past experience and makes predictions about future experience. The "better"—the more completely, consistently, and elegantly—a theory accounts for past experience, and the more accurate its predictions about future experience, the stronger or more robust it is, and thus the more useful it is. The writer's personal theory of writing—their conceptions of what happens when they write, what ought to be happening, why that does or does not happen—shapes both their actions while writing and their interpretations of the results of their writing activities. This theory of writing and the set of conceptions that make it up are how a writer—in our case, an FYC student—understands "the game" of writing. (110)

In the next chapter, J. Blake Scott and Elizabeth Wardle's account of how threshold concepts can inform the design of a major in rhetoric and composition, we see a plan for students to take up threshold concepts in a more sophisticated way, as is appropriate for a major in the field involving several courses. Scott and Wardle's narrative of their experience at the University of Central Florida raises two sets of questions about the role threshold concepts can play in the design of a major: What are our threshold concepts, assuming we agree there are such concepts, and if named, what assumptions does their naming reveal? and How can they function as a framework for curriculum design?

Like Downs and Robertson, Scott and Wardle did not begin their curricular design process "by directly considering threshold concepts" but rather "have come to believe that doing so could have been a helpful addition to [their] curriculum planning" (123). More specifically, like Estrem, Scott and Wardle see the value of threshold concepts in curricular planning in their use as an adaptive framework, in the "flexible alignment" provided by threshold concepts, in contrast to what they see as the "standardization" of outcomes: "*The nature of threshold concepts —* not goals, not learning outcomes, but foundational assumptions that inform learning across time—makes them *flexible* tools for imagining a progression of student learning across a curriculum rather than at one specific moment or in one short period of time" (123). In creating their design for the major, the writing department at UCF employed multiple frameworks, each of which is keyed to the overarching threshold concept that writing and rhetoric is a subject of study:

> We began by identifying three overlapping strands of the field's scholarship: rhetorical studies, writing studies, and literacy and language studies, the latter including linguistics. We also categorized the field in another way—naming pedagogical, historical, and theoretical scholarship as important overlapping dimensions of the field's work. (124)

Moreover, in drawing on threshold concepts, the UCF group created variations of them through three processes: modification, extension, and boundary marking. Thus, for example, in designing the curriculum, the UCF group was implicitly guided by two related threshold concepts discussed in part 1 of this collection—that Writing Is a Rhetorical and Social Activity (1.0) and that Writing Speaks to Situations through Recognizable Forms (2.0)—along with the premise that *practice adapting writing in various types of contexts is an effective way to improve writing competencies*, a variation of the threshold concept that Learning to Write Effectively Requires Different Kinds of Practice, Time, and Effort (4.3, 126).

Ultimately, the major at UCF will ask students, much like Downs' and Robertson's students, to create their own theory of writing, in this case using an electronic portfolio inside the capstone as the reflective site for this work.

In considering doctoral education in rhetoric and composition, Kara Taczak and I take up another site where threshold concepts are integral: the question is how they might be so.

More specifically, as this volume explains and illustrates, given that faculty can identify threshold concepts they believe locate the field, it's reasonable to expect we would also see them informing doctoral education given the nature of such education: they introduce students to, and in some ways socialize them into, the field, whether explicitly or more implicitly (142).

Using the Florida State University doctoral program in rhetoric and composition as a site for analysis, Kara and I use three integrated doctoral curricula—the delivered, lived, and experienced curricula—as lenses for inquiry.

The *delivered form of the curriculum*, which we take up first, is defined . . . as the curriculum "we design. We see it in syllabi, where course goals are articulated. . . . We see it in assignments, where students deal with the specifics of the curriculum. We see it in readings, where students enter a specific discourse and specific ways of thinking" (Yancey 2004, 17). In the case of the FSU doctoral program in writing studies, we would expect to find threshold concepts in courses—in descriptions, syllabi, and assignments—as well as in nonclassroom sites like preliminary exams and the dissertation (142).

The second kind of curriculum, . . . the "lived curriculum," is the set of "prior courses and experiences and connections that contextualize the delivered curriculum" (Yancey 2004, 16) as well as the curriculum into which students will graduate: as our review of the FSU doctoral program in RC shows, its purpose is to prepare students through the delivered curriculum for the lived curriculum of the field.

But of course, students will make their own sense of the curriculum, and that's a third and final curriculum, the *experienced curriculum*, "what some call the de facto curriculum—that is, the curriculum that *students construct* in the context of the delivered curriculum we seek to share" (Yancey 2004, 58). This curriculum, then, is the enactment of the delivered curriculum by the students themselves. (142)

In sum, the three different curricula provide different opportunities to encounter and work with different threshold concepts.

In the context of the other curricula discussed in this volume, one of the more interesting dimensions of this model of education is the kind of opportunity we see for learning inside the lived curriculum, given that "it operates in a context outside of the program and sometimes . . . outside of the academy" (Taczak and Yancey, 146). It's here that "students are more inclined to experience another threshold concept, that of failure" (146), a threshold concept defined by Collin Brooke and Allison Carr:

xxiv   COMPOSITION/RHETORIC, THRESHOLD CONCEPTS & A DISCIPLINARY CORE

As students progress throughout their educational careers and the expectations for their writing evolve from year to year and sometimes course to course, there is no way that we can expect them to be able to intuit these shifting conditions. They must have the opportunity to try, to fail, and to learn from those failures as a means of intellectual growth. (63)

How to help students learn from *failures as a means of intellectual growth* is particularly important as graduate students cross the threshold from doctoral education into faculty positions in the field.

Addressing writing assessment as she opens the second section of chapters, Enacting Threshold Concepts about Writing across the University, Peggy O'Neill considers how threshold concepts from two disciplines contribute to a cross-disciplinary field, in this case the field of writing assessment, located in assessment and in writing. As O'Neill explains, neither set of concepts is subordinate to the other; to work effectively, practitioners need to understand both.

> While writing studies' threshold concepts are central to understanding writing assessment, they are not sufficient to such understanding because writing assessment lies at the intersection of threshold concepts specific to writing studies and those specific to educational assessment. Understanding writing assessment therefore requires understanding both sets of concepts and how they interact. Writing studies professionals who design and administer assessments must learn to understand critical concepts of validity and reliability associated with psychometrics since these concepts are widely used across disciplines and assessment contexts and have established power in the discourse of education and assessment. Conversely, assessment specialists, who may be responsible for designing and evaluating assessments across a variety of disciplines and contexts, must understand the threshold concepts associated with writing (articulated in part I) if they are working in writing assessment. Both sets of concepts are required to create assessments that produce valid results and to use those results effectively and responsibly. (158)

In developing this line of thinking, O'Neill makes two other important points. First, she observes that writing assessment addresses many situations, from classroom to program. Second, she points out that it's through tapping the interdisciplinary threshold concepts that we can develop new practices and make new knowledge.

Rebecca S. Nowacek and Bradley Hughes take up the question of how threshold concepts might enhance the tutoring of writing, focusing on three areas: writing-tutor education, writing-tutor practice, and the development of threshold concepts at the intersection of writing studies and tutoring. Nowacek, for example, raises the issue of priorities as a way of deciding what to include in a course preparing students to tutor, and, like many of the chapter authors, she begins with questions.

The notion of threshold concepts implies that writing tutors will be better equipped for their work if they learn to see with and through the threshold concepts of writing. If that is the case, how should a tutor-education program sequence the work of grappling with those threshold concepts? Are some threshold concepts more central to writing center work than others? Asking these TC-inspired questions has helped [me] better understand three dimensions of the tutor education program at Marquette: choosing what to prioritize during the initial tutor-education course and what to defer until ongoing tutor education, making clearer decisions about hiring processes, and revising the content of the tutor-education course. (174)

As important, once fully engaged in writing center practice, tutors may find threshold concepts useful in understanding practice, especially that occurring within the less successful tutorial; as Nowacek and Hughes put it, threshold concepts can be helpful in "illuminating possible explanations for writers' resistance" (178). Last but not least and perhaps most intriguing, they propose the category of writing center-specific threshold concepts. As an illustration, they nominate "tutors need to learn that *experienced, effective conversational partners for writers regularly inhabit the role of 'expert outsider,'* and tutors need to learn the skills necessary for inhabiting that role" (181). Here, then, the role of expert outsider is identified as a rhetorical situation through which practice can be understood.

Linda Adler-Kassner and John Majewski take up another issue, the role threshold concepts can play "in the service of professional development." Borrowing Jan H. F. Meyer's trajectory of faculty engagement, Adler-Kassner and Majewski add two other frameworks for a robust approach:

The trajectory [of professional development] includes four phases: (1) describing threshold concepts of their discipline; (2) using threshold concepts as an "interpretive framework" through which to consider teaching; (3) reflexively incorporating them into teaching practices; and (4) conducting research on teaching and understanding teaching as research (Meyer 2012, 11). Meyer's study echoes elements of other literature focusing on professional development, such as Middendorf and Pace's (2004) Decoding the Disciplines (DtD) process, which leads faculty through a seven-step process beginning with identification of "learning bottlenecks" (points where students get stuck in a course), which leads to an examination of expert knowledge related to the bottleneck, finally resulting in the design and assessment of pedagogical activities that address the sticking point (decodingthedisciplines.org). In the frameworks of both Meyer and Joan Middendorf and David Pace, teaching is intimately connected to creative application of expert knowledge in a manner similar to academic research. As Sarah Bunnell and Daniel

Bernstein argue, the application of this knowledge (here, represented in threshold concepts) to teaching is a "scholarly enterprise" that includes understanding teaching as an "active, inquiry-based process" and seeing teaching as a "public act contributing to 'community property'" that leads to "open dialogue about teaching questions and student work." (Meyer 2012, 15; 186)

At the heart of this approach are two kinds of expertise: first, threshold concepts in the discipline; and second, "expertise associated with knowledge about how to learn and represent threshold concepts" (Adler-Kassner and Majewski, 187).

Professional development, of course, is predicated on the idea that something will change; as Adler-Kassner and Majewski put it, "A key question is how an introduction to threshold concepts [can] change actual teaching practice" (196). More specifically, focusing on Majewski's general education class in history, the coauthors point to the role of explicitness as critical for such change, the ways it can highlight disciplinarity, and how, working together, the two can assist learners:

> More emphasis was put on teaching skills specific to a history course, such as reading primary sources or connecting historical evidence to arguments. To illustrate the way historians read and the importance of identifying context, for instance, students viewed a video of a think-aloud exercise in which John struggled to interpret a primary source document from ancient Rome. In a similar fashion, students were instructed in lecture on specific ways historians craft arguments, especially how to approach an analytical thesis and how to directly link evidence to argument. The necessity of having a meaningful argument was repeatedly emphasized—to write history, students could not just summarize facts but had to interpret facts in ways that made them significant. To do so, they had to write analytical narratives that flowed chronologically but still made an overall argument. The course thus explicitly reminded students that their analytical narratives were particular to the threshold concepts of history and reinforced these concepts through lecture and hands-on activity. They were writing in a particular context that would develop a different set of skills than would courses in other disciplines. (198)

In the final chapter, Chris Anson considers how writing as it occurs across a campus can be enhanced through the use of threshold concepts. Defining writing as a disciplinary activity, Anson explains the role that six threshold concepts can play in this work:

- defining writing as a disciplinary activity;
- reconceptualizing the social and rhetorical nature of writing;
- distinguishing between writing to learn and writing to communicate;

- establishing shared goals and responsibilities for improvement;
- understanding the situated nature of writing and the problem of transfer; and
- viewing student writing developmentally. (205)

As important, Anson points out how important it is to work with threshold concepts in what we might call their *fullness*. When we don't, when for example "threshold concepts are reduced from verbs to nouns, from their fully articulated, active form (along with plentiful explanation) to buzzwords and catch phrases, many faculty will balk, and resistance can follow" (216). As a corrective to this, Anson notes the relationship of a single maxim to a full set of threshold concepts. Much as we see in the explanation of the threshold concepts in the first part of *Naming What We Know*, each one is in relation to several others; to understand it, we have to understand it in the context of the others.

> During some campus visits, my hosts have counseled me never to use a specific word among the faculty, such as *outcomes* or *rubric* or even *WAC*, usually because some earlier curricular disaster or failed innovation poisoned the entire campus to whatever the term meant at the time. Although it is less likely, certain threshold concepts introduced too glibly can trigger false assumptions, resistance, or confusion among faculty. An example familiar to most WAC leaders takes the problematically reduced form of advice not to focus first (or even at all) on the surface features of students' writing: "students' grammatical mistakes are not as important as what they are trying to say" or even "don't focus on grammar." Unpacking this assertion means delving into the relationship between form and meaning, the effects of certain pedagogies on students' self-efficacy and further writing behaviors, the relationship among writing assignments and learning goals, students' linguistic backgrounds, and a host of other complicated issues. (216)

***

Reading across these chapters, we can see eight points of agreement. First, we agree on the metaconcept that writing is an activity and a subject of study. This threshold concept thus expands the field's historical focus on practice to include writing as a subject of study as well. For some colleagues, as Blake Scott and Elizabeth Wardle suggest, this is a provocative claim; not all faculty agree that there are threshold concepts in the field, much less agree on what they might be. At the same time, what we also see in the claim that writing is a subject of study is that writing has a content, a claim that the rest of the threshold concepts detail. If this is so, we need have Fulkerson's content envy no longer.

Second, we agree that a threshold concept functions as both propositional statement and heuristic for inquiry, a heuristic we can, in

Heidi Estrem's terms, see with and through. Their value as propositions is twofold: we articulate what we know, and we can use that articulation as a point of departure for additional scholarly investigation.

Third, we agree that threshold concepts provide a way of thinking, a framework for multiple kinds of work, be it the design of general education or the foundational principles for writing across the curriculum.

Fourth, we agree that threshold concepts aren't fixed but are rather contingent and flexible, and that to be helpful, they need to be so. Entailed in this agreement is a sense that outcomes, which have offered both promise and help to writing programs, have become rigid and standardized; as such, they provide a foil to threshold concepts.

Fifth, we agree that threshold concepts are neither acontextual nor arhetorical, but are specific to a discipline and community of practice; they often function as a kind of boundary object in dialogue with local situations and/or other frameworks, including those connected to the discipline, as in Downs and Robertson's design for FYC, and to other fields, as we see in O'Neill's discussion of writing assessment.

Sixth, we agree, as Scott and Wardle and Nowacek and Hughes illustrate, that as threshold concepts are employed in a given setting, variants of the threshold concepts can develop, ones that themselves toggle between more general threshold concepts and understandings informing the local.

Seven, we agree, as Adler-Kassner and Majewski argue, that we need to be explicit in working with both faculty and students, and that such explicitness, as explained in *How People Learn*, facilitates transfer.

And eighth, we agree that all of us—including students—can use threshold concepts to inquire, analyze, interpret, and, ultimately, make knowledge.

***

We have long been interested in mapping our field. In 1984, for example, Janice Lauer took up that task, beginning by identifying the core features of a discipline to contextualize her argument that at that time, rhetoric and composition was an emerging discipline.

> At its deepest level, a discipline has a special set of phenomena to study, a characteristic mode or modes of inquiry, its own history of development, its theoretical ancestors and assumptions, its evolving body of knowledge, and its own epistemic courts by which knowledge gains that status. (Lauer 1984, 20)

Some twenty years later, then-*CCC Online* editor Collin Brooke employed databases and linking to create another kind of map; and nearly ten years after that, Derek Mueller (2012) plotted the long tail of composition, and graduate students at CUNY began sharing their academic genealogy project. The exploration into threshold concepts and their uses presented in this volume provides yet another approach to the field's larger mapping project, here a process identifying not only the map, but also *what* there is to map. In this sense, threshold concepts are kairotic: they articulate the substance of the field as a mechanism for mapping the field itself.

It may also be that threshold concepts, as presented here, mark another kind of threshold for the field, an idea that's occurred to me as I've participated in articulating key concepts, in providing definitions for two of the threshold concepts, in coauthoring a chapter, in reading this volume, and in writing this introduction. In reviewing the list of contributors to threshold concepts, for example, I was interested in the timeline we might draw, collectively accounting for their scholarly contributions. A back-of-the-envelope calculation might begin with Andrea Lunsford's "Classical Rhetoric and Technical Writing," published in a 1976 issue of *College Composition and Communication*, and continue through the 2015 publication of this volume: that's nearly forty years of a sixty-five year history of the discipline.

But my review of the list of chapter authors prompted another insight, in part because I had just read Robert Connors's observations about "generations" of "modern composition specialists": he dates the first generation as occurring between the "late 1940s and the early 1960s" and the second occurring in the 1960s into the 1970s, and he notes that the specialists of both these generations "retool[ed] as writing specialists after literary doctorates" (Connors 1999, 9). The third generation—and he counts himself in that generation—took their doctorates in rhetoric and composition at a limited number of institutions,[3] and Connors cites this generation as something of a dividing line, in the development of the field, between those who retooled to found a field and those who entered a field already in progress. I'm not sure precisely how I would date the generations, but there's no doubt that early leaders of the field took their doctoral work in literature and English education;[4] and there's no doubt that these early leaders—and leaders in some of the succeeding generations as well—were attracted to the field in large part because it wasn't established and they thus could make significant contributions to what they saw as an emerging field (Craig et al. forthcoming). The assumption underlying *Naming*, of course, is that the field *is* now established, and it thus would be a useful enterprise to consider together what it is that we do know. This established field, of course, is the field that most of the chapter contributors entered: teacher-scholars who saw not only an established field, but a field so established that it includes defined subfields—among them writing centers, writing assessment, and WAC—often providing their own pathways into the larger field; who chose graduate study in rhetoric and composition from one of more than eighty institutions currently offering the doctorate in rhetoric and composition; and whose education was not necessarily taken in English departments nor, even when it was, defined by literature. It occurred to me, in other words, that the literary context so prominent in so many accounts of our history and even in accounts of our pedagogy, as Fulkerson explains, is, for these contributors, as for new generations, no longer our default context—or, and at least as important, our default *content*. And it also occurred to me that our shared interest in threshold concepts, which is an expression of an interest in disciplinarity, is a logical next step when a field has matured, as ours has.

If this is so, then by means of this project, we are entering another threshold for the field, one with enormous potential to help shape the field's future.

Notes

1. The field has intermittently taken up the question of the content of composition, most recently in 2006 and sponsored by the CCCC, though it was quite clear that not everyone agreed that there is such a content. For a summary of the CCCC-sponsored discussion, see http://compfaqs.org/ContentofComposition/HomePage.

2. It's worth noting that taken together, the chapters address the full set of responsibilities a faculty member in the discipline of rhetoric and composition might take up, including the one program that has now completed the set, the major in rhetoric and composition. In 1999, Robert Connors made the argument that to coalesce as a discipline, composition needed two "elements": "methods of intellectual tradition in a great burgeoning of journals and books" and a "method of scholarly reproduction" (Connors 1999, 8), by which he meant doctoral programming. In 2004, I argued that for the field to become a discipline, another element was needed, the major in rhetoric and composition: "In other words, it is past time that we fill the glaringly empty spot between first-year composition and graduate education with a composition major" (Yancey 2004, 308).

3. There were several other programs predating the ones on Connors's list, including the well-known doctoral program at the University of Iowa.

4. See, for example, Stock's 2011 edited *Composition's Roots in English Education*.

References

Connors, Robert. 1999. "Composition History and Disciplinarity." In *History, Reflection, and Narrative: The Professionalism of Composition*, edited by Debra Journet, Beth Boehm, and Mary Rosner, 1963–1983: 3–23. Stanford, CA: Ablex.

Craig, Jacob, Matt Davis, Christine Martorana, Josh Mehler, Kendra Mitchell, Antony N. Ricks, Bret Zawilski, and Kathleen Blake Yancey. Forthcoming. "Against the Rhetoric and Composition Grain: A Microhistorical View." In *Microhistories of Composition*, edited by Bruce McComiskey. Logan: Utah State University Press.

Fulkerson, Richard. 2005. "Composition at the Turn of the Twenty-First Century." *College Composition and Communication* 56 (4): 654–87.

Gerber, John. 1950. "The Conference on College Composition and Communication." *College Composition and Communication* 1 (1):12.

Lauer, Janice. 1984. "Composition Studies: Dappled Discipline." *Rhetoric Review* 3 (1): 20–29. http://dx.doi.org/10.1080/07350198409359074.

Meyer, Jan H. F. 2012. "Variation in Student Learning as a Threshold Concept." *Journal of Faculty Development* 26 (3): 9–13.

Meyer, Jan H. F., and Ray Land. 2003. "Threshold Concepts and Troublesome Knowledge: Linkages to Ways of Thinking and Practising." ETL Project Occasional Report 4. http://www.etl.tla.ed.ac.uk/docs/ETLreport4.pdf.

Mueller, Derek. 2012. "Grasping Rhetoric and Composition by Its Long Tail: What Graphs Can Tell Us about the Field's Changing Shape." *College Composition and Communication* 64 (1): 195–223.

Stock, Patricia, ed. 2011. *Composition's Roots in English Education*. Portsmouth, NH: Heineman.

Yancey, Kathleen Blake. 2004. "Made Not Only in Words: Composition in a New Key." *College Composition and Communication* 56 (2): 297–328. http://dx.doi.org/10.2307/4140651.

Yancey, Kathleen Blake, Liane Robertson, and Kara Taczak. 2014. *Writing Across Contexts: Transfer, Composition, and Sites of Writing*. Logan: Utah State University Press.

NAMING WHAT WE KNOW

NAMING WHAT WE KNOW
The Project of This Book

Linda Adler-Kassner and Elizabeth Wardle

Reading across the last fifty years of research, it is possible to make a case that our field has in many ways been concerned with its constitution *as* field. Researchers and teachers have reflected on what the field is, whether it is a field, and so on—and on a fairly regular basis. That these are fraught questions is evident in our difficulty even settling on a name for the field. Within the last ten or so years, we seem to have settled on three terms—*composition, rhetoric,* and *writing studies,* individually or in combination with one another—to speak to the collective efforts of the discipline.

But while we have engaged in what James Carey, perhaps slightly misquoting John Dewey, refers to as "the neurotic quest for certainty" (Carey 1989, 89) in pursuit of these questions about the external boundaries of the field, researchers and teachers *in* the field have, at the same time, focused on questions related to a common theme: *the study of composed knowledge.* Within this theme, our work has been expansive. To name just a few areas of practice within it, we have studied what composed knowledge looks like in specific contexts; how good and less-than-good qualities of composed knowledge are defined, by whom, and with what values associated with those definitions and qualities; how to help learners compose knowledge within specific contexts and with what consequences for learner and context; the relationships between technologies and processes for composing knowledge; connections between affordances and potential for composing knowledge; and how composed knowledge can be best assessed and why.

As we have taken on these questions associated with composed knowledge, writing researchers, instructors, and programs have simultaneously attempted to participate in discussions—with one another and with others (such as departmental colleagues, administrators, parents,

DOI: 10.7330/9780874219906.c000b

and policymakers)—about what students should learn about writing, how they should learn those things, and how those things should be taught and assessed. These responses have taken two forms. One involves drafting concise, usable statements about best practices extending from the field's knowledge that are intended to be used for policy and practice. This perspective is represented by documents like *The Framework for Success in Postsecondary Writing* or the CCCC *Position Statement on Dual Credit/Concurrent Enrollment Composition: Policy and Best Practices.* Another involves attempts to identify and clarify the boundaries of the discipline as a way of containing, instantiating, and reifying types of writing-related knowledge (e.g., Bizzell 1986; Cook 2011; Kopelsen 2008; Phelps, Wiley, and Gleason 1995; Worsham 1999a, 1999b).

These efforts to outline best practices and outline and clarify the field's boundaries are important. But they sidestep a pressing point: whatever we call ourselves, wherever we may be on the continuum of disciplinarity, fifty (plus) years of research has led us to know some things about the subject of composed knowledge and the questions we ask related to this broad term. This book represents an effort to bring together those things we know using a particular frame, that of threshold concepts.

Threshold concepts are concepts critical for continued learning and participation in an area or within a community of practice. This lens of threshold concepts emerged from a research project in the United Kingdom on the characteristics of effective teaching and learning environments in undergraduate education (Cousin 2006). Jan H. F. Meyer and Ray Land began by studying concepts economists felt were central to the study of their discipline; this lens has now been effectively used to consider threshold knowledge in many other discipline. According to Meyer and Land, threshold concepts have several common characteristics:

- Learning them is generally transformative, involving "an ontological as well as a conceptual shift . . . becoming a part of who we are, how we see, and how we feel" (Cousin 2006).

- Once understood, they are often irreversible and the learner is unlikely to forget them.

- They are integrative, demonstrating how phenomena are related, and helping learners make connections.

- They tend to involve forms of troublesome knowledge, what Perkins refers to as knowledge that is "alien" or counterintuitive (qtd. in Meyer and Land 2006, 3).

While much of the discussion about threshold concepts has been related to how people learn and participate in specific disciplinary communities, threshold concepts of writing studies speak both to and beyond our disciplinary community. This is because the subject of our discipline—composed knowledge—is widely relevant. Consider the ubiquity of some of the field's most widely examined questions: How is "good" composed knowledge (and its opposite) defined? How are students taught to produce composed knowledge? How is composed knowledge assessed? What values are associated with judgments about composed knowledge? and What consequences are attached to the teaching, production, and/or assessment of composed knowledge? Certainly, then, there are threshold concepts of writing studies that are central to participation in the discipline of writing studies; but there are also threshold concepts *from* writing studies that can assist writers and teachers of all sorts, whatever their disciplinary or professional affiliations. The concepts named in this portion of the collection, then, can be positioned differently for different audiences—a first-year writing course, a graduate class, a conversation about writing with a colleague from another department or an administrator, a discussion about writing with a stakeholder outside of the academy. The threshold concepts here also might be considered relevant for audiences inside and beyond the discipline. In this way, both the concepts and our discussions of them in this book differ somewhat from some of the threshold concepts literature that has preceded it, which has been directed almost exclusively toward a disciplinary audience. It also differs from literature in writing studies focusing on reflexive practice, which has been concerned primarily with how to help writers foster a more thorough understanding of their own processes.

COMPOSING PART 1: HOW WE NAMED WHAT WE KNOW

Part 1 of *Naming What We Know* is intended to serve as a sort of crowd-sourced encyclopedia of threshold concepts of writing studies. Any attempt to name what a field knows must be a project taken up by numerous members of the field, and that is what we attempted to elicit with this project. We first identified a group of prominent writing researchers and teachers whose scholarship we believed had made important contributions to the field in a variety of areas, from genre studies to digital composing, from assessment to considerations of identity and diversity in composing. We invited forty-five of those teacher-scholars to participate on a wiki (PBWiki, to which we are enormously grateful for their easy-to-use and stable platform), proposing ideas, phenomena, knowledge, or orientations they considered to be threshold concepts of writing studies. Over several months, twenty-nine of the original forty-five invited participants read the introduction to *Overcoming Barriers to Student Understanding* by Meyer and Land (2006), made fifty-one suggestions regarding what they considered to be threshold concepts, and wrote 139 comments regarding the concepts proposed by others. The two of us then met and analyzed the wiki contributions. We distilled one metaconcept, Writing Is an Activity and a Subject of Study, and five overarching concepts that each seemed to unfold into somewhere between three and nine constituent elements. We circulated this draft among the participants, and after their revisions and approval, we assigned contributors to write extended definitions (one-thousand-word definitions for overarching concepts and five-hundred-word definitions for the subconcepts). Some of these authors took on coauthors at this stage who had not participated in previous stages but who were experts in the concept at hand. Resulting drafts were revised and posted to the wiki. Several concepts were revised, moved, integrated with others, or deleted altogether before the current concepts and categories were finalized. In the end, the members of the group who engaged in this process have identified a total of thirty-seven threshold concepts as "what we know"—from research in writing studies and aligned fields (i.e., linguistics, learning theory, and psychology).

The communities of practice/threshold concepts approach used here is predicated upon the idea that within a community of practice (see Wenger 1999) there is sufficient consensus around these shared ideas; that our writing studies community of practice existed at all was a sort of hypothesis that was tested during the online discussion that led to the development of this section of *Naming What We Know*. To this end, rather than beginning by attempting to outline the boundaries of the field or speak to particular issues, the participants set about looking at the research and theory to determine what they could agree we collectively know. In this regard, this process parallels Bob Broad's idea of "dynamic criteria mapping" to some extent, an "organic" (Broad 2003) attempt to work from the inside out rather than the other way around. And these efforts led to a surprising amount of agreement.

In the end, both of us—along with the twenty-nine contributors to the wiki—are comfortable identifying these as final-for-now definitions of *some* of what our field knows. But we want to stress the contingent changing nature of knowledge. As a group, we've come to some consensus about some of what we know and agree on at this time in our field's history and development. The concepts and definitions here represent what we know for now; their existence as known concepts is currently critical for epistemological participation in our disciplines, and many of them are, we think, critical for anyone who wants to help learners write more effectively, whatever their disciplines or professions may be. That this knowledge will continue to change, and that what we see as most important will continue to evolve, is inevitable and desirable if we are to continue to grow as a field.

WHY WE NAMED WHAT WE KNOW— AND NEED TO KEEP DOING SO

Perhaps the value of stopping to name what we know is obvious, but we anticipate that these efforts to have done so will be contentious. Thus, it seems worth taking a little space here to explicitly argue for the need to have engaged in this project, and for the need to continue to engage in it in the coming decades.

There are a number of individuals and groups asserting definitions of what "good writing" is and how it should be developed in schools; this is nothing new. From *Why Johnny Can't Read* (Flesch 1955), published in 1955, to "Why Johnny Can't Write" (Sheils 1975) published in 1975, to *A Nation at Risk* (National Commission on Excellence in Education 1983) in 1983, to the report of the Spellings Commission on the Future of Higher Education that appeared in 2006 (Miller 2006), literacy instruction has long been the subject of scrutiny. What *is* new, though, is the combination of message, funding, and power shared among those involved in this latest round of discussions (see, for instance, Hall and Thomas 2012; Strauss 2013). From this vantage point, then, naming what we know seems particularly important. Broadly, we see a push to standardize ideas about what "good writing" means, extending from what we think of as the college and career readiness agenda. While the Common Core State Standards (2013) (with their focus on three text types: argumentative writing, informative/explanatory writing, and narrative writing) are the most visible evidence of this agenda, the push for writing curricula (and assessments) at the postsecondary level that do not necessarily reflect writing studies research (or the experience of its practitioners) are being felt by some writing faculty in states where legislatures have more control over curricular guidelines, as in Florida, and are hovering just beyond in many other states (such as New York, where the CUNY and SUNY systems have signed an agreement to use Common Core assessments as part of their placement mechanism for students). As both of us (Adler-Kassner 2012; 2014; Downs and Wardle 2007; Wardle 2009; 2012) and others (Applebee 2013; Hesse 2012) have noted, these efforts do *not* always consistently reflect what we know.

In the current educational and policy climate, then, writing carries a heavy burden. It continues both to serve as a vehicle through which knowledge is both generated and demonstrated and to draw the attention of many stakeholders who, regardless of their expertise, weigh in on what "good writing" is, how it should be taught and learned and by whom, and how that learning should be assessed. We hope this effort to begin naming *what we know*—what research about writing, writers, and the act of inscribing knowledge can tell us about fostering knowledge about writing and writing performance that is (still) critical for writers. We also hope this collection can provide a basis for writing studies professionals to describe what we know in ways that are accessible to educated readers (and listeners) who are not necessarily specialists in our discipline. As, however, with any communication between expert practitioners (like writing researchers and teachers) and those with less experienced-based expertise, that communication may take some translating and reframing. For instance, the threshold concept that Habituated Practice Can Lead to Entrenchment (5.3) holds a great deal of meaning to experts, but that meaning is gleaned from deep understandings of the nature of genre, prior knowledge, and identity (as in concepts 2.2, 3.2, and 3.3). We offer the following as a few examples of what this translation or reframing for nonexperts might look like:

Table 0.1

Habituated Practice Can Lead to Entrenchment (5.3).	"Good writing" looks different in different contexts. If writers learn to write one thing or in one way, and they practice just that one thing or way over and over, they might think all writing is like the writing they do, and they might not recognize that good writing looks different and happens differently across different contexts.
Disciplinary and Professional Identities Are Constructed through Writing (3.4).	Faculty use writing (mostly in the form of publications) to share ideas with others and demonstrate that they understand both the ideas of others (research and current issues) and appropriate ways of talking about those ideas in their disciplines. As students delve more deeply into disciplines (as they move, for instance, toward majors or advanced degrees), they are expected to use writing in the ways members of their disciplines do, to engage with others in their disciplinary communities in ways that demonstrate that they understand the work these people do and how to communicate with them, as one of them.

continued on next page

Table 0.1—*continued*

Failure Can Be an Important Part of Writing Development (4.2).	Sometimes, learning what does not work and why it doesn't work can help writers grow, learn, and write more effectively the next time. Learning is not always a process of sequentially mastering skills but is sometimes a messy process that requires revisiting something and having to try again.

The explanations of the threshold concepts in this book are specifically designed to help readers think through what the concepts mean and what their consequences are. They are designed to assist people in the field in explaining them to others. We urge readers to consider how they can best use this content when and if they draw on it for conversations with those outside of our field.

Ultimately, then, the argument here is that our field knows a lot about its subject of study. We know much about how writers write and learn to write, and how best to assess writing. Yet we continue to lose the battle over discussions of writing to stakeholders who have money, power, and influence but little related expertise. If we want to actively and positively impact the lives of writers and writing teachers, we must do a better job of clearly stating what our field knows and helping others understand how to use that knowledge as they set policy, create programs, design and fund assessments, and so on.

UNDERSTANDING AND USING *NAMING WHAT WE KNOW*

We offer this book as a step toward the goal of clearly stating what we know and bring to the table. The collection has two parts. The first is a sort of "encyclopedia" of thirty-seven of the field's threshold concepts arranged in five categories, all of which fall under the metaconcept Writing Is an Activity and a Subject of Study. The second focuses on threshold concepts in action in eight specific sites of writing instruction and writing development. Throughout the book, readers will find references to concepts in the first part of the collection (e.g., 1.4, 3.1, 4.2). These are, in essence, two-dimensional hyperlinks, referencing readers to other, related threshold concepts they might want to think about in relationship to the one about which they are currently reading. If these cross-references become distracting, we urge readers to skip over them or return to them later.

While there are many productive reasons to name what we know, several caveats and cautions are in order regarding how to understand and use the work in this book. First, we want to reiterate that the threshold concepts in this book do not and cannot represent the full set of threshold concepts for our field; in fact, we do not believe it is possible or desirable to try to name, once and for all, all such concepts. Even as we were finalizing categories and threshold concepts after months of dialogue and debate, contributors were noting concepts and indeed entire areas of study they thought had been elided, given short shrift, or left out entirely. We offer these thirty-seven concepts as an effort to begin to name what we know and to invite readers to continue this effort at their own institutions and at conferences and in journals.

Second, these threshold concepts should in no way, shape, or form be used as a checklist—for the development of curriculum, for instance, or to check students' learning. As Kathleen Blake Yancey explains in concept 3.2, Writers' Histories, Processes, and Identities Vary, there has historically been a desire to make "the teaching of writing uniform—mapped across grade levels . . . [in the hopes that] a single approach would enfranchise all writers" (53). There is a difference between naming and describing principles and practices that extend from the research base of a discipline, as this book begins to do, and stripping the complexity from those principles in order to distill them into convenient categories to which generic attributes can be associated or attached. Any attempt to create a "learning checklist" with these (or any other) threshold concepts would, in fact, engage in this complexity stripping (see Land and Meyer 2010 for their discussion of the dangers of "assessment regimes" for the use of threshold concepts).

Heidi Estrem's chapter in part 2 of this collection takes up the more complicated relationship between threshold concepts and learning outcomes, an intersection that also raises questions about the nature of these two ideas. One reason it is not appropriate to conflate learning outcomes and threshold concepts is that threshold concepts are liminal, and learning them happens over time at varied levels of understanding. They often cannot be taught directly by explication but must be experienced and enacted over time with others before they are fully understood. In other words, we cannot expect that students in a single class—first-year composition, for example—would master the threshold concepts outlined in this book. They might be introduced to some of these concepts, they might encounter them, they most certainly will engage in practices that assume some of these threshold concepts to be true. But they will not and cannot be expected to master threshold concepts in a single term or class, and there is no assessment mechanism that can determine whether they have productively encountered them. Learning threshold concepts amounts to learning some of the assumptions of a community of practice, and that only productively happens across time. This type of learning is messy, time consuming, and unpredictable. It does not lend itself to shortcuts or checklists or competency tests.

Rather than become concerned with creating threshold concepts assessments or stripped-down threshold concepts checklists, teachers might more productively consider which threshold concepts inform (or should inform) their classes—particularly looking at sets of classes across time—and whether their curricula and activities are productively acting out of and introducing students to those threshold concepts. In other words, rather than construct a threshold concepts curriculum or a threshold concepts-assessment, readers might consider how these threshold concepts *inform* curriculum or assessment. How, for instance, might the idea that Writing Is an Activity and a Subject of Study contribute to the development of a writing class? What might it look like when learners at multiple levels understand writing as both of these things? Readers might ask themselves whether the writing assessments they are designing act out of generally agreed-upon writing studies threshold concepts, such as Writing Mediates Activity or Writing Is a Way of Enacting Disciplinarity, or whether they are unintentionally enacting harmful conceptions of writing, such as writing is only scribal skills or any piece of writing can be effectively assessed out of context.

In sum, while this book is an effort to name what we know to ourselves and to students and faculty new to our discipline, it is also an effort and a call to extend discussions about what we know to audiences beyond ourselves. As we stressed earlier here, *who* we are and what we call ourselves is less important than *what we know* and the impact that knowledge has. Advocating for writers and writing and making change through knowledge are what matters. We hope this collection proves a productive mechanism for enacting change in writing classrooms, assessments, and policy-writing sessions around the country.

References

Adler-Kassner, Linda. 2012. "The Companies We Keep *or* The Companies We Would Like to Keep: Strategies and Tactics in Challenging Times." *WPA Journal* 36: 119–40.

Adler-Kassner, Linda. (Forthcoming). "Liberal Learning, Professional Training, and Disciplinarity in the Age of Education 'Reform': Remodeling General Education." *College English.*

Applebee, Arthur. 2013. "Common Core State Standards: The Promise and the Peril in a National Palimpsest." *English Journal* 103 (1): 25–33.

Bizzell, Patricia. 1986. "On the Possibility of a Unified Theory of Composition and Literature." *Rhetoric Review* 4 (2): 174–80. http://dx.doi.org/10.1080/073501986093 59121.

Bransford, John D., James W. Pellegrino, and M. Suzanne Donovan, eds. 2000. *How People Learn: Brain, Mind, Experience, and School: Expanded Edition.* Washington, DC: National Academies Press.

Broad, Bob. 2003. *What We Really Value: Beyond Rubrics in Teaching and Assessing Writing.* Logan: Utah State University Press.

Carey, James. 1989. Communication as Culture: Essays on Media and Society. Boston: Unwin and Hyman.

Common Core State Standards. 2013. http://www.corestandards.org/.

Cook, Paul. 2011. "Disciplinarity, Identity Crises, and the Teaching of Writing." In *Who Speaks for Writing?* edited by Ethna D. Lay and Jennifer Rich, 87–102. New York: Peter Lang.

Cousin, Glynis. 2006. "An Introduction to Threshold Concepts." *Planet* 17 (December): 4–5. http://dx.doi.org/10.11120/plan.2006.00170004.

Downs, Doug, and Elizabeth Wardle. 2007. "Teaching about Writing, Righting Misconceptions: (Re)Envisioning FYC as Intro to Writing Studies." *College Composition and Communication* 58 (4): 552–84.

Flesch, Rudolph. 1955. *Why Johnny Can't Read.* New York: Harper & Row.

Fulkerson, Richard. 1990. "Composition in the Eighties." *College Composition and Communication* 41 (4): 409–29. http://dx.doi.org/10.2307/357931.

Hall, Cassie, and Scott L. Thomas. 2012. "'Advocacy Philanthropy' and the Public Policy Agenda: The Role of Modern Foundations in American Higher Education." Paper prepared for the 93rd annual meeting of the American Educational Research Association, Vancouver, Canada.

Hesse, Doug. 2012. "Who Speaks for Writing? Expertise, Ownership, and Stewardship." In *Who Speaks for Writing: Stewardship for Writing Studies in the 21st Century,* edited by Jennifer Rich and Ethna D. Lay, 9–22. New York: Peter Lang.

Kopelson, Karen. 2008. "Sp(l)itting Images; or, Back to the Future of (Rhetoric and?) Composition." *College Composition and Communication* 59 (4): 750–80.

Land, Ray, and Jan H. F. Meyer. 2010. "Threshold Concepts and Troublesome Knowledge (5): Dynamics of Assessment." In *Threshold Concepts and Transformational Learning,* edited by Jan H. F. Meyer, Ray Land, and Caroline Baillie, 61–79. Amsterdam: Sense.

Meyer, Jan H. F., and Ray Land. 2006. "Threshold Concepts and Troublesome Knowledge: An Introduction." In *Overcoming Barriers to Student Understanding,* edited by Jan H. F. Meyer and Ray Land, 3–18. London: Routledge.

Miller, Charles, et al. 2006. *Report of the Commission on the Future of Higher Education.* Washington, DC: US Department of Education.

National Commission on Excellence in Education. 1983. *A Nation at Risk.* Washington, DC: US Department of Education.

Phelps, Louise Wetherbee, Mark Wiley, and Barbara Gleason, eds. 1995. *Composition in Four Keys: Inquiring into the Field.* New York: McGraw-Hill.

Sheils, Merrill. 1975. "Why Johnny Can't Write." *Newsweek*, December 8, 58–65.

Strauss, Valerie. 2013. "Gates Gives 150 Million in Grants for Common Core Standards." *Answer Sheet* (blog), May 12. http://www.washingtonpost.com/blogs/answer-sheet/wp/2013/05/12/gates-gives-150-million-in-grants-for-common-core-standards/.

Wardle, Elizabeth. 2009. "'Mutt Genres' and the Goal of FYC: How Can We Help Students Write the Genres of the University?" *College Composition and Communication* 60 (4): 765–88.

Wardle, Elizabeth. 2012. "Creative Repurposing for Expansive Learning: Considering 'Problem-Exploring' and 'Answer-Getting' Dispositions in Individuals and Fields." *Composition Forum* 26. http://compositionforum.com/issue/26/creative-repurposing.php.

Wenger, Etienne. 1999. *Communities of Practice: Learning, Meaning, and Identity.* Cambridge: Cambridge University Press.

Worsham, Lynn. 1999a. "Critical Interference and the Postmodern Turn in Composition Studies." *Composition Forum* 10: 1–29.

Worsham, Lynn. 1999b. "On the Rhetoric of Theory in the Discipline of Writing: A Comment and a Proposal." *JAC: A Journal of Rhetoric.* 19: 389–409.

PART 1

Threshold Concepts of Writing

METACONCEPT
Writing Is an Activity and a Subject of Study

Elizabeth Wardle and Linda Adler-Kassner

Writing is created, produced, distributed, and used for a variety of purposes. In this sense, it is an *activity* in which individuals and groups engage. However, the production, consumption, circulation, distribution, and use of writing are also areas of inquiry. Researchers in a number of fields (including, but not limited to, rhetoric and composition, linguistics, and literacy studies) investigate questions about writing. These include:

- How have forms of writing developed over time?
- What conceptions of writing do people have, and what values are suggested by these conceptions? What writing practices and processes are encouraged by these conceptions? Where do these conceptions come from?
- How is writing produced by individuals and groups, for what purposes, and with what implications or consequences?
- How are attitudes toward the production and uses of writing shaped by individuals and groups within specific contexts?
- How have different approaches to shaping the production of writing taken form, with what motivations, and to what ends?
- How is writing a technology, and how do writing technologies impact how writing happens and what can be done with writing?

Outside of scholars involved in the study of writing, the idea that writing is not only an activity in which people engage but also a subject of study often comes as a surprise, partially because people tend to experience writing as a finished product that represents ideas in seemingly rigid forms but also because writing is often seen as a "basic skill" that a person can learn once and for all and not think about again.

Research in writing and rhetoric has demonstrated that these ideas about writing do not match the ways that writing actually works and happens, but this more complex view of writing is not one that is widely shared or understood beyond the field. In fact, to be considered "successful," all writers must learn to study expectations for writing within specific contexts and participate in those to some degree.

The threshold concept that writing is a subject of study *as well as* an activity is troublesome because it contravenes popular conceptions of writing as a basic, ideology-free skill. When teachers and learners recognize writing as complex enough to require study, and recognize that the study of writing suggests they should approach, learn, and teach writing differently, they are then invited to behave differently and to change their conceptions of what writing is and their practices around writing that extend from those conceptions.

CONCEPT 1
Writing Is a Social and Rhetorical Activity

1.0
WRITING IS A SOCIAL AND RHETORICAL ACTIVITY
Kevin Roozen

It is common for us to talk about writing in terms of the particular text we are working on. Consider, for example, how often writers describe what they are doing by saying "I am writing an email" or "I'm writing a report" or "I'm writing a note." These shorthand descriptions tend to collapse the activity of writing into the act of single writer inscribing a text. In doing so, they obscure two foundational and closely related notions of writing: writers are engaged in the work of making meaning for particular audiences and purposes, and writers are always connected to other people.

Writers are always doing the rhetorical work of addressing the needs and interests of a particular audience, even if unconsciously. The technical writers at a pharmaceutical company work to provide consumers of medications with information they need about dosages and potential side effects. The father writing a few comments on a birthday card to his daughter crafts statements intended to communicate his love for her. Sometimes, the audience for an act of writing might be the writer himself. A young man jotting in his diary, for example, might be documenting life events in order to better understand his feelings about them. A child scribbling a phrase on the palm of her hand might do so as a way of reminding herself to feed the family pets, clean her room, or finish her homework. Writing, then, is always an attempt to address the needs of an audience.

In working to accomplish their purposes and address an audience's needs, writers draw upon many other people. No matter how isolated a writer may seem as she sits at her computer, types on the touchpad of her smartphone, or makes notes on a legal pad, she is always drawing upon the ideas and experiences of countless others. The technical writers at a pharmaceutical company draw collaboratively upon the ideas of others

DOI: 10.7330/9780874219906.c001

they work with as they read their colleagues' earlier versions of the information that will appear on the label. They also connect themselves to others as they engage with the laws about their products written by legislatures and the decisions of lawsuits associated with medications that have been settled or may be pending. The father crafting birthday wishes to his daughter might recall and consciously or unconsciously restate comments that his own parents included on the birthday cards he received as a child. As I work to craft this explanation of writing as a social and rhetorical activity, I am implicitly and explicitly responding to and being influenced by the many people involved in this project, those with whom I have shared earlier drafts, and even those whose scholarship I have read over the past thirteen years.

Writing puts the writer in contact with other people, but the social nature of writing goes beyond the people writers draw upon and think about. It also encompasses the countless people who have shaped the genres, tools, artifacts, technologies, and places writers act with as they address the needs of their audiences. The genres of medication labels, birthday wishes, and diary entries writers use have undergone countless changes as they have been shaped by writers in various times and places. The technologies with which writers act—including computer hardware and software; the QWERTY keyboard; ballpoint pens and lead pencils; and legal pads, journals, and Post-It notes—have also been shaped by many people across time and place. All of these available means of persuasion we take up when we write have been shaped by and through the use of many others who have left their traces on and inform our uses of those tools, even if we are not aware of it.

Because it conflicts with the shorthand descriptions we use to talk and think about writing, understanding writing as a social and rhetorical activity can be troublesome in its complexity. We say "I am writing an email" or "I am writing a note," suggesting that we are composing alone and with complete autonomy, when, in fact, writing can never be anything but a social and rhetorical act, connecting us to other people across time and space in an attempt to respond adequately to the needs of an audience.

While this concept may be troublesome, understanding it has a variety of benefits. If teachers can help students consider their potential audiences and purposes, they can better help them understand what makes a text effective or not, what it accomplishes, and what it falls short of accomplishing. Considering writing as rhetorical helps learners understand the needs of an audience, what the audience knows and does not know, why audience members might need certain kinds of information, what the audience finds persuasive (or not), and so on. Understanding the rhetorical work of writing is essential if writers are to make informed, productive decisions about which genres to employ, which languages to act with, which texts to reference, and so on. Recognizing the deeply social and rhetorical dimensions of writing can help administrators and other stakeholders make better decisions about curricula and assessment.

1.1

WRITING IS A KNOWLEDGE-MAKING ACTIVITY

Heidi Estrem

Writing is often defined by what it *is*: a text, a product; less visible is what it can *do*: generate new thinking (see 1.5, "Writing Mediates Activity"). As an activity undertaken to bring new understandings, writing in this sense is not about crafting a sentence or perfecting a text but about mulling over a problem, thinking with others, and exploring new ideas or bringing disparate ideas together (see "Metaconcept: Writing Is an Activity and a Subject of Study"). Writers of all kinds—from self-identified writers to bloggers to workplace teams to academic researchers—have had the experience of coming upon new ideas as a result of writing. Individually or in a richly interactive environment, in the classroom or workplace or at home, writers use writing to generate knowledge that they didn't have before.

Common cultural conceptions of the act of writing often emphasize magic and discovery, as though ideas are buried and the writer uncovers them, rather than recognizing that "the act of *creating* ideas, not finding them, is at the heart of significant writing" (Flower and Hayes 1980, 22; see also 1.9, "Writing Is a Technology through Which Writers Create and Recreate Meaning"). Understanding and identifying how writing is in itself an act of thinking can help people more intentionally recognize and engage with writing as a creative activity, inextricably linked to thought. We don't simply think first and then write (see 1.6, "Writing Is Not Natural"). We write *to* think.

Texts where this kind of knowledge making takes place can be formal or informal, and they are sometimes ephemeral: journals (digital and otherwise), collaborative whiteboard diagrams, and complex doodles and marginalia, for example. These texts are generative and central to meaning making even though we often don't identify them as such. Recognizing these kinds of texts for their productive value then broadens our understanding of literacy to include a rich range of everyday and workplace-based genres far beyond more traditionally recognized ones. Naming these as writing usefully makes visible the roles and purposes of writing (e.g., Barton and Hamilton 1998; Heath 2012).

Understanding the knowledge-making potential of writing can help people engage more purposefully with writing for varying purposes. In higher education, for example, faculty from across the curriculum now often include a wider range of writing strategies in their courses. That is, beyond teaching the more visible disciplinary conventions of writing in their fields, faculty also integrate writing assignments that highlight what is less visible but highly generative about writing in many contexts: writing's capacity for deeper understandings and new insights (see Anson 2010 for one historical account of the shift in how faculty from across campus teach writing). Beyond the classroom, people can employ exploratory, inquiry-based writing tasks like freewriting, planning, and mapping—sometimes individual and often collaborative. These strategies can help all writers increase their comprehension of subject material while also practicing with textual conventions in new genres. Through making the knowledge-making role of writing more visible, people gain experience with understanding how these sometimes-ephemeral and often-informal aspects of writing are critical to their development and growth.

1.2

WRITING ADDRESSES, INVOKES, AND/OR CREATES AUDIENCES
Andrea A. Lunsford

Writing is both relational and responsive, always in some way part of an ongoing conversation with others. This characteristic of writing is captured in what is referred to as the classic *rhetorical triangle*, which has at each of its points a key element in the creation and interpretation of meaning: writer (speaker, rhetor), audience (receiver, listener, reader), and text (message), all dynamically related in a particular context. Walter Ong (1975) referred to this history in his 1975 "The Writer's Audience is Always a Fiction," connecting the audience in oral performances with readers of written performances and exploring the ways in which the two differ. For Ong, the audience for a speech is immediately present, right in front of the speaker, while readers are absent, removed. Thus the need, he argues, for writers to fictionalize their audiences and, in turn, for audiences to fictionalize themselves—that is, to adopt the role set out for them by the writer.

Scholars in rhetoric and writing studies have extended this understanding of audience, explaining how writers can address audiences—that is, actual, intended readers or listeners—and invoke, or call up, imagined audiences as well. As I am writing this brief piece, for example, I am imagining or invoking an audience of students and teachers even as I am addressing the actual first readers of my writing, which in this case are the editors of this volume.

The digital age has brought with it the need for even closer consideration of audiences. We can no longer assume, for example, that the audience members for an oral presentation are actually present. And, especially in a digital age, writing cannot only address and invoke but also create audiences: as a baseball announcer in the film *Field of Dreams* (based on W. P. Kinsella's *Shoeless Joe*) says, "If you build it, they will come." Writers whose works have "gone viral" on the web know well what it means to create an audience that has been unintended and indeed unimagined. Perhaps even more important, the advent of digital and online literacies has blurred the boundaries between writer and audience significantly: the points of the once-stable rhetorical triangle seem to be twirling and shifting and shading into one another. When consumers of information can, quite suddenly, become producers as well, then it's hard to tell who is the writer, who the audience. In addition, the deeply collaborative and social nature of literacy in a digital age not only calls into question earlier distinctions but allows for greater agency on the part of both writers and audiences.

Such shifting and expanding understandings of audience and of the ways writers interact with, address, invoke, become, and create audiences raise new and important questions about the ethics of various communicative acts and call for pedagogies that engage students in exploring their own roles as ethical and effective readers/audiences/writers/speakers/listeners in the twenty-first century.

1.3

WRITING EXPRESSES AND SHARES MEANING TO BE RECONSTRUCTED BY THE READER

Charles Bazerman

The concept that writing expresses and shares meaning is fundamental to participating in writing—by writing we can articulate and communicate a thought, desire, emotion, observation, directive, or state of affairs to ourselves and others through the medium of written words.

The potential of making and sharing meaning provides both the motive and guiding principle of our work in writing and helps us shape the content of our communications. Awareness of this potential starts early in emergent literacy experiences and continues throughout one's writing life but takes on different force and depth as one continues through life.

The expression of meanings in writing makes them more visible to the writer, making the writer's thoughts clearer and shareable with others, who can attempt to make sense of the words, constructing a meaning they attribute to the writer. While writers can confirm that the written words feel consistent with their state of mind, readers can never read the writer's mind to confirm they fully share that state of mind. Readers share only the words to which each separately attributes meanings. Thus, meanings do not reside fully in the words of the text nor in the unarticulated minds but only in the dynamic relation of writer, reader, and text.

While a writer's meanings arise out of the expression of internal thought, the meanings attributed by a reader arise from the objects, experiences, and words available to that reader. For readers, the words of the text index or point to accessible ideas, thoughts, and experiences through which they can reconstruct meanings based on what they already know (see 3.3, "Writing Is Informed by Prior Experience").

Although meaning is philosophically complex, children readily grasp it in practice as they learn that they can share their experiences through writing about it. As their writing develops, they can express or articulate meanings more fully and precisely concerning a wider range of experiences, with wider audiences and with greater consequences.

The idea that writing expresses and shares meaning to be reconstructed by the reader can be troublesome because there is a tension between the expression of meaning and the sharing of it. Often, we view our expressions as deeply personal, arising from inmost impulses. We may not be sure others will respond well to our thoughts or will evaluate us and our words favorably. Therefore, every expression shared contains risk and can evoke anxiety. Writers often hesitate to share what they have expressed and may even keep private texts they consider most meaningful. Further, writers may resist the idea that their texts convey to readers something different than what the writers intended. Feedback from readers indicating that the writer's words do not convey all the writer hoped is not always welcomed (see 4.1, "Text Is an Object Outside of One's Self that Can Be Improved and Developed"; 5.2, "Metacognition Is Not Cognition"; and 4.4, "Revision Is Central to Developing Writing").

Awareness that meaning is not transparently available in written words may have the paradoxical effect of increasing our commitment to words as we mature as users of written language. As writers we may work on the words with greater care and awareness of the needs of readers so as to share our expressions of meaning as best as we can with the limited resources of written language. As readers we may increase our attention to reconstructing writers' meanings despite the fragility of words. The vagaries of meaning also may become a resource for us as writers, whether we are poets evoking readers' projections of personal associations or lawyers creating loopholes and compromises.

1.4

WORDS GET THEIR MEANINGS FROM OTHER WORDS

Dylan B. Dryer

This threshold concept is best illustrated with an example of how a particular word is defined and understood. If asked on the spot to define the word *cup*, an English speaker might say, "Well, it's a smallish drinking vessel, something you'd use for hot drinks like coffee or tea, so probably ceramic rather than glass; usually it has a little handle so your hand doesn't too hot." This is a perfectly serviceable definition, but the way it has been phrased glosses right over this threshold concept. To say that "a cup is a small ceramic drinking vessel" cannot be literally true, after all; the object used to serve hot drinks is not called into being by this sound, nor is there any reason for the phonemes symbolized by the three characters *c*, *u* and *p* to refer to this object (or to refer to it in English, at any rate; in German that object is referred to as *die Tasse*; in Mandarin as *Cháwǎn*; and so on.) Even English speakers don't always use that sound to mean a smallish ceramic drinking vessel. In the kitchen, *cup* is probably a unit of measure; in certain sporting circles, *cup* is the diminutive for the championship trophy (e.g., the Stanley Cup). *Cup* can even mean to hold something gingerly by not closing one's fingers about it, as one would cup an eggshell.

Cup does not have an especially elaborate range of meanings (consider words like *go* or *work* or *right*), but it adequately illustrates Ferdinand de Saussure's great insight: "In language itself, there are only differences" (Saussure 1983, 118). Saussure meant that because there is no necessary connection between any sounds or clusters of symbols and their referents (otherwise different languages would not exist), the meanings of words are relational—they acquire their meanings from other words. Any definition relies on words to explain what other words mean; moreover, words in a sentence or paragraph influence and often determine each other's meaning (which is why children are often advised to puzzle out an unfamiliar vocabulary word from its context). Slang terms for *good* and *bad* are particularly vivid examples of the ways context drives meaning—although these terms change practically overnight, their meanings are usually obvious because of the context of enthusiasm or disparagement in which they're uttered.

While the realization that words cannot be permanently linked to specific meanings can be disconcerting, the effects of this threshold concept are familiar. Most of us, for example, have had the unpleasant feeling that someone else has twisted our words or taken them out of context; we might have bristled at an excessively technical loophole someone finds in a seemingly sensible and obvious rule; we might have been startled by an interpretation of a familiar poem or a text we hold sacred (Meyer and Land 2006, 5). These experiences are reminders that the relations that imbue a sentence with particular meanings come not just from nearby words but also from the social contexts in which the sentence is used. For example, not only does each word in the four-word question "Ready for the cup?" combine with the other three to make the utterance understandable, but social context makes this question mean one thing in a kitchen and another thing while changing the channel at a sports bar. "Language," says Mikhail Bakhtin, "lies on the borderline between oneself and the other. The word in language is half someone else's" (Bakhtin 1981, 293).

This phenomenon works the other way, too: if meanings of words shift in response to changes in social contexts, it's also possible to infer changes in social contexts from changes in the meanings of words. In everyday usage, *text* is now almost exclusively a verb as the ubiquity of cell phones has changed our communication practices; changes in our thinking about gender representation have virtually eliminated the word *mankind* from public discourse; *green* has acquired a complex set of meanings in political, economic, and engineering contexts, and so on. And writers often give semantic drift deliberate shoves of their own, either by working to change what a word is perceived to mean (for example, "queer") or by placing familiar words in new contexts to provoke a new perspective; for example, Gloria Anzaldúa and Linda Brodkey have likened writing to "compustura" (Lunsford 1998, 9) and "stitching" (1994, 545–7), respectively—seaming together something different from existing material.

There are three important implications of understanding this threshold concept. First, when writers understand that meanings are not determined by history or *Webster's* prescriptions alone, but also by language users' contexts and motives, they gain a powerful insight into the causes of communicative success and failure. When readers and writers share a workplace, a close relationship, a broad set of assumptions, or the same field of study, they can rely on these social contexts to fill in the blanks with shared understanding (specialists conversing in technical jargon or lovers speaking in their private language, for example). But when readers and writers don't share close, intense contexts like these, they can have surprising reactions to even seemingly self-evident words like *justice, research, freedom, essay,* or *evidence.* To work with another simple example, Saussure used a drawing to represent the concept of tree evoked by the Latin word *arbor* and the equally arbitrary English *tree.* Suppose then that we surround the word *tree* with two different clusters of words, some drawn from communities reliant on the timber industry (*living wage, local economy, tradition,* and *skill*) and others drawn from communities reliant on tourism (*nature, habitat, preservation,* and *recreation*). It's not at all far from the truth to say we are speaking of two different trees. Even if we can agree in very broad particulars what *justice* means, our personal sense of what it means, the contexts in which we might use it, and the examples we might use to illustrate it will seldom map precisely onto readers' equally complex private sets of connotations for this word.

Second, since we must often communicate with those outside of our close social contexts, this threshold concept also helps us see how we can reduce the likelihood of misunderstandings. Certainly students are often exhorted to define their terms, but this concept helps explain why particular meanings for key terms in their writing can require careful framing. Part of this understanding involves a sense of when readers might need their expectations for certain words managed and/or redirected. These moves will not guarantee perfect understanding, but they can help increase the chances that readers will produce the particular meaning the writer intended. Instructors, too, should remember that common assignment verbs like *analyze, interpret, explain,* and *respond* have discipline-specific contexts.

Finally, and most excitingly, writers who understand that the definitions of any word develop from its usage realize that they, too, are part of this process; every instance of their language use works to preserve certain meanings and to advance others.

1.5

WRITING MEDIATES ACTIVITY

David R. Russell

Writing is a technology, a tool (see 1.9, "Writing Is a Technology through Which Writers Create and Recreate Meaning"). It is, in a material sense, nothing more than making marks on surfaces, whether of paper, stone, liquid-crystal screens, or a child's hand (the girl reminding herself to feed her dog we met in 1.0, "Writing Is a Social and Rhetorical Activity"). The marks may represent the sounds of speech (as in alphabetic scripts like English) or ideas (as in ideographic scripts like Chinese) or pictures (as in pictographic scripts like Cuneiform). But as we've seen in 1.1 and 1.3 ("Writing Is a Knowledge-Making Activity" and "Writing Expresses and Shares Meaning to be Reconstructed by the Reader"), the marks do not "contain" ideas or emotions or even meaning. People make something of them. They must read them and interpret them to act on them or think with them.

This physical presence of writing mediates—comes between, intervenes in—the activity of people (Russell 1995; Russell 1997). The white marks $S\ T\ O\ P$ on a red hexagonal surface mediate the activity of the drivers who arrive at the intersection at about the same time. (Those written marks also help mediate the activity of a scofflaw driver with the police and the courts.)

Writing occupies an intermediate or middle position to form a connecting link that people use to coordinate their activity. Sometimes this is obvious, like the stop sign or laws or the constitution of a club or a nation. Sometimes writing mediates activity that is conflictual, like court proceedings—or even massively violent, like wars fought over interpretations of holy scripture. Sometimes it mediates the deepest human bonds (like the father writing a birthday card in 1.0, "Writing Is a Social and Rhetorical Activity").

Although other forms of communication (like speaking) also mediate activity, writing has several advantages (and disadvantages) over those forms. Depending on the surface and the writing instrument used, writing lasts longer than speech (unless a recording device "writes" the sound waves). More importantly, the marks can be copied and distributed over great distances, unlike (unrecorded) speech and most other symbols. Thus, writing can coordinate the activity of far more people over much longer periods of time. For example, the Ten Commandments, first written on stone, have shaped human activity for some three thousand years now.

People can also return to writing over and over, revise it and shape it relatively easily (though more easily with a word processor than a quill pen or chisel!). In this way writing is very useful for mediation of cognitive processes—thinking. Writing can mediate the *internal* activity of thought and emotion as well as *external* behavior. Internal thoughts and feelings can be externalized relatively quickly in writing, manipulated and revised rather easily (individually or with other people), then reinternalized, or stored for later comparison. People can compare earlier states of mind to later states and act accordingly (like the young man with his journal in 1.0, or scientists in a lab examining successive printouts from an instrument). In this way, the mediation of writing has been central to the development of knowledge, in science and the arts, and to education, as people write to learn as well as learn to write.

The concept that writing mediates human activity is troublesome because it goes against the usual concepts of writing as "just" transcribing ("writing down" or "writing up") thought or speech (see 1.6, "Writing Is Not Natural"). But it is a concept people unconsciously use every time they choose a medium of communication because of its properties (a text rather than a phone call, for example)—or forget those properties (when an affair is discovered by means of work emails that the lovers thought were "just" their intimate conversation). More importantly, it is a concept that lies behind the durable, and seemingly permanent, structures of our modern human institutions, whose ongoing activity would be impossible without the medium of writing. The institutions that form our modern lives—government, commerce, industry, the arts, sciences, and so on—are mediated by written marks in databases, laws, regulations, books, the Internet.

1.6

WRITING IS NOT NATURAL

Dylan B. Dryer

English speakers routinely talk about writing as if it were speech, characterizing their inability to understand a text as difficulty understanding what that text is "saying," speaking of a writer's "voice" or "tone," describing readers as an "audience," and so forth. This habit conceals an essential difference: speech is natural in the sense that as modern homo sapiens, we've been speaking to one another for nearly two hundred thousand years. Our speech has been bound up in complex feedback loops with our physiology (evidence suggests that our larynxes adapted during these millennia, gradually acquiring an extraordinary expressive range) and our cognition (note how quickly and easily almost all children acquire expressive fluency in their native language[s] and how eagerly and seemingly involuntarily most adults participate in children's efforts at language acquisition). It is at this point exceptionally difficult to tease human socialization and language apart (see Burke 1966). But it's essential to remember that while many older children and adults also routinely write, they do so by combining arrays of symbols *for* those sounds.

These symbols can do many things, as this collection illustrates, but they cannot "record" speech or thought in their original forms; they *translate* speech and thought into inscriptions. Others (if they know the code) must then try to reactivate these symbols into meaning. Writing is not even inevitable: after all, not all languages have writing, and no particular system of inscribing symbols (alphanumeric, ideographic, syllabic, abjadic, etc.) is an obvious complement to any particular family of languages. And even more to the point, we haven't been doing it all that long: as far as anyone can tell, inscriptive systems didn't start cropping up here and there until about 3000 BCE, and only a few members of those cultures would have used those systems. The century or so in which some cultures have attempted to teach inscriptive systems at a nearly universal scale is definitely not long enough to be able to identify specific selective effects this technology has had on our cognitive architecture or overall physiology.

Words like *inscriptions, symbols, code,* and *arrays* are intended to emphasize the *technological* dimension of writing, first systematically explored by Walter Ong over thirty years ago. While we usually reserve the word *technology* for recent innovations, any cultural artifact that mediates activity is a technology, including those that have become invisible through long use: roofs, coats, hammers, electric lighting, cooking pots, and so forth. While some typists no longer need to peek at their QWERTY keyboards, and most children gradually stop "drawing" letters and start "writing" them as the symbols for certain sounds become interiorized, these writers have naturalized their relationship with technological arrays, not taken the next logical or organic step in language acquisition and practice. Keyboards and other tools of inscription—pens, pencils, chalk, dry-erase markers, software for computers and cellphones—fade from consciousness through use, and it becomes hard to remember that even a stick used to scratch *L-O-V-E* in the sand is using a technology of conventionalized symbols for sounds. However, neither writing produced with technologies—all writing, in other words—nor written language itself can be said to be "natural" in the way that speech is.

While counterintuitive, denaturalizing writing is not difficult: the startling experience of attempting to sign a document with one's nondominant hand, for example, can be a disconcerting reminder of the time before muscle memory and cognitive routine habituated us to certain symbol shapes. Pairing a familiar translation with its original-language version or an hour spent learning to read short texts in a simple code like Wingdings font can expose the arbitrariness of symbol-phoneme relationships. But why do this at all, especially since habituated fluency with these symbols and their technologies of inscription are generally considered important indexes of our maturity as writers?

It's useful to remember that writing is not natural because writers tend to judge their writing processes too harshly—comparing them to the ease with which they usually speak. Speech, however, employs an extensive array of modalities unavailable to writing: gesture, expression, pacing, register, silences, and clarifications—all of which are instantaneously responsive to listeners' verbal and nonverbal feedback. Once it is understood that writing *itself* is a technology, comparisons to speech become obviously limited or downright misleading since no inscriptive system could possibly capture a language's full range of communicative potential.

Writers can also benefit from the realization that they needn't blame themselves for the shortcomings of the system they've inherited. The limitations of this system—confounding illogicalities in pronunciation and spelling (*choose* but *loose*; *wood* and *would*; *clout* but *doubt*); exasperating inconsistencies in what constitutes an "error" and for whom; the persistent gulf between writers' intentions and readers' interpretations—are simply inherent to a piecemeal technology encumbered with centuries of patchwork solutions to antiquated designs. This is not to say that these limitations are unimportant or ignorable. It is to say, however, that all writers are negotiating workarounds to the limitations of a technology they have inherited rather than bungling an obvious complement to the speech in which they have been naturally adept since childhood.

1.7

ASSESSING WRITING SHAPES CONTEXTS AND INSTRUCTION
Tony Scott and Asao B. Inoue

In school settings, writing assessment refers to the formulation of a judgment or decision based on the reading of student writing with a particular set of expectations or values in mind. Assessment thus encompasses a range of activities, from responding with revision in mind to evaluation or grading of final products to large-scale programmatic assessments.

Writing assessments are a social activity and can be shaped by a variety of individual or institutional factors, including stated goals for writing education; disciplinary philosophies of literacy and learning; political agendas; efficiency imperatives; or common cultural assumptions about writers and literacy. Because the judgments reflected in assessments are informed by factors like these, assessment is not neutral: it shapes the social and rhetorical contexts where writing takes place, especially in school. Any assessment or evaluation applies specific values and also encourages writers to adopt those values. How teachers or others assess student writing, what products those assessment processes produce (e.g., grades, comments on papers, decisions about students, responses to peers' drafts, etc.), and the consequences of those products all can *create* the very competencies any writing assessment says it measures (Gould 1981; Hanson 1993).

In other words, whatever is emphasized in an assessment produces what is defined as "good writing" in a class, a program, or a curriculum. Likewise, what is not emphasized becomes less important and may not be considered characteristic of good writing. For example, a classroom activity that asks students to identify and comment on the critical thinking occurring in peers' drafts emphasizes critical thinking as a part of what is good writing. By asking students to look for and evaluate critical thinking in drafts, teachers signal that they value critical thinking and encourage students to value it, possibly more than other elements one might find in drafts.

Writing assessment constructs boundaries for learning and student agency in learning environments and frames how students understand writing and their own abilities. It can therefore affect curricula, students' senses of their legitimacy and chances of success, and a teacher's job status, intellectual and creative agency, and merit.

Finally, assessment shapes relationships and power between teachers, students, and institutions. Depending on the institutional setting, teachers and students have varying degrees of agency to determine the character of their work, and teachers and students negotiate their relative authority, in part, through the ways students' writing is evaluated and the consequences associated with those evaluations. Institutions can use assessments to inform teachers and students while lending them agency, or they can align prescribed curricula with assessment outcomes to determine the focus of teaching and circumscribe the scope of students' writing. Writing assessment can thereby function as an intentional means of controlling the labor and creative latitude of teachers and students.

The assessment of writing shapes contexts and learning environments: it is a set of practices enacted by people in specific circumstances for specific purposes that have consequences for both the people whose writing is being judged and for those who are judging.

1.8
WRITING INVOLVES MAKING ETHICAL CHOICES
John Duffy

We tend to think of writing as an activity that involves communicating information, or making an argument, or expressing a creative impulse, even when we imagine it as something that creates meaning between writers and readers (see 1.2, "Writing Addresses, Invokes, and/or Creates Audiences"). Writing is indeed all those things. But writing is equally an activity that involves ethical choices that arise from the relationship of writer and reader.

Writing involves ethical choices because every time we write for another person, we propose a relationship with other human beings, our readers. And in proposing such relationships we inevitably address, either explicitly and deliberately, or implicitly and unintentionally, the questions that moral philosophers regard as ethical: What kind of person do I want to be? How should I treat others? How should I live my life? (Shafer-Landau 2007). For writers, these questions may be rephrased: What kind of writer do I wish to be? What are my obligations to my readers? What effects will my words have upon others, upon my community?

To say that writing involves ethical choices is not to suggest that individual writers should be judged as ethical or unethical in the sense of being moral, upright, honest, and so forth. Nor it is to say that writers necessarily reflect on ethical concerns as they write. They may or may not. Neither is it to assert, finally, that every text can be regarded as ethical or unethical based on its content. Many texts, perhaps most, are devoid of the subject matter typically associated with ethics.

Rather, to say writing involves ethical choices is to say that when creating a text, the writer addresses others. And that, in turn, initiates a relationship between writer and readers, one that necessarily involves human values and virtues. A writer attempting to communicate an idea or persuade an audience, for example, may write in ways that privilege honesty, accuracy, fairness, and accountability. These qualities imply an attitude toward the writer's readers: in this case, attitudes of respectfulness, open-mindedness, goodwill, perhaps humility. Conversely, an informational or persuasive text that is unclear, inaccurate, or deliberately deceptive suggests a different attitude toward readers: one that is at best careless, at worst contemptuous. (A close examination of what are commonly referred to as *logical fallacies* will show that these are better understood as ethical dispositions rather than as lapses of logic.) Writers of fiction or poetry, to take a different kind of example, may write in ways that privilege other virtues, such as playfulness, opacity, or originality. These, too, speak to the writer's conception of the reader and therefore to the ethical considerations that follow when entering a relationship with another human being.

The understanding of writing as an act of ethical decision making unsettles conceptions of writing as solely instrumental, polemical, or aesthetic. Beyond these, writing is also and perhaps ultimately understood as an activity that engages us with others and thus with problems associated with the moral life: What shall I say? To whom do I speak? What obligations follow from my words? What are the consequences? Whether or not the writer voices such questions, they are inherent in the act of communicating with another (see 1.3, "Writing Expresses and Shares Meaning to be Reconstructed by the Reader").

When we see writing this way, as an activity involving ethical choices arising from the human relationship of writer and readers, we cross a threshold that both expands and complicates our understandings of what it means to write.

1.9

WRITING IS A TECHNOLOGY THROUGH WHICH WRITERS CREATE AND RECREATE MEANING
Collin Brooke and Jeffrey T. Grabill

I. A. Richards once observed, "A book is a machine to think with" (Richards 2001). While we may think about texts differently than we do our automobiles or kitchen appliances, there is something suggestive about Richards's comparison that is worth pursuing. Writing is a technology, and thinking of it in this fashion can be productive for both students and teachers of writing.

Writing has always been a technology for thinking and communicating. Early inscription technologies enabled the organization of social practices (like commerce), and innovations in the organization of writing itself, such as the emergence of the book, helped create new social relationships. Whether we are talking about sound waves, physical marks on a page, or pixels rendered on the screen of a computer, tablet, or phone, writing makes material some version of the thoughts and ideas of its composer (see 1.1, "Writing Is a Knowledge-Making Activity"). The audience for such writing must similarly devote material resources to understanding it, even if simply in the form of attention (see 1.2, "Writing Addresses, Invokes, and/or Creates Audiences"). Meaning doesn't just happen.

The tools we use to produce writing (pens, keyboards) and those media where writing takes place (pages, books, screens) are all a part of what we mean when we describe writing as a technology. Tools and media shape what we are able to write and the ideas we can express, and they condition the expectations of those who read our writing. We might describe these qualities as the affordances of particular technologies (and environments), those features that permit certain actions (while perhaps limiting others). Writing an essay on a computer, for example, affords certain actions, such as the quick erasure or manipulation of text from words to sentences to paragraphs. Media carry different affordances. We think little of seeing hashtags in a Twitter feed, for instance, but many of us would find it quite distracting to read a novel with such language practices. Likewise, the ability to click on a hashtag in a tweet (and to see all the posts tagged thusly) is not an affordance of the printed page.

With the emergence and diffusion of digital technologies, however, the impact of technology on the making of meaning has never been more visible, socially and culturally. The power of networks can perhaps be most easily understood in terms of connectivity: the ability to connect readers to writers, to turn anyone with a network connection into a publisher. Connectivity allows writers to access and participate more seamlessly and quickly with others and to distribute writing to large and widely dispersed audiences. Many writing technologies have streamlined the writing process, but the computer network has had a dramatic social impact. Consider, for example, platforms like Facebook and *Wikipedia*, arguably two of the most significant collaborative writing projects in human history. The affordances of particular writing technologies participate in the construction of new and changing rhetorical contexts.

Writers may prefer different tools and/or environments depending on their affordances, yet it has become more difficult to separate the scene of writing from the tools we use to produce it. This is because writing, as it always has been, is a technology for thinking, and so it may be the case that we interiorize the technology of writing itself to shape the possibilities for meaning.

References

Anson, Chris. 2010. "The Intradisciplinary Influence of Composition and WAC, 1967–1986." *WAC Journal* 21: 5–19.

Bakhtin, M. M. 1981. "Discourse in the Novel." In *The Dialogic Imagination*, edited by Michael Holquist. Translated by Caryl Emerson and Michael Holquist., 259–422. Austin: University of Texas Press.

Barton, David, and Mary Hamilton. 1998. *Local Literacies: Reading and Writing in One Community*. London: Routledge. http://dx.doi.org/10.4324/9780203448885.

Brodkey, Linda. 1994. "Writing on the Bias." College English 56 (5): 527–47.

Burke, Kenneth. 1966. "Definition of Man." In *Language as Symbolic Action: Essays on Life, Literature, and Method*, ed. Kenneth Burke, 3–24. Berkeley: University of California Press.

Flower, Linda, and John Hayes. 1980. "The Cognition of Discovery: Defining a Rhetorical Problem." *College Composition and Communication* 31 (1): 21–32.

Gould, Stephen J. 1981. *The Mismeasure of Man*. New York: W. W. Norton.

Hanson, F. Allan. 1993. *Testing Testing: Social Consequences of the Examined Life*. Berkeley: University of California Press.

Heath, Shirley Brice. 2012. *Words at Work and Play: Three Decades in Family and Community Life*. Cambridge: Cambridge University Press.

Lunsford, Andrea A. 1998. "Toward a Mestiza Rhetoric: Gloria Anzaldúa on Composition and Postcoloniality." *JAC: A Journal of Composition Theory* 18 (1): 1– 27.

Meyer, Jan H. F., and Ray Land. 2006. "Threshold Concepts and Troublesome Knowledge: An Introduction." In *Overcoming Barriers to Student Understanding*, edited by Jan H. F. Meyer and Ray Land, 3–18. London: Routledge.

Ong, Walter. 1975. "The Writer's Audience is Always a Fiction." *PMLA* 90 (1): 9–21.

Richards, I. A. 2001. *Principles of Literary Criticism*. 2nd ed. London: Routledge.

Russell, David R. 1995. "Activity Theory and Its Implications for Writing Instruction." In *Reconceiving Writing, Rethinking Writing Instruction*, edited by Joseph Petraglia, 51–77. Mahwah, NJ: Erlbaum.

Russell, David R. 1997. "Rethinking Genre in School and Society: An Activity Theory Analysis." *Written Communication* 14 (4): 504–54. http://dx.doi.org/10.1177/0741088 397014004004.

Saussure, Ferdinand de. 1983. *Course in General Linguistics*. Translated by Roy Harris. Chicago: Open Court.

Shafer-Landau, Russ, ed. 2007. *Ethical Theory: An Anthology*. Malden: Blackwell.

CONCEPT 2
Writing Speaks to Situations through Recognizable Forms

2.0
WRITING SPEAKS TO SITUATIONS
THROUGH RECOGNIZABLE FORMS
Charles Bazerman

A fundamental problem in communication precedes the choosing of any words or shaping of any message: identifying the situation we are in and the nature of the communication we wish to make. Are salespeople offering us a deal and do we want to accept? Are our acquaintances amusing each other with jokes and are we amused? Are our trusted advisors asking us to reconsider our behaviors and do we resist? The situation frames our understanding of the communicative action of others and gives us the urgency and motive to respond because somehow we sense our words will satisfy our needs in the situation or otherwise make the situation better for us. In face-to-face life, this problem is solved through our recognizing the geographic locale we are in, the people we are talking to, our relationship to them, the events unfolding before us, and our impulses to do something. Through long practical experience we learn to recognize spontaneously what appears to be going on around us and how it affects us. Our impulses to act communicatively emerge as doable actions in the situation, in forms recognizable to others—we accept the offer, we laugh at the joke, we agree to change. Conscious thought is warranted only if we have reason to believe things are not as they appear to be, if confusions arise within the situation, or if we want to suppress our first impulse and pursue a less obvious strategic path—laughing to appear congenial though we find the joke offensive.

Writing, as well, addresses social situations and audiences organized in social groups and does so through recognizable forms associated with those situations and social groups. But with writing we have fewer here-and-now clues about what the situation is, who our audiences are, and how we want to respond. Written messages can circulate from one material and social situation to another, and in fact are usually intended to.

DOI: 10.7330/9780874219906.c002

A newspaper report about events in one city is read in another, even in another country, and further events have evolved between writing and reading. A poem written for a small circle of friends is read centuries later in a literature classroom.

The technical concept of rhetorical situation brings together recognition of the specifics of the situation, the exigency the situation creates, and our perception that by communication we can make the situation better for ourselves (Bitzer 1968). Awareness of rhetorical situation is the beginning of reflection on how we perceive the situation, what more we can understand about it, how we can formulate our goals, and what strategies we may take in our utterances. It helps us put in focus what we can accomplish in a situation, how we can accomplish it, and what the stakes are. But this awareness also puts a reflective distance between our perception of the situation and our responses, which may disrupt spontaneous impulses and our sense of being in the moment. This disruption can thus can be troublesome and require a fundamental reorientation toward our experiences, which we may at first resist. Recognizing we are being accused of misdeeds may make us aware we need to answer but also aware that we must frame our words carefully so as to defend ourselves persuasively and so as not to lead to further trouble or accusations.

With writing, the need for understanding the rhetorical situation is even greater than in speaking because there are fewer material clues with which to locate ourselves spontaneously. To engage in a disciplinary discussion in chemistry, we not only need to know the chemistry, we need to know how each text is entering into a debate or accumulating past findings or projecting future plans (see 2.3, "Writing Is a Way of Enacting Disciplinarity"). It is through genre that we recognize the kinds of messages a document may contain, the kind of situation it is part of and it might migrate to, the kinds of roles and relations of writers and readers, and the kinds of actions realized in the document (see 1.2, "Writing Addresses, Invokes, and/or Creates Audiences," and 2.2, "Genres Are Enacted by Writers and Readers"). Genre recognition provides a necessary clue for locating and making sense of any piece of paper or any digital display that comes before our eyes. Perhaps even more complexly, we may need to understand how documents move from among and between spaces, including from real spaces to enduring virtual spaces, which then may return to specific material spaces. So, teachers may collect records of students within a classroom for immediate classroom-management needs, but these records then may enter the school records for school-management purposes and then may be combined with school medical and other records to create a file on the student, creating an enduring characterization of the student that may reappear in a court proceeding. Thus, to understand the full range of situations a document in a particular genre may be used in and the full set of meanings that might be attributed to it, we also need to understand the activity system it is part of (Russell 1997) (see 1.0, "Writing Is a Social and Rhetorical Activity," and 1.5, "Writing Mediates Activity").

Yet while writing may require more awareness of genres, the associated situations, and the activity systems those genres are part of, several factors limit conscious, reflective examination of genres and an understanding of their implications for the variability of writing. First, much learning of writing is in school, where stylized and repetitive classroom relations and situations, teacher authority, and student display of competence prevail. People often take school-based assumptions with them long after they leave school, associating writing with particular kinds of school assignments and finding their main motives to be avoiding correction and getting a good grade.

Later, after schooling, if they become deeply embedded in a set of writing practices associated with their profession or career, they may then assume, with little conscious attention to how complex and varied situations, exigencies, motives, and genres may be, that what they learn in that specific context are general rules and models for effective writing—with the result that they overgeneralize the practices they have learned. Further, they may think of the writing practices they develop through long professional experience to be part of their profession and may think of how they produce their texts as a matter of just doing good science, or being a good salesman, or knowing how to keep good records of what happens. Their writing knowledge, knowledge of situations, and sense of genres becomes deeply tacit and less accessible to conscious reflection. However, bringing such things to reflective attention through the concepts of rhetorical situation, genre, and activity systems is a necessary step to understanding their writing and making deeper choices.

2.1

WRITING REPRESENTS THE WORLD, EVENTS, IDEAS, AND FEELINGS

Charles Bazerman

It is no surprise to people that they can talk or write about things they see or do, what they feel, and what they think. But it is something of a surprise to realize that how each of these is represented in the writing or speaking—in other words, in the communication—changes what is shared about each of them and thus what our common knowledge is. I may think if I write about a mountain that the mountain is there for all to see, so the words I use are not that important. But when I realize that all my readers are likely to know of the mountain, particularly on a sunny early spring afternoon after an overnight snow storm ending in sleet so the crust breaks through unpredictably beneath the feet, is through the words I write, I begin to take greater care in choosing my words. I want to represent facts, the world, or my imaginings as precisely and power-fully as I can. We may resist this idea because we think the world and the meaning of our ideas are more robust than the words we choose, or because grappling with words is hard and frustrating work, and we may feel that our words are always a reduction, always lose something. That is indeed so. But because words are such thin and frail communicators, writers must work hard to make them do the best they can do.

A further troublesome corollary is that what we can share with each other through writing is limited by our ability to represent the world through language and the ability of our readers to make sense of our representations in ways congruent to our intentions (see 1.2, "Writing Addresses, Invokes, and/or Creates Audiences," and 1.3, "Writing Expresses and Shares Meanings to Be Reconstructed by the Reader"). Writers often have great ambitions about the effects and power of what they write and their ability to capture the truth of realities or conjure imagined realities, but they are constantly caught up short by what they can bring into shared reality through words. Recognizing the limita-tions of our representations can lead us to appropriate modesty and caution about what we and others write and about decisions and cal-culations made on the basis of the representations. Alfred Korzybski stated this concept vividly by noting "the map is not the territory" (Korzybski 1958, 58). Yet knowledge of this concept helps us work more effectively from our verbal maps in the way we view and contemplate the world represented.

Despite the limits of language, most of what we consider knowledge comes from the representation of the world and events in texts (see 1.1, "Writing Is a Knowledge-Making Activity"). Will Rogers famously said, "All I know is what I read in the newspapers." The humor and humil-ity in his statement are precisely in the recognition that most of our knowledge comes from the texts we read. If people don't share those texts (or other texts derivative of the primary representation), they don't share the knowledge. The recognition that different statements representing knowledge circulate in different groups does not mean all representations are equal, but it focuses our attention on the procedures and criteria by which these representations enter a communicative network and are evaluated, held accountable, and established as credible. People may resist this recognition as it destabilizes the absoluteness of knowledge and seems to undermine certainty of truth, but recognition of this concept provides a path to a more detailed understanding of how things reach the status of truth within different communities and the criteria by which truth is held. Knowing this can help us write more carefully and effectively to represent the world, events, and ideas credibly within and across communities and to discuss the representations of others in relation to the social worlds the knowledge circulates within.

2.2

GENRES ARE ENACTED BY WRITERS AND READERS

Bill Hart-Davidson

One of the more counterintuitive ideas in writing studies has to do with the nature of a genre—not just how the term is defined but also about what genres are. Common-sense notions of *genre* hold that that the term describes a form of discourse recognizable as a common set of structural or thematic qualities. People may speak about detective novels as a genre distinct from romance novels, for instance. We can also recognize nonliterary forms as genres, such as the scientific article.

In writing studies, though, the stabilization of formal elements by which we recognize genres is seen as the visible effects of human *action*, routinized to the point of habit in specific cultural conditions. The textual structures are akin to the fossil record left behind, evidence that writers have employed familiar discursive moves in accordance with reader expectations, institutional norms, market forces, and other social influences.

The idea that genres are enacted is associated most strongly, perhaps, with Carolyn Miller's argument in a 1984 article in the *Quarterly Journal of Speech* titled "Genres as Social Action." Miller's (1984) argument was influenced by Mikhail Bakhtin (1986), and has been developed over the last thirty years by a number of scholars studying writing in organizational settings such as David Russell (1991), Charles Bazerman (1988), and Catherine Schryer (1993), among many others.

This view holds that genres are habitual responses to recurring socially bounded situations. Regularities of textual form most lay people experience as the structural characteristics of genres emerge from these repeated instances of action and are reinforced by institutional power structures. Genres are constructions of groups, over time, usually with the implicit or explicit sanction of organizational or institutional power.

This view of genre has several interesting implications most newcomers to the idea find challenging and fascinating. One is that no single text is a genre; it can only be an instance of that genre as it enters into contexts (activity systems) where it might be taken up as such an instance. Readers and users of texts have as much to do with a text becoming an instance of a genre as writers do (see 1.2, "Writing Addresses, Invokes, and/or Creates Audiences,"). And because creating a genre is not something an individual writer does, but rather is the result of a series of socially mediated actions that accumulate over time, genres are only *relatively* stable. Generic forms are open to hybridization and change over time. This is why Schryer refers to the textual features of genres as "stable for now" forms, acknowledging that they can evolve.

JoAnneYates (1993) offers a fascinating historical account of this sort of genre hybridization in the context of the rise of American industrialization. In this account, we learn that standard features of genres, such as the header block of a business memo appearing in the upper left corner, become stable in use situations. When documents were stored in vertical stacks rather than in file cabinets, the memo block allowed for easy search and retrieval. This convention remains today even in email though we no longer need to flip through hard copies to find a message. As we might expect, the convention is less stable due to changes in the use context; users can choose to hide or minimize headers, for instance, in many email programs.

2.3

WRITING IS A WAY OF ENACTING DISCIPLINARITY
Neal Lerner

The central claim of this threshold concept is that disciplines shape—and in turn are shaped by—the writing that members of those disciplines do. In sum, the relationship between disciplinary knowledge making and the ways writing and other communicative practices create and communicate that knowledge are at the heart of what defines particular disciplines.

As an example of the relationship between writing and disciplinarity, consider the use of citations. On the most visible level, citation practices vary by discipline—and often within subdisciplines. Whether the practice is an author-last-name parenthetical system, author-last-name-plus-date parenthetical citation, footnotes, or numbered references, disciplinary distinctions are clearly marked, and readers in those disciplines have clear expectations for what type of citation formats they will encounter. Different formats also convey different disciplinary values. For example, formats that include the date in a parenthetical citation (e.g., APA) convey to readers that timeliness is important to that discipline; in contrast, formats that only include authors' last names (e.g., MLA) convey the value that references are timeless in certain ways.

Citation practices also enact disciplinarity on more subtle levels (see, e.g., Bazerman 1987; Connors 1999; Hyland 1999; Swales 1990). The mechanics used to introduce previously published work—for example, a parenthetical reference or footnote versus an attributive phrase—convey distinct disciplinary values. Citations tell us something about the discipline's values and practices while also recreating them by enacting them.

On a larger discourse level, any disciplinary genre speaks to the processes by which members of a discipline shape, make distinct, and value its forms and practices of knowledge creation and communication, and these processes, in turn, are shaped by the histories of those genres (see 2.0, "Writing Speaks to Situations through Recognizable Forms"). For example, the experimental report in science has evolved over several hundred years into the IMRD format—introduction, methods, results, discussion—an organizational scheme meant to mimic the scientific research process, particularly as that process has become more codified (Bazerman 1988). In contrast, while a short story also has specific features meant to function in specific ways for a specific disciplinary audience, readers would be hard pressed to confuse a short story with an experimental report. Many distinct disciplinary genres—e.g., legal briefs, SOAP notes, mathematical proofs—reflect the values those disciplines assign to particular kinds of evidence, particular forms of argument, and particular expectations for the transaction between readers and writers in particular rhetorical situations (see 2.0, "Writing Speaks to Situations through Recognizable Forms").

Of course, disciplinary boundaries can sometimes be quite fluid rather than fixed and stable. Such fluidity offers further evidence that disciplinary knowledge making is a social process and subject to changing norms, practices, and technologies (Thaiss and Zawacki 2006; also see 1.9 "Writing Is a Technology through Which Writers Create and Recreate Meaning"). Ultimately, writers and readers come to writing in their disciplines with histories, intentions, and expectations, all shaping the disciplines themselves and, in turn, shaping the writing that members of those disciplines do.

2.4

ALL WRITING IS MULTIMODAL

Cheryl E. Ball and Colin Charlton

Multimodal means "multiple + mode." In contemporary writing studies, a mode refers to a way of meaning making, or communicating. The
New London Group (NLG) outlines five modes through which meaning
is made: linguistic, aural, visual, gestural, and spatial. Any combination
of modes makes a multimodal text, and all texts—every piece of communication a human composes—use more than one mode. Thus, all
writing is multimodal (New London Group 1996).

Historically, rhetoric and composition studies is often assumed to
focus on writing (and sometimes speech) as solely alphanumeric-based
communication—what the NLG would label as part of the linguistic
mode of communication. The term *mode*, within this historical perception, was reserved for defining the rhetorical modes of exposition,
argumentation, description, and narration. In multimodal theory, the
definition of *mode* is complicated to distribute equal emphasis on how
meanings are created, delivered, and circulated through choices in
design, material composition, tools and technologies, delivery systems,
and interpretive senses (see 1.3, "Writing Expresses and Shares Meaning
to Be Reconstructed by the Reader," and 1.9, "Writing Is a Technology
through Which Writers Create and Recreate Meaning"). That is, *mode*
isn't just words (in the linguistic sense of NLG's framework) but sound,
texture, movement, and all other communicative acts that contribute to
the making of meaning.

While the concept of multimodality has enjoyed increased circulation since the turn of the twenty-first century and has been associated
with new media or new technologies, rhetoric and composition's historic approach to the teaching of writing has almost always included
the production of multimodal texts. This understanding can be traced
from classical rhetorical studies of effective speech design including
body and hand gestures to current concerns with infographics and
visual rhetorics.

With this context in mind, there are still two major misconceptions
associated with multimodality. First, some assume all multimodal texts
are digital. While it's true that most writing and design work in the
twenty-first century is mediated through digital technologies such as
computers, smartphones, or tablets, many texts that might be produced
with digital technologies aren't necessarily distributed with digital technologies (e.g., posters, flyers, brochures, memos, some reports, receipts,

magazines, books, scholarly print-based articles, etc.). In addition, many texts are not digital in their production *or* distribution ('zines, paintings, scrapbooks, etc.).

Second, some assume that the opposite of multimodal is monomodal. In fact, there is no such thing as a monomodal text. This assumption is a throwback to the romantic version of writing as focusing solely on alphanumeric textual production and analysis and is often used by scholar-teachers new to multimodal theory as a way to distinguish between "old" ways of researching and teaching writing and "new," multimodal ways (see the discussion of writing and disciplinarity in 2.3, "Writing Is a Way of Enacting Disciplinarity"). An example of a text often referred to as being monomodal is the traditional first-year-composition research essay (see 2.0, "Writing Speaks to Situations through Recognizable Forms"). Yet such a text is recognized from its linguistic mode and its visual and spatial arrangement on the page (title, name block, double spacing, margins, default font size, formulaic structure, etc.).

Monomodality, then, is used (incorrectly) to signify a lack of multiple media or modes when really what a user might mean is that a structure like a five-paragraph essay *privileges* the linguistic mode over the spatial or visual modes. Thus, writing as a knowledge-making activity (see 2.0, "Writing Speaks to Situations through Recognizable Forms") isn't limited to understanding writing as a single mode of communication but as a multimodal, performative (see 1.5, "Writing Mediates Activity," and 2.5, "Writing Is Performative") activity that takes place within any number of genres (see 2.2, "Genres Are Enacted by Writers and Readers") and disciplines.

2.5

WRITING IS PERFORMATIVE
Andrea A. Lunsford

Students are sometimes puzzled by the notion that writing is performative. Yet some discussion usually clarifies the concept as students quickly see that their writing performs for a grade or other reward for an audience of academics (mostly teachers; see 1.7, "Assessing Writing Shapes Contexts and Instruction"). In these pieces of writing, students might adopt a role or persona—of the "good student," for example. But writing is performative in other important senses as well. Kenneth Burke's concept of "language as symbolic action" helps explain why (Burke 1966). For Burke and other contemporary theorists, language and writing have the capacity to act, to do things in the world. Speech act theorists such as J. L. Austin (1962) speak of "performatives," by which they mean spoken phrases or sentences that constitute an action: a judge saying "I now pronounce you husband and wife" or "I sentence you to X" actually performs these acts. Other examples ("I bequeath" in a will or "I name this ship the Enterprise") carry such performativity (see 2.6, "Texts Get Their Meaning from Other Texts").

But we can see other ways in which writing performs: from the Declaration of Independence to the petition that results in a change of policy to a Kickstarter site whose statements are so compelling that they elicit spontaneous donations, writing has the capacity to perform. At its most basic, saying that writing is performative means that writing *acts*, that it can make things happen. This is what students in the Stanford Study of Writing, a longitudinal exploration of writing development during the college years, meant when they told researchers over and over again that "good writing is writing that makes something good happen in the world."

There is yet a third way in which writing can be said to be performative, and that is in relation to another threshold concept, that writing is *epistemic*. That is to say that writing does not simply record thought or knowledge but rather that writing has the capacity to actually produce thought and knowledge (see 3.0, "Writing Enacts and Creates Identities and Ideologies"). Most writers have experienced this performative aspect of writing—a time when you are writing away and the writing suddenly gives rise to new ideas, new insights into your topic. In the moment of producing such insights, writing is, again, performative.

2.6
TEXTS GET THEIR MEANING FROM OTHER TEXTS
Kevin Roozen

If I were to ask a writer or reader what the text in front of her means, it would be easy to assume that *text* refers only to the text immediately at hand. This assumption, though, overlooks the fact that whatever meaning a writer or reader makes of a particular text is not a result of their engagements with that particular text alone. Rather than existing as autonomous documents, texts always refer to other texts and rely heavily on those texts to make meaning. Although we commonly refer to *a* text or *the* text, texts are profoundly intertextual in that they draw meaning from a network of other texts. As a field, writing studies has developed a number of names for the networks of texts writers and readers create and act with, including *landscapes, sets, systems, ecologies, assemblages, repertoires,* and *intertexts.*

Some of the texts that contribute to the creation of meaning—for both writers and readers—are those that already exist. Thomas Jefferson's crafting of the Declaration of Independence, for example, was informed explicitly and implicitly by a vast network of previous texts that included Locke's writings on social contract theory, resolutions written by the First Continental Congress and other political bodies, political pamphlets, newspaper articles, a colonial play, the writings of Euripides, and the drafts and revisions offered by other members of Congress. Writers and readers rely on these kinds of intertextual linkages to make meaning of all kinds of texts. Children reading *Winnie the Pooh* for the first time might think about other books they have read or that have been read to them about forests, stuffed bears, or animals. Shoppers jotting grocery lists might rely on previous lists they have created and used or seen others use. Insurance processors adjusting claims might draw upon their previous encounters with the particular forms they need to read and fill out. Other texts drawn into an intertextual network are those the reader or writer might anticipate acting with in the future. A student taking notes while attempting to understand a philosophy text might also be thinking toward the essay exam at the end of the semester. A Supreme Court justice writing an opinion likely to be challenged in the future might craft it in a way that heads off particular legal arguments but leaves open others. The meaning writers and readers work to make of a given text at hand, then, is a function of the interplay of texts from their near and distant pasts as well as their anticipated futures.

Texts even rely upon a range of nonwritten texts. Readers and writers, for example, might draw upon visual images as they engage with a focal text. The child's reading of *Winnie the Pooh* might be informed by pictures or video images she has seen of the characters and scenes from the book. The shopper might use the images on coupons as a way to remember which items to include on next week's grocery list. Texts might also be linked to inscriptions such as charts, diagrams, and tables. Adjusting the insurance claim might involve the processor in looking up pricing data in a set of Excel charts, creating a digital drawing of an automobile accident, or interpreting schematics of automobile parts. Texts might also emerge from instances of talk. The philosophy student's notes, for example, might include comments offered by classmates during a class discussion or by a roommate. In drafting an opinion, the Supreme Court justice might draw upon conversations with clerks or with other justices.

The concept of texts getting their meaning from other texts may conflict with dominant Western notions of authorship, creativity, and originality, but it is an important one for a number of stakeholders. For teachers, recognizing that texts work in conjunction with other texts is a key first step toward creating opportunities for students to engage with a wide variety of texts, perhaps even ones that might not be privileged in formal educational settings. It is also a key step toward teachers acknowledging, valuing, and fostering connections with the different kinds of texts that animate learners' lives beyond the classroom. For learners, recognizing that texts get their meaning from other texts is the first step toward thinking carefully and creatively about how forging and reconfiguring linkages to other texts and even other contexts can shift meaning in ways both subtle and profound. This realization, in turn, can lead learners toward strategies for writing and reading that foreground the role of other texts. For administrators, conceptualizing the intertextual nature of writing and reading provides the foundation for thinking carefully and systematically about the kinds of texts learners need to encounter at particular points throughout the curriculum. For writing researchers, recognizing the intertextual nature of meaning making is the vital first step toward developing theoretical perspectives and methodological approaches for tracing the textual connections persons and collectives employ in the continual making and remaking of knowledge, selves, and societies.

References

Austin, J. L. 1962. *How to Do Things with Words*. Oxford: Clarendon Press.

Bakhtin, M. M. 1986. "The Problem of Speech Genres." In *Speech Genres and Other Late Essays*, edited by Caryl Emerson and Michael Holquist. Translated by Vernon W. McGee, 60–102. Austin: University of Texas Press.

Bazerman, Charles. 1987. "Codifying the Social Scientific Style: The APA Publication Manual as a Behaviorist Rhetoric." In *The Rhetoric of the Human Sciences*, edited by John Nelson, Allan Megill, and Donald McCloskey, 125–44. Madison: University of Wisconsin Press.

Bazerman, Charles. 1988. *Shaping Written Knowledge: The Genre and Activity of the Experimental Article in Science*. Madison: University of Wisconsin Press.

Bitzer, Lloyd F. 1968. "The Rhetorical Situation." *Philosophy & Rhetoric* 1 (1): 1–14.

Burke, Kenneth. 1966. *Language as Symbolic Action*. Berkeley: University of California Press.

Connors, Robert J. 1999. "The Rhetoric of Citation Systems: Part 2, Competing Epistemic Values in Citation." *Rhetoric Review* 17 (2): 219–45. http://dx.doi.org/10.1080/07350 199909359242.

Hyland, Ken. 1999. "Academic Attribution: Citation and the Construction of Disciplinary Knowledge." *Applied Linguistics* 20 (3): 341–67. http://dx.doi.org/10.1093/applin /20.3.341.

Korzybski, Alfred. 1958. *Science and Sanity: An Introduction to Non-Aristotelian Systems and General Semantics.* Brooklyn: Institute of General Semantics.

Miller, Carolyn. 1984. "Genre as Social Action." *Quarterly Journal of Speech* 70 (2): 151–67. http://dx.doi.org/10.1080/00335638409383686.

New London Group. 1996. "A Pedagogy of Multiliteracies: Designing Social Futures." *Harvard Educational Review* 66 (1). http://wwwstatic.kern.org/filer/blogWrite44ManilaWebsite/paul/articles/A_Pedagogy_of_Multiliteracies_Designing_Social_Futures .htm.

Russell, David R. 1991. *Writing in the Academic Disciplines, 1870–1990: A Curricular History.* Carbondale: Southern Illinois University Press.

Russell, David R. 1997. "Rethinking Genre in School and Society: An Activity Theory Analysis." *Written Communication* 14 (4): 504–54. http://dx.doi.org/10.1177/0741088 397014004004.

Schryer, Catherine F. 1993. "Records as Genre." *Written Communication* 10 (2): 200–34. http://dx.doi.org/10.1177/0741088393010002003.

Swales, John. 1990. *Genre Analysis: English in Academic and Research Settings.* Cambridge: Cambridge University Press.

Thaiss, Chris, and Terri Zawacki. 2006. *Engaged Writers, Dynamic Disciplines.* Portsmouth: Heinemann, Boynton/Cook.

Yates, JoAnne. 1993. *Control through Communication: The Rise of System in American Management.* Vol. 6. Baltimore: Johns Hopkins University Press.

CONCEPT 3
Writing Enacts and Creates Identities and Ideologies

3.0

WRITING ENACTS AND CREATES IDENTITIES AND IDEOLOGIES
Tony Scott

An ideology is a system of ideas and beliefs that together constitute a comprehensive worldview. We make sense of the world around us *through* the ideologies to which we have been exposed and conditioned. Ideologies are both formed and sustained by a variety of factors, including religions, economic systems, cultural myths, languages, and systems of law and schooling. A common assumption in humanities theory and research is that there is no ideology-free observation or thought. Our conceptions of everything—gender identities and roles, people's proper social statuses, what it means to love, the proper basis for separating what is true from what is false—are inescapably shaped by ideologies. To be immersed in any culture is to learn to see the world through the ideological lenses it validates and makes available to us. Writing is always ideological because discourses and instances of language use do not exist independently from cultures and their ideologies.

Linguist James Paul Gee points out that those who seek to create any education program in reading and writing must ask a question: "What sort of social group do I intend to apprentice the learner into?" (Gee 2008, 48). This seemingly innocent question is actually quite loaded because it starts from the premise that there is no general literacy: literacy is always in some way involved in the negotiation of identities and ideologies in specific social situations. Vocabularies, genres, and language conventions are a part of what creates and distinguishes social groups, and thus learning to write is always ongoing, situational, and involving cultural and ideological immersion. This thinking represents a fundamental shift in how many writing scholars now see literacy education, from a view that is individualistic and focused on the acquisition of discrete, universal skills to one that is situated and focused on social involvement and consequences (see 1.0, "Writing Is a Social and

DOI: 10.7330/9780874219906.c003

Rhetorical Activity"). Writers are not separate from their writing and they don't just quickly and seamlessly adapt to new situations. Rather, writers are socialized, changed, through their writing in new environments, and these changes can have deep implications. For instance, when students learns to write convincingly as undergraduate college students in an introductory writing class, they enact that identity based on their reading of the expected and acceptable social norms. So in their writing, they might be inquisitive, deliberative, and given to founding their opinions on careful reasoning and research. In displaying these characteristics in their writing, they enact an identity in response to social expectations for who they are and what they should be doing.

This social view of ideology in writing studies has been influenced by the work of Lev Vygotsky (1978) and Mikhail Bakhtin (1986). Drawing on research on language acquisition in children, Vygotsky described how external speech becomes internalized and then comes to frame how we think, self-identify, and act in the world. As we are immersed in discourses through reading and dialogue with others, we begin to name and understand *through* those discourses, internalizing the ideologies they carry. Indeed, language learning and use is a primary means through which ideologies are conveyed, acquired, and made to seem "natural," without obvious alternatives or need of explanation. As ideological activity, writing is deeply involved in struggles over power, the formation of identities, and the negotiation, perpetuation, and contestation of belief systems. We can see obvious ideological tensions all around us in public political discourse: Do you use *climate change* or *global warming*? Does the United States have an issue with "illegals" or "undocumented immigrants"? Perhaps less obvious but highly consequential examples are embedded in everyday writing. In writing in professional contexts, for instance, writers can gain credibility and persuasive power through showing they understand and share the beliefs and values that are commonplace, and markers of fuller socialization, within their professions. When lawyers write effective briefs, or engineers write technical reports, the genres, conventions, and vocabularies they use reflect the ideologies of their professions and settings.

The research-driven shift toward this cultural, ideological view of writing creates tensions with the structures and practices that continue to prevail in many educational institutions. The first-year writing requirement, for instance, was historically based on the premise that writing is a universal skill set and singular discourse individuals can master if they are determined and taught well. In this view, literacy is an ideologically neutral tool, a stable, transposable set of codes and conventions that can be acquired and then deployed in virtually any setting. Writing is thus seen as separate from other learning, from ideological differences and struggle, and from the socialization processes that operate in learning environments. Required writing courses and gatekeeping assessments that similarly purport to certify generic literate readiness have been placed at thresholds to higher education based on these assumptions.

The understanding that writing is an ideological, socially involved practice and thus inescapably implicated in identity making has vexed the project of writing education and the institutional structures that facilitate it—like first-year writing and placement tests. In scholarship in rhetoric and composition, much conversation has centered on "academic writing" because educating students to be proficient academic writers continues to be a common goal for postsecondary writing classes. Writing researchers have investigated how institutional projects of teaching academic writing have historically situated students in relation to literacy according to unacknowledged ideological assumptions. When we seek to "apprentice" students into academic writing, what ideological imperatives are being asserted in the ways we choose to conceive of academic writers and writing? Other researchers have positioned writing within sites of complicated ideological exchange and struggle as their research considers writing and writers in relation to diaspora, race, global economics and the consciousnesses, social statuses and embodied histories of writers. This work explores the ways conventions, meanings, power, identities—even notions of the functions and authority of authorship and texts—are culturally produced and socially negotiated.

Among professional educators in writing studies, awareness of writing as ideological enactment has led to efforts to understand and take responsibility for the ideological assumptions and consequences of pedagogical practices.

3.1

WRITING IS LINKED TO IDENTITY

Kevin Roozen

Common perceptions of writing tend to cast it as the act of encoding or inscribing ideas in written form. To view writing in this manner, though, overlooks the roles writing plays in the construction of self. Through writing, writers come to develop and perform identities in relation to the interests, beliefs, and values of the communities they engage with, understanding the possibilities for selfhood available in those communities (see 3.0, "Writing Enacts and Creates Identities and Ideologies"). The act of writing, then, is not so much about using a particular set of skills as it is about becoming a particular kind of person, about developing a sense of who we are.

Our identities are the ongoing, continually under-construction product of our participation in a number of engagements, including those from our near and distant pasts and our potential futures. Given that our participation with our multiple communities involves acting with their texts, writing serves as a key means by which we act with and come to understand the subject matter, the kinds of language, the rhetorical moves, the genres, the media and technologies, and the writing processes and practices at play in our various sites of engagement, as well as the beliefs, values, and interests they reflect (see 1.0, "Writing Is a Social and Rhetorical Activity"). Writing, then, functions as a key form of socialization as we learn to become members of academic disciplines (see 3.4, "Disciplinary and Professional Identities Are Constructed through Writing"), professions, religious groups, community organizations, political parties, families, and so on.

Writing also functions as a means of displaying our identities. Through the writing we do, we claim, challenge, perhaps even contest and resist, our alignment with the beliefs, interests, and values of the communities with which we engage. The extent to which we align ourselves with a particular community, for example, can be gauged by the extent to which we are able and willing to use that community's language, make its rhetorical moves, act with its privileged texts, and participate in its writing processes and practices. As we develop identities aligned with the interests and values of the communities in which we participate, we become more comfortable making the rhetorical and generic moves privileged by those communities.

Understanding the identity work inherent in writing is important for many stakeholders. For teachers and learners, it foregrounds the need to approach writing not simply as a means of learning and using a set of skills, but rather as a means of engaging with the possibilities for selfhood available in a given community. It also means recognizing that the difficulties people have with writing are not necessarily due to a lack of intelligence or a diminished level of literacy but rather to whether they can see themselves as participants in a particular community. For administrators, this threshold concept highlights the demand for structuring the curriculum in ways that allow learners to develop a sense of what it means to become a member of an academic discipline and creating models of assessment that address learners' identity work. For researchers interested in literate activity, it underscores the importance of theoretical perspectives and methodological approaches that make visible the construction of self.

3.2

WRITERS' HISTORIES, PROCESSES, AND IDENTITIES VARY

Kathleen Blake Yancey

Although human beings often seem to share histories, engage in similar composing processes, and have identities that are at the core human, each writer is unique: indeed, each writer is a combination of the collective set of different dimensions and traits and features that make us human.

Writers, developing in the contexts of family, schooling, and culture, continue that development as they write in increasingly multiple and varying contexts—of larger personal relationship structures, in workplace sites, in the civic sphere, and in cultural contexts that themselves are always changing. Initially, as children learning language and writing—a process that continues throughout our lives—people write their ways into a "variety of complex, interwoven social systems" (Brown and Duguid 2000, 140). In the process, each writer begins a lifelong process of balancing individual perspectives and processes with the opportunities, demands, constraints, and genres of specific rhetorical situations and contexts of the larger culture. The ways in which individual writers do this, however, are influenced by their individual histories, processes, and identities.

Writers' identities are, in part, a function of the time when they live: their histories, identities, and processes are situated in a given historical context. Millennia ago, before formal schooling provided instruction in composing, writers employed their own composing processes, drawing on caves, composing hieroglyphics for tombstones, and writing petroglyphs on the walls of canyons. Later, as formal schooling developed in various parts of the world, male children in the upper classes were *instructed* in the art of writing, in the west, for example, learning, in part through a rhetoric keyed to the civic sphere, the five canons of rhetoric: invention, memory, arrangement, style, and delivery. In more recent times, as our knowledge about writing has deepened, we have understood that composing processes also vary according to at least three factors—the individual writer, the genre being composed, and the rhetorical situation. This new knowledge has also shaped understandings about the invention, drafting, reviewing, revising, editing, and publishing of composing. Likewise, although composition has been a school subject in the US university for over a century, the development of models of composing in the 1970s and 1980s, based in the practices of writers, changed the teaching of writing: teachers have shifted from teaching writing through analysis of others' texts to teaching writing through engaging students in composing itself.

Equally important, as composing becomes increasingly digitized and people worldwide learn to compose in multiple spaces and with multiple devices without any formal instruction (Yancey 2004), we are reminded that school is merely one historical context; there are many. In addition, because of the multiple affordances of digital technologies, composers routinely work with images, sounds, and video, as well as with words, to make meaning, and in using these materials to make meaning, individual writers are able to express their own identities and histories.

Writers' identities vary as well, in part through individual and collective identity markers such as gender, race, class, sexual orientation, and physical abilities; in part through individuals' relationships with family and friends; and in part through experiences that both attract and influence identity. Writing itself, especially through genres, also anticipates and, to a certain extent, enforces an identity.

The threshold concept that writers' histories, processes, and identities vary is troublesome because it speaks to the complexity of composing itself and to the complexity of the task of helping students learn to compose. People who want the teaching of writing to be uniform—mapped across grade levels, for instance, with all students inventing in the same way, drafting in the same way, and using the same language—find this threshold concept frustrating, in part because they had hoped a single approach would enfranchise all writers; the failure of such an approach speaks to the differentiation of composing itself given writers' histories and identities. The variation in students' composing processes, like the variation in their histories and identities, thus makes the teaching of writing a complex, sophisticated task. At the same time, it's worth noting the inherently paradoxical nature of writing—that we write as both individuals and as social beings, and that helping writers mature requires helping them write to others while expressing themselves. Put another way, writing is paradoxical because of its provision both for the social and the conventional and for the individual: individuals participating in multiple contexts account for social aspects of writing (see 2.0, "Writing Speaks to Situations through Recognizable Forms," and 4.3, "Learning to Write Effectively Requires Different Kinds of Practice, Time, and Effort"), and at the same time writing is located in an individual who is necessarily distinct (see 4.1, "Text Is an Object Outside of One's Self that Can Be Improved and Developed," and 5.1, "Writing Is an Expression of Embodied Cognition"). In addition, neither writers nor their contexts are static: both change over time, which introduces yet another source of variation and which also means that variation is the normal situation for composing and composers.

3.3

WRITING IS INFORMED BY PRIOR EXPERIENCE

Andrea A. Lunsford

If no one is an island, as poet John Donne famously argued, then no writing is isolated and alone either. Writing is, first of all, always part of a larger network or conversation; all writing is in some sense a response to other writing or symbolic action. Even when writing is private or meant for the writer alone, it is shaped by the writer's earlier interactions with writing and with other people and with all the writer has read and learned. Such interactions form a network or conversation that comes from knowledge and from all the experience the writer has had. Here's an example that may help to illuminate this claim: for over two decades, I asked people all over the United States to recall their earliest memories of writing. Many described learning to write their own names: that act seems to signal a significant moment in cognitive and emotional development. But others—left-handers, for example—reported something painful associated with writing: being made to sit on their left hands so they had to write right-handed. Many others spoke of being made to write "I will not X" a hundred times in punishment for some mistake; still others remembered being ridiculed or somehow humiliated for something they had or had not written. For many people, it turned out, prior experience with writing had been negative, and this attitude and these feelings went with them throughout their lives so that they dreaded writing or felt inadequate when faced with a writing task. Luckily, such associations or prior experiences can be mitigated or changed, and that often happens as writers become more confident or encounter more positive experiences with writing. But those early experiences can still linger on.

In addition to drawing on memories of writing, writers also draw on personal knowledge and lived experience in creating new texts (see 2.2, "Genres Are Enacted by Writers and Readers"; 2.3, "Writing Is a Way of Enacting Disciplinarity"; and 2.6, "Texts Get Their Meaning from Other Texts"). Assigned to write an essay, for example, writers summon up the features of an essay they've used in the past or learned about by reading and talking about the essay genre. Likewise, a student writing an argument draws on prior knowledge or experience with producing such a text, including perhaps how to organize an argument for maximum effect. Other writers may draw on something written in the past for a new purpose.

In some instances, prior knowledge and experience are necessary and often helpful; in others they can work against writers. When writers call on strategies they have used before when approaching a new writing task, those strategies may or may not work well in the current situation. In studying college student writers' responses to first-year assignments, for example, Linda Flower found that students tended to rely on a strategy she called "gist and list" (essentially making a point [the gist] and then listing a series of supporting statements) whether that strategy was an effective one or not (Flower et al. 1990). When writers can identify how elements of one writing situation are similar to elements of another, their prior knowledge helps them out in analyzing the current rhetorical situation. But when they simply rely on a strategy or genre or convention out of habit, that prior knowledge may not be helpful at all.

3.4
DISCIPLINARY AND PROFESSIONAL IDENTITIES ARE CONSTRUCTED THROUGH WRITING
Heidi Estrem

While people can negotiate how identities are constructed through writing in a variety of contexts (see 3.1, "Writing Is Linked to Identity"), many first encounter unfamiliar disciplinary (or professional) discourse in college. In most American colleges and universities in the United States, students complete-general education courses (introductory courses designed to introduce students to both ways of thinking and disciplinary perspectives within the university) before continuing on to specialized courses within their chosen disciplines or fields. This increasingly discipline-specific learning process involves both the simple acquisition of new knowledge and an "expansion and transformation of identity, of a learner's 'sense of self'" (Meyer and Land 2006, 11). Writing—as a means of thinking, a form of inquiry and research, and a means for communication within a discipline—plays a critical role in that identity transformation and expansion. Disciplines have particular ways of asking and investigating questions enacted through and demonstrated in writing; teachers or researchers demonstrate their memberships in disciplines by using writing in ways validated by disciplines. It is thus through writing that disciplines (and writers [see 2.3, "Writing is a Way of Enacting Disciplinarity"]) are both enacted and encountered by writers—first as students, and then as professionals throughout their careers.

Identities are complex expressions and embodiments of who someone is (see 3.1, "Writing Is Linked to Identity"). For many students in college encountering disciplinary writing for the first time, discipline-specific writing threatens their sense of self because these ways of thinking and writing are so distinct from other more familiar reading and writing practices, such as those valued at home or in other communities in which the students are members (see 3.0, "Writing Enacts and Creates Identities and Ideologies," and 3.5, "Writing Provides a Representation of Ideologies and Identities"). As writers continue to work in the academy and beyond, they negotiate (and challenge) disciplinary identities via writing, finding ways to traverse the differing implicit and explicit writing expectations. The process of learning to manage these tensions contributes to the formation of new identities, for as people progress through their major discipline(s), writing increasingly complex texts in the process, they are also writing themselves into the discipline(s) (see 2.3, "Writing Is a Way of Enacting Disciplinarity"). That process of identity formation is interwoven with learning the writing conventions, practices, habits, and approaches of their discipline.

For many people, the idea that writing is not merely a matter of recording one's research or thoughts, but is in fact a process linked to the development of new, professional identities, is troublesome. Writing can appear to be an act of transcription or representation of processes, not an expression of identity. Many prevalent descriptions of the relationship between writing and research neutralize and generalize disciplinary or professional writing into a last step in the research project, one in which research results are "written up" (see 1.0, "Writing Is a Social and Rhetorical Activity," and 1.1, "Writing Is a Knowledge-Making Activity"). Approaching disciplinary writing as an act of identity and affiliation illuminates how writing in new contexts is not only about learning abstract conventions but also about learning how to *be* within a group with social conventions, norms, and expectations (see 3.0, "Writing Enacts and Creates Identities and Ideologies").

3.5

WRITING PROVIDES A REPRESENTATION
OF IDEOLOGIES AND IDENTITIES

Victor Villanueva

Writing provides a means whereby identities are discovered and constituted. Yet those are never clear cut. We carry many identities, choosing to foreground one (or some) over others depending on the context, the audience, and the rhetorical task at hand (see 3.2, "Writers' Histories, Processes, and Identities Vary"). If I am writing to a school board about a new policy, for example, I will likely foreground my identity as a parent. If I am writing about writing, as I am here, I will foreground my identity as a professor of writing and rhetoric. In like manner, we also carry any number of political identities, identities that reflect particular ideological predispositions. We can write as a liberal or a conservative, as a woman recognizing particular power dynamics, as a person of color. Identity politics—the idea that one's self-defined identities drive one's choices as they engage in discussions, actions, and interactions—entails a conscious decision by the individual to enter into what critical theorist Gyatri Spivak (1987) terms a "strategic essentialism," a reduction of complex political and economic relations in order to present a political statement.

Identity politics tends toward the construction of a single identity. But we know that identit*ies* are multifaceted. One can be liberal on social issues but a conservative on fiscal issues. None of us is ideologically "pure." Or one can be a gay man of color, wherein sets of different conflicts and different power relations can occur. Even as there is a great deal of value to identity politics, then, when writing from an overtly political or cultural position there is a risk in identity politics of reducing cultures, races, ethnicities, genders, sexualities, or class relations to their "natures," especially when writers do this as they imagine their audiences and their identities.

There are limits to what can be anticipated about what readers know, assume, or believe. To write from the position of one who is "color blind," for example, could be read as a denial of complex histories and current hierarchical differences in power and economic relations. To write about a gay relationship in terms of husbands and wives is to maintain conventional conceptions of gender roles. In other words, because all writing is inflected by power dynamics shaped by identities and ideologies, writers must become aware of the how those identities and ideologies are represented in their writing.

Compositionist James Berlin (1987) points to a way in which representation can be brought into the writing classroom. In his taxonomies of epistemological assumptions about writing, he provides essentially three conceptions of how writing can be seen to work: as reflective, a mirror of an objective reality; as intentional, conveying what an author intends so that the reader's job is to discern that intention; or as or constructed, so that there is a negotiation within the writer with his or her ways of seeing the world and a negotiation within the reader between his or her own worldviews and the perceived worldviews of the writer. Students (maybe even most nonspecialists) accept the first two assumptions, that writing is transparent and/or that it conveys exactly what a writer meant to say. A "pedagogy of representation" (Giroux 1994) disrupts these two perceptions and asks students to do the critical work of discovering the kinds of cultural, political, and economic assumptions contained within their own writing and within popular culture. Guiding questions would be what's being said? and what's left unsaid? These two simple questions can begin to uncover the power dynamics contained in all writing.

References

Bakhtin, M. M. . 1986. *Speech Genres and Other Late Essays*. Austin: University of Texas Press.

Berlin, James. 1987. *Rhetoric and Reality*. Carbondale: Southern Illinois University Press.

Brown, John Seely, and Paul Duguid. 2000. *The Social Life of Information*. Boston, MA: Harvard Business School Press.

Flower, Linda, Victoria Stein, John Ackerman, Margaret J. Kantz, Kathleen McCormick, and Wayne C. Peck. 1990. *Reading-to-Write: Exploring a Cognitive and Social Process*. New York: Oxford University Press.

Gee, James Paul. 2008. *Social Linguistics and Literacies: Ideology in Discourses*. 3rd ed. New York: Routledge.

Giroux, Henry A. 1994. "Living Dangerously: Identity Politics and the New Cultural Racism." In *Between Borders: Pedagogy and the Politics of Cultural Studies*, edited by Henry A. Giroux and Peter McLaren, 1–27. New York: Routledge.

Meyer, Jan H. F., and Ray Land. 2006. *Overcoming Barriers to Student Understanding: Threshold Concepts and Troublesome Knowledge*. London: Routledge.

Spivak, Giyatri. 1987. *In Other Worlds: Essays in Cultural Politics*. London: Taylor and Francis.

Vygotsky, L. S. 1978. *Mind in Society: The Development of Higher Psychological Processes*. Cambridge: Harvard University Press.

Yancey, Kathleen Blake. 2004. "Made Not Only in Words: Composition in a New Key." *College Composition and Communication* 56 (2): 297–328. http://dx.doi.org/10.2307/4140651.

CONCEPT 4
All Writers Have More to Learn

4.0

ALL WRITERS HAVE MORE TO LEARN

Shirley Rose

Many people assume that all writing abilities can be learned once and for always. However, although writing is learned, all writers always have more to learn about writing.

The ability to write is not an innate trait humans are born possessing. Humans are "symbol-using (symbol-making, symbol-misusing) animals," and writing is symbolic action, as Kenneth Burke has explained (Burke 1966, 16). Yet learning to write requires conscious effort, and most writers working to improve their effectiveness find explicit instruction in writing to be more helpful than simple trial and error without the benefit of an attentive reader's response. Often, one of the first lessons writers learn, one that may be either frustrating or inspiring, is that they will never have learned all that can be known about writing and will never be able to demonstrate all they do know about writing.

Writers soon discover that writing strategies that are effective for them in one context are often inappropriate and ineffective in another context in which they need or want to write; even when strategies work, writers still struggle to figure out what they want to say and how to say it. They struggle because writing is not just transcribing preformed ideas but also developing new ones; thus a writer never becomes a perfect writer who already knows how to write anything and everything. This difficulty and imperfectability of writing, and the fact that it is not a "natural" phenomenon (see 1.6, "Writing Is Not Natural") is one reason formal writing instruction is typical of schooling in the United States at all levels. But learning about writing doesn't happen only in school. For example, James Gee (2004) showed how a teenage writer of fan fiction learned about writing outside school through the practice, advice, and modeling provided by her online community of other writers. Likewise, instruction in writing does not necessarily end when formal schooling ends. Writers encounter new

DOI: 10.7330/9780874219906.c004

contexts, genres, tasks, and audiences as they move among workplaces and communities beyond formal schooling, and these new contexts call for new kinds of writing.

With experience, writers do discover that some writing habits developed in one context can be helpful in another. For example, habits such as writing multiple drafts or setting aside regular, frequent periods for writing in a place free of distractions often prove effective regardless of the writing task or context. Likewise, writing strategies useful in one context, such as using explicit transitional words to signal organization or using illustrations to develop an idea, will work well in many different writing contexts for many different purposes. However, these same writing habits and strategies will not work in all writing situations (see 5.3, "Habituated Practice Can Lead to Entrenchment"). There is no such thing as "writing in general"; therefore, there is no one lesson about writing that can make writing good in all contexts (see 2.0, "Writing Speaks to Situations through Recognizable Forms," and 2.2, "Genres Are Enacted by Writers and Readers"). Writers must struggle to write in new contexts and genres, a matter of transferring what they know but also learning new things about what works in the present situation. The difficulty of drawing on prior knowledge in this way has spawned a thread of research on transfer of knowledge about writing (see Wardle 2012). The working knowledge that enables a writer to select the practices and strategies appropriate for a particular writing context and task is learned over time through experience as a writer and as a reader of writing. Therefore, a demonstration of one's ability to write effectively in one context cannot constitute proof of one's ability to write in other contexts.

Writers—and teachers of writing—might sometimes wish all writing abilities could be learned once and for always, just as one can learn how to spell a particular word correctly or how to punctuate a quotation correctly once and for always. However, many writing abilities, such as choosing the most appropriate and precise word, and exercising good judgment in deciding whether to quote directly or to paraphrase in any given writing situation, cannot be learned just once. This imperfectability of writing ability is even more evident when a writer must learn how to choose and use evidence to make an effective argument in an unfamiliar situation.

This threshold concept can be difficult to understand because the content of most school subjects is divided into categories and levels of difficulty and sequenced in a way that assumes students must learn the content or skills of one level or stage before moving on to the next level. Unlike these subjects, formal writing instruction is usually designed to repeat the same principles or lessons over and over as student writers encounter new situations for writing and learning.

This is an important threshold concept for educators to understand because it enables us to recognize that it is impossible to make a valid judgment of a student writer's ability by examining a single sample of his or her writing, particularly a sample of writing that does not address a specific rhetorical situation (see 1.7, "Assessing Writing Shapes Contexts and Instruction"). For these same reasons, one cannot assume that a student who has demonstrated the ability to write a literary critical analysis of *Romeo and Juliet* as a senior in high school will also be able to write a paper outlining issues currently being discussed in response to new developments in research on childhood diabetes for a college course.

This threshold concept is helpful for all writers to understand because it will enable them to recognize that encountering difficulty in a writing situation is an indication that they are ready to learn something new about writing.

Writers never cease learning to write, never completely perfect their writing ability, as long as they encounter new or unfamiliar life experiences that require or inspire writing.

4.1

TEXT IS AN OBJECT OUTSIDE OF ONESELF THAT CAN BE IMPROVED AND DEVELOPED

Charles Bazerman and Howard Tinberg

In the course of writing, whether preliminary notes, a sketch, or a full draft, a writer inscribes signs that now exist on paper, digital display, or some other medium. While these signs may have their origin in meanings within the mind of the writer and the initial spontaneous choice of words, they now have been externalized into an independent artifact that can be examined, revised, or otherwise worked on by the writer, collaborators, or other people.

For writers, this externalization decreases the amount of material they must remember and attend to while composing (reducing cognitive load) and allows them to focus attention on limited issues. Externalization also allows writers to look at the text produced so far to see how clearly it reads, what it conveys, whether it can be improved in any way. This working on a text now external to the writer allows a more technical examination, distancing the writer from an idealized sense of meaning and what they feel internally in order to see what the words actually convey. The writer potentially can take the part of the reader. This distancing, however, is not automatic, as the writer may assume the words convey all that they imagine. Thus, becoming aware that the text exists outside the writer's projection and must convey meaning to readers is an important threshold in developing a more professional attitude toward the act of writing and what is produced. Insofar as writers see the text as not yet fulfilling initial ambitions, they can work to improve the text to convey as much as their technical skill and craft allow.

Collaborators, team members, supervisors, editors, and others who may share the work of producing text do not share the initial writer's attachment to the anticipated meaning and have only what the inscribed words bring; they thus provide better measures of what the text actually conveys. While they may view the text with a cooler eye, noting its limitations and failures to convey, they also may lack a sense of all the text may become and of the initial author's intentions. The emerging and changing text then becomes a site of negotiated work to produce the final document.

In response to the view that writing is expressionistic—revealing primarily writers' thoughts and emotions—composition scholars have over the last several decades promoted a view of writing as socially constructed, "crowd-sourced" we'd say these days (Flower 1994; Gere 1987; LeFevre 1987; Lunsford and Ede 1990). More fundamentally, this view is an extension of George Herbert Mead's (1934) understanding that we form our sense of the self through taking the part of the other in our struggle to make ourselves understood. Such a view, while no longer positing that the author is dead, does encourage us to see the text as existing independently of the author and thus capable of being changed and perfected by the author and others.

4.2

FAILURE CAN BE AN IMPORTANT PART OF WRITING DEVELOPMENT

Collin Brooke and Allison Carr

It may seem counterintuitive to suggest that the teaching of writing should focus as much on puzzling out failure as it does on rewarding success. We often forget, however, that successful writers aren't those who are simply able to write brilliant first drafts; often, the writing we encounter has been heavily revised and edited and is sometimes the result of a great deal of failure (see 4.4, "Revision Is Central to Developing Writing," and 4.3, "Learning to Write Effectively Requires Different Kinds of Practice, Time, and Effort"). As renowned writer

Anne Lamott observes, "Almost all good writing begins with terrible first efforts. You need to start somewhere" (Lamott 1995, 303).

As students progress throughout their educational careers and the expectations for their writing evolve from year to year and sometimes course to course, there is no way we can expect them to be able to intuit these shifting conditions. They must have the opportunity to try, to fail, and to learn from those failures as a means of intellectual growth. Edward Burger (2012), professor of mathematics and coauthor of *The 5 Elements of Effective Thinking*, explains that "in reality, every idea from every discipline is a human idea that comes from a natural, thoughtful, and (ideally) unending journey in which thinkers deeply understand the current state of knowledge, take a tiny step in a new direction, almost immediately hit a dead end, learn from that misstep, and, through iteration, inevitably move forward."

In the writing classroom, when assessment is tied too completely to final products, students are more likely to avoid risking failure for fear of damaging their grades, and this fear works against the learning process. They focus instead on what the teacher wants and simply hope to be able to get it right on the first try. Burger (2012) advocates building "quality of failure" into his courses and reports that his students are willing to take greater risks and to examine their missteps for what they can change about them.

One of the most important things students can learn is that failure is an opportunity for growth. As sites of language development, writing classrooms, especially, should make space for quality of failure, or what Lamott describes as "shitty first drafts," by treating failure as something all writers work through, rather than as a symptom of inadequacy or stupidity. Writers need the time and space to explore Thomas Edison's proverbial ten thousand ways that won't work in order to find the ways that do. Such practices will enable writing teachers and students to develop a healthy dialogue around the experience of failure, perhaps leading to the development of what we might call *pedagogies of failure*, or ways of teaching that seek to illuminate the myriad ways writing gets done by examining all the ways it doesn't. Embracing failure in the writing classroom in these ways makes failure speakable and doable.

Outside of the classroom, the capacity for failure (and thus success) is one of the most valuable abilities a writer can possess. The ability to write well comes neither naturally nor easily; the thinkers we praise and admire are not the lucky few born with innate talent. Rather, they are the ones who are able to make mistakes, learn from them, and keep writing until they get it right. J. K. Rowling (2008), for example, is quite open about how she "failed on an epic scale" before she was able to write the *Harry Potter* series. In her 2008 commencement address at Harvard University, she explained, "It is impossible to live without failing at something, unless you live so cautiously that you might as well not have lived at all—in which case, you fail by default."

4.3

LEARNING TO WRITE EFFECTIVELY REQUIRES DIFFERENT KINDS OF PRACTICE, TIME, AND EFFORT

Kathleen Blake Yancey

When someone wants to swim, they get into the water: if we want to write, we put pen to paper, fingers to keyboard, or fingertips to touch screen.

Through practice, we become familiar with writing; it becomes part of us. What we practice is who we are; if we want to be writers, we need to write. And in the practice of writing, we develop writing capacities, among them the ability to adjust and adapt to different contexts, purposes, and audiences.

One kind of practice provides fluidity. Much like a swimmer becoming familiar with the water, writers become familiar with writing—with the feel of a pen in the hand; with the sense of putting individual words on a page that then come together to form larger blocks of meaning, whether sentences, paragraphs, full texts; and with the habit of reviewing what we have just written to see how it fits with what we thought we were writing and with what it is we thought we wanted to say and to share—whether, from our perception, the writing will speak to situations and contexts using conventions of a genre and medium we recognize and think our audience(s) will, too (see 2.0, "Writing Speaks to Situations through Recognizable Forms").

Another kind of practice can refine technique, whether that be dialogue in a narrative, citations for a scientific research paper, or a rhetorical appeal to an elected official. With practice, we can create what seems otherwise out of reach or totally foreign, can compose a text—of words or of words and other elements—shaped by and in response to context. Practice can focus on the whole of a composing process or on different aspects of composing: inventing, researching, drafting, revising, sharing, editing, and publishing.

Practice can involve writing in different spaces, with different materials, and with different technologies. Some writers prefer to write at the same time of day in the same location; others like to change locations;

some like to compose with the same pencil or in the same writer's notebook. As digital technologies have become ubiquitous, writers have become more aware of all technologies, from a pen designed for calligraphy on a piece of fine paper to the dynamic touch screen of a cellphone, and the ways these affordances may influence writing. Likewise, writers necessarily also work in multiple modalities—whether the modality be on the page through document design or on the networked screen bringing words, images, videos, and sound into a single text. In an age when so many spaces and affordances are available, writers need considerable practice keyed not only to fluidity and technique but also to differentiated practice across different spaces of writing, working with different technologies of writing.

Practice can also involve other people, who can help us see what is working in a text and what is not; with their responses, we can revise so as to communicate more clearly. In school, organized around disciplines, practices can vary, and this is yet another sense of the word *practice*: a set of recurring activities located in a specific community. The practice of writing a poem may require no research; the practice of completing a research project in anthropology may require research in the field, and research in the library as the project is being drafted. These practices support participation in different areas of inquiry, themselves situated in what Jean Lave and Etienne Wenger call "communities of practice" (Lave and Wenger 2000).

The threshold concept that learning to write effectively, especially in different contexts or communities of practice, takes different kinds of practice, and such practice takes time and effort, is troublesome for three reasons. First, writers are often assumed simply to be "born": that is, a good writer is assumed to be a good writer "naturally" (see 1.6, "Writing Is Not Natural," and 4.0, "All Writers Have More to Learn"). In this view of writing, the amount and kind of practice is irrelevant and superfluous because practice would make no difference. Second, some people believe that when we learn to write in one genre, we have learned to write in all; but to write in any genre, we need practice in that genre and in the conventions defining that genre. Third, this threshold concept locates writing specifically as a practice situated within communities, which suggests how complex writing is and how, as an activity, it spans a lifetime.

Research has demonstrated that for effective writers and writing, practice is the key: engaging in the different kinds of practices identified above—to acquire fluency, to focus on techniques and strategies, and to engage with other humans—is the way for all human beings to develop into competent writers.

4.4

REVISION IS CENTRAL TO DEVELOPING WRITING

Doug Downs

To create the best possible writing, writers work iteratively, composing in a number of versions, with time between each for reflection, reader feedback, and/or collaborator development. The revision implied in this process—that is, significant development of a text's ideas, structure, and/or design—is central to developing writing. (*Revision* here is distinct from line editing or copyediting to "polish" a text.) In the same way that writing is not perfectible, writing also is not in the category of things that are often right the first time (see 5.1, "Writing Is an Expression of Embodied Cognition"). This principle also implies two corollaries. First, unrevised writing (especially more extended pieces of writing) will rarely be as well suited to its purpose as it could be with revision. Second, writers who don't revise are likely to see fewer positive results from their writing than those who build time for feedback and revision into their writing workflows. When we teach the centrality of revision to writing development, therefore, we must also teach writers to develop workflows that anticipate and rely on revision and to discover what methods of revision best suit their own writing processes.

Revision works because writing shares a characteristic of other language-based endeavors: using language not only represents one's existing ideas, it tends to generate additional language and ideas (see 3.0, "Writing Enacts and Creates Identities and Ideologies"). Writing something usually gives the writer something new, more, or different to say. Therefore, while writing, writers usually find something to say that they didn't have to say before writing. This phenomenon creates an effect analogous to driving with headlights. The headlights reach only a fraction of the way to the destination; a writer can only begin writing what they "see" at the beginning. Driving to the end of the headlights' first reach—writing the first draft—lets the headlights now illuminate the next distance ahead. A writer at the end of their first draft now sees things they did not when they began, letting them "drive on" through another draft by writing what they would have said had they known at the beginning of the first draft what they now know at the end of it (see 4.1, "Text Is an Object Outside of One's Self that Can Be Improved and Developed").

From another angle, revision works by building into the textual-production process time and space for further consideration of a writing problem by the writer, for garnering additional perspectives from other readers and collaborating writers, and for review of a draft against specific criteria (e.g., the directness of a claim or the strength of evidence for it). The expectation of revision—the building of time into a writing process (see 4.3, "Learning to Write Effectively Requires Different Kinds of Practice, Time, and Effort")—creates both the opportunity for, and sometimes directed prompting for, looking at the text again, differently.

The threshold concept that revision is central to developing writing can be difficult in a number of ways. Novice or unreflective writers, especially students, may see revision as punishment for poor performance. Being told to write again or write more, especially if the assigned writing has little intrinsic value to the writer or is used primarily to judge them, may hardly seem like a positive opportunity. Teachers may heighten this effect by making revision optional (rather than every bit as expected a phase of the writer's workflow as drafting) and even reserving the option only for weak pieces of writing. ("I let them revise if they get a low grade.") Students, teachers, writers, and educational policymakers must understand the implication of this threshold concept: revising, or the need to revise, is not an indicator of poor writing or weak writers but much the opposite—a sign and a function of skilled, mature, professional writing and craft.

4.5

ASSESSMENT IS AN ESSENTIAL COMPONENT OF LEARNING TO WRITE

Peggy O'Neill

Assessment is often associated with external mandates and formal accountability systems. Yet, assessment is also a critical component of writing and learning to write. Assessment conceived of in this way is not about grades, exams, or standardized tests but rather about teaching and learning (Shepard 2000). In writing, it is essential for writers to learn to assess texts written by others as well as their own work—both the processes used to create the texts and products that result. Brian Huot calls this pedagogical approach "instructive evaluation" and explains that it "involves the student in the process of evaluation, making her aware of what it is she is trying to create" and it "requires that we involve the student in all phases of the assessment of her work" (Huot 2002, 69).

In this sense, assessment is essential in all stages of the writing process. Through the prewriting, drafting, revision, editing, and publishing of a text, writers assess various components of the rhetorical situation as well as a variety of texts (their own and, frequently, others'). They must assess options and make decisions based on those assessments. For example, writers assess the situation to determine the purpose of the writing, its audience(s), and the context. They select the appropriate genre, writing technology, and publishing medium (see 2.2, "Genres Are Enacted by Writers and Readers," and 2.4, "All Writing Is Multimodal"). Writers must also evaluate their own processes. They may need to examine their approaches to a task, such as searching for information, to determine if it is effective or if a different approach would be more productive (e.g., Is this database useful for my topic? Am I using the appropriate search terms?). Writers must also assess feedback on writing, asking whether suggestions are useful and how they might respond. Once texts are drafted, a writer must assess the product, considering issues such as the appropriateness of style and content, the persuasiveness of evidence, the extent to which conventions of grammar and usage have been followed. Writers also assess texts written by others: for accuracy, legitimacy, and bias, for genre conventions, or for the audience's expectations.

To learn and improve, writers need to develop assessment abilities; therefore, students benefit when teachers integrate assessment throughout the learning process through a variety of activities. These assessment activities can be open, fluid, and tentative (Huot 2002), as in feedback on an early draft that may include a few critical questions or a conversation in which the writer explains why they made a particular choice. The assessment activities may also be more formalized, such as a structured protocol for a self-assessment of a text. By teaching students how to assess both the product and processes of their work, writing teachers are helping students prepare for future writing tasks and opportunities.

4.6

WRITING INVOLVES THE NEGOTIATION OF LANGUAGE DIFFERENCES
Paul Kei Matsuda

All writing entails language—or more specifically, the internalized knowledge of words, phrases, and sentences and how they are put together to create meaning. This statement may seem obvious to some. Yet, language is often taken for granted in the discussion of writing, especially when writers and writing teachers assume that all writers share more or less the same intuitive knowledge of language structures and functions—a condition described by Paul Kei Matsuda as the "myth of linguistic homogeneity" (Matsuda 2006). In reality, however, the knowledge of language held by individual language users varies. No one is a perfect language user, and writers from distinct sociolinguistic contexts (i.e., regional, socioeconomic, ethnic) often come with noticeably different language features in their heads—and in their writing. Furthermore, in today's globalized world, where the audience for writing is increasingly multilingual and multinational, it is more important than ever to see the negotiation of language as an integral part of all writing activities.

As writers strive to use a shared code that allows for effective communication, it is important for all writers and readers to develop the awareness that we are all participating in the process of negotiating language differences. In any writing context, the audience will likely include translingual individuals—those who grew up using different varieties of the target language or another language altogether. For this reason, language features (e.g., vocabulary, idioms, sentence structures) as well as rhetorical features (e.g., persuasive appeals, cultural references and reader-writer positioning) that were once unmarked may need to be negotiated by writers and writing teachers. For instance, writers cannot assume that the phrase *to beat a dead horse* will be understood by all readers universally; to be effective, writers may need to consider embedding contextual clues or even building in some redundancies.

By the same token, readers and writing teachers cannot assume that what were once considered errors are indeed errors; they may reflect language practices perfectly acceptable in some parts of the world—or even in different parts of the same country. For example, including some Spanish words or phrases into sentences is perfectly acceptable for an audience of English-Spanish bilingual writers or users of English-Spanish contact varieties—as long as they do not violate the language rules shared by both users. For a mixed audience that includes non-Spanish users (which is often the case in international academic writing), writers may need to provide additional information (translation, footnote, etc.) in order to facilitate the rhetorical goal of writing (see 1.0, "Writing Is a Social and Rhetorical Activity").

This renewed realization about the changing nature of language and the presence of language differences has several implications. Teachers who use writing as part of their instruction must develop an understanding of the nature of language, principles of language development, and language features situated in various contexts of use. Such knowledge is especially important in facilitating the development of communicative competence (Bachman 1990) among writers who come from nondominant language backgrounds. Teachers also must become more aware of the fuzzy boundary between appropriate usage and inappropriate usage (i.e., errors) to help students understand when and how language differences become negotiable. To help students negotiate language differences successfully—including making principled decisions about whether or not to adopt dominant language practices—teachers must understand various strategies for negotiating language differences. Finally, teachers must help students understand the risks involved in negotiating language differences. Beyond the classroom, all writers today need to fully understand the diversity within a language as well as how languages continue to change.

References

Bachman, Lyle. 1990. *Fundamental Considerations in Language Testing.* Oxford: University of Oxford Press.

Burger, Edward. 2012. "Teaching to Fail." *Inside Higher Ed*, August 21. https://www.inside highered.com/views/2012/08/21/essay-importance-teaching-failure.

Burke, Kenneth. 1966. *Language as Symbolic Action.* Berkeley: University of California Press.

Flower, Linda. 1994. *The Construction of Negotiated Meaning: A Social Cognitive Theory of Writing.* Carbondale: Southern Illinois University Press.

Gee, James Paul. 2004. *Situated Language and Learning: A Critique of Traditional Schooling.* New York: Routledge.

Gere, Ann Ruggles. 1987. *Writing Groups: History, Theory, and Implications.* Carbondale: Southern Illinois University Press.

Huot, Brian. 2002. *(Re)Articulating Writing Assessment for Teaching and Learning.* Logan: Utah State University Press.

Lamott, Anne. 1995. *Bird by Bird: Some Instructions on Writing and Life.* New York: Anchor Books.

Lave, Jean, and Etienne Wenger. 2000. *Communities of Practice.* Cambridge: Cambridge University Press.

LeFevre, Karen Burke. 1987. *Invention as a Social Act.* Carbondale: Southern Illinois University Press.

Lunsford, Andrea, and Lisa Ede. 1990. *Singular Texts/Plural Authors.* Carbondale: Southern Illinois University Press.

Matsuda, Paul Kei. 2006. "The Myth of Linguistic Homogeneity in U.S. College Composition." *College English* 68 (6): 637–51. http://dx.doi.org/10.2307/25472180.

Mead, George Herbert. 1934. *Mind, Self, and Society: From the Standpoint of a Social Behaviorist.* Chicago: University of Chicago Press.

Rowling, J. K. 2008. "The Fringe Benefits of Failure, and the Importance of Imagination." *Harvard Magazine.* http://harvardmagazine.com/2008/06/the-fringe-benefits-failure-the-importance-imagination.

Shepard, Lorrie A. 2000. "The Role of Assessment in a Learning Culture." *Educational Researcher* 29 (7): 4–14. http://dx.doi.org/10.3102/0013189X029007004.

Wardle, Elizabeth. 2012. "Understanding 'Transfer' from FYC: Preliminary Results of a Longitudinal Study." *WPA: Writing Program Administration* 31 (1/2): 6–85.

CONCEPT 5
Writing Is (Also Always) a Cognitive Activity

5.0
WRITING IS (ALSO ALWAYS) A COGNITIVE ACTIVITY
Dylan B. Dryer

Behind the claim by Linda Adler-Kassner and Elizabeth Wardle in "Metaconcept: Writing Is an Activity and a Subject of Study" in this volume that "writing can never be anything but a social and rhetorical act" are decades of research inspired by what is now known as the *social turn.* Those applying insights from the social turn to the study of writing found again and again that any act of writing is situated in complex activity systems that enmesh any writer's motives with other spaces, traditions, values, ideologies, other humans, previous iterations of the genre, and the constraints and affordances of language itself (see 1.5, "Writing Mediates Activity"; 2.1, "Writing Represents the World, Events, Ideas, and Feelings"; 2.3, "Writing Is a Way of Enacting Disciplinarity"; and 3.2, "Writers' Histories, Processes, and Identities Vary"). But if writing is always a social and rhetorical act, it necessarily involves cognition. While contemporary advanced research on writing is profoundly and productively oriented to influences on writing outside the skull, as it were, the four concepts in this chapter signal the beginnings of a convergence as potentially transformative as the "social turn" itself (after all, the "social turn" was in part a rejection of prior attempts to conceptualize writing as a solely cognitive phenomenon). To see this potential clearly, we must revisit what is known about composing processes inside the skull.

Well before the social turn, writing researchers in the late 1960s were examining cognitive aspects of writing, and their work became particularly relevant to those teaching in the open-admissions campuses of the 1970s. Many students came to those campuses with writing experiences and composing strategies that perplexed and dismayed their instructors; some faculty declared that many of these students could not write at all (for more on this era, see Bizzell 1982; Lu 1999;

DOI: 10.7330/9780874219906.c005

Soliday 2002). Even as some faculty members and researchers attributed students' writing struggles to mental and even cultural "deficits," others were trying to map mental processes in a more descriptive way (Flower and Hayes 1981; Perl 1979). By observing writers who had been asked to verbalize what they were thinking while they were drafting and revising, these researchers found evidence for a writing process that extends before and after the moment of text production. The models these researchers produced helped break the grip of still-dominant assumptions that writing was simply a matter of transcribing thought while avoiding error (for more on this, see 1.4, "Words Get Their Meaning from Other Words" and 1.9, "Writing Is a Technology through Which Writers Create and Recreate Meaning"). Researchers in cognition and writing attempted to diagnose and develop interventions for issues still important today: What makes writers "blocked," or causes them to stall once they get going? What can writers do to overcome anxiety? Why do writers interrupt higher-order attempts to shape meaning to correct lower-order issues of spelling and punctuation, and does it matter? What happens when writers' plans for the texts they hope to produce or the readers they hope to reach are changed by the texts they've already produced? What are writers *doing* when they pause while writing? Is there a relationship between syntactical complexity and "maturity" of thought? How do the strategies of skilled writers differ from those of novices? Can thinking *about* thinking enhance writing, reading, and/or revision practices? All of these questions are about cognition although, as previous threshold concepts demonstrated, we know they are not only about cognition.

This early cognitive research produced findings that continue to underpin our field's beliefs and activities. For example, anxiety (about error, imagined audience, or perfectionism) can overwhelm composing processes and can be mitigated with low-stakes, generative writing (Bloom 1981; Elbow 1981; Rose 1985); revision strategies depend on what writers think revision is (Bridwell 1980; Sommers 1980); composing and revising processes are malleable and genre specific (Britton et al. 1975); composing practices can transform as well as transcribe knowledge (Bereiter and Scardamalia 1987); and, perhaps most generally, the ways people think about approaching a writing task affect their experiences with it.

Researchers in the cognitive sciences who happen to study writing have independently and empirically validated much of that early work: neural processes essential to writing must be successfully coordinated across different areas of the brain; revision, even for seemingly uncomplicated "errors," is cognitively quite complex; and writers' syntactical fluency improves in tight correspondence with knowledge of their topics. Perhaps most important, writers' brains have structural limitations on what is known as *working memory*—where fleeting and mutable bits of information, images, to-do lists, or immediate plans are held, juggled, and discarded. Unfortunately, working memory appears to be fairly inelastic and zero-sum. This limitation is why unfamiliar task loads (as alluded to in 1.6, "Writing Is Not Natural") can reduce performance in other, usually high-competency, areas; why rates of surface error rise predictably when students attempt a new genre for the first time (see also Quinlan et al. 2012); and why field researchers find writers creatively rigging up makeshift additional capacity for their working memories (Angeli 2015; Barber et al. 2006; MacKay 1999).

What's more, there is now substantial evidence that composing practices measurably influence other mental processes (recall, goal setting, attention span, knowledge acquisition, processing time, etc.) as well as psychosocial and even *physiological* phenomena (stress and anxiety levels, recovery from trauma, immunological response, pain sensitivity, postoperative recovery, etc.). As 5.1 ("Writing Is an Expression of Embodied Cognition") makes clear, writing is cognitive not only because it "draws on the full resources of our nervous system" but because it actively influences our nervous system as well (Berninger and Richards 2012; Berninger and Winn 2006). Evidently, as Marilyn Cooper argues in a review of recent work in neurophenomenology, what we write literally helps make us who we are (Cooper 2011, 443). This phenomenon helps explain why writers constrained to "repeated practice of the same genres" may, as explained in 5.3, become "entrenched" in particular approaches or conventions. Although neuroplasticity (the capacity of the brain to create and reinforce new neural connections through learning and use) is only now becoming part of the conversation in US writing studies, our most progressive composition pedagogies have long emphasized metacognition and reflection for just this reason. That is, not only do compositionists want writers to "demonstrate consciousness of process that will enable them to reproduce success" (see 5.3, "Habituated Practice Can Lead to Entrenchment") and to "begin assessing themselves as writers, recognizing and building on their prior knowledge about writing" (see 5.4, "Reflection Is Critical for Writers' Development"), they hope to ensure that writers receiving instruction in one context are also equipped to fend off the cognitive entrenchment of repetition and overgeneralization.

As long as teachers keep this caution about entrenchment in mind, working memory and the benefits of automaticity are set to become powerful enabling concepts for modern writing studies. All writers can increase fluency and performance through naturalizing routines; just as letter shapes recede from children's consciousness (or more specifically, the frontal lobes) and free up working memory for higher-order composing goals, so too will even the most structurally elaborate academic and workplace genres eventually become assimilated into writers' routines (see 2.1, "Writing Represents the World, Events, Ideas, and Feelings"). Teachers and supervisors alike should remember that automaticity takes time, perhaps at a temporary cost to other skill sets (see 4.2, "Failure Can Be an Important Part of Writing Development," and 4.3, "Learning to Write Effectively Requires Different Kinds of Practice, Time, and Effort") and that writers taking on a new task are attempting to forge neurological connections that literally *aren't there yet* (see James and Engelhardt 2012; Richards et al. 2011).

In sum, insights from the social turn and insights from what some are calling the *neurological turn* appear to be converging, as can be seen in this recent definition from two cognitive researchers: "The writing process is supported by a single system—the writer's internal mind-brain interacting with the external environment (including technology tools)" (Berninger and Winn 2006, 108).

5.1

WRITING IS AN EXPRESSION OF EMBODIED COGNITION
Charles Bazerman and Howard Tinberg

Writing is a full act of the mind, drawing on the full resources of our nervous system, formulating communicative impulses into thoughts and words, and transcribing through the work of the fingers. Writers at the computer or desk carry the tension of thought throughout their full posture, can grimace at the difficult contradiction, and can burst into laughter at the surprising discovery or the pleasure of an elegant phrase.

This is as true of the reasoned and evidence-grounded academic writer as of the impassioned writer of love letters. The emotional engagement of scientific writers for their subject may entail careful attention to evidence and reasoning grounded in prior work in the field and an understanding of the theory and methodological principles of the field; yet without a passion for the subject that turns a writer's full mind and thought to the task of producing new words and ideas, little of value would get written.

If cognition assumes complex mental processes at work, then embodied cognition draws in addition upon the physical and affective aspects of the composing process. While there is still much to learn about how the brain and mind work when engaged in the complex task of writing, it was evident to theorists as early as James Moffett (1968) and Ann Berthoff (1978; 1981) that writing comes from full engagement of the entire writer, which is developed across many years of a developing self. Both drew on the work of Lev Vygotsky (1986) who, in the early years of the twentieth century, explored the role of language internalization and externalization in the social formation of mind and emotions (see Bazerman 2012). More recently, psychologists such as Ron Kellogg (2008) have documented the extensive concentration and long time it takes a writer to develop. Howard Gardner (2008) as well has called for recognition of the full, human dimension of both readers and writers in the construction of meaning. Finally, a number of teachers drawing on psychoanalytic traditions have considered how writing challenges and exposes elements of emotions and psychological structures (e.g., Alcorn 2002).

5.2
METACOGNITION IS NOT COGNITION
Howard Tinberg

"Do you know your knowledge?" asks Samuel Taylor Coleridge, trying to point out the difference between knowing what we know and knowing that we know (qtd. in Berthoff 1978, 233). The first calls upon cognition while the second requires metacognition. In other words, to think through a solution to a problem differs from an awareness of how we came to resolve that problem, or, as Kara Taczak notes in this collection, writers engage in cognition when they reflect on "what they are doing in that particular moment" but display metacognition when they consider "why they made the rhetorical choices they did" (78). For those of us who teach writing, the objective is not just to have our students produce effective writing—that is, to respond in logical and thoughtful ways to the question posed. We also want our students to demonstrate consciousness of process that will enable them to reproduce success. Metacognition is not cognition. Performance, however thoughtful, is not the same as awareness of how that performance came to be.

Cognition refers to the acquisition and application of knowledge through complex mental processes. Writers draw upon cognitive processes when they

- demonstrate an understanding of the question;
- deploy accurately and purposefully concepts, knowledge sets, and terms that reveal genuine expertise;
- meet the needs of their audience;
- fulfill the requirements of genre; or
- exhibit a control over language, grammar, and mechanics.

But the effective accomplishment of writing tasks over time requires even more. It calls upon metacognition, or the ability to perceive the very steps by which success occurs and to articulate the various qualities and components that contribute in significant ways to the production of effective writing, such as

- discerning the structure of a draft;
- delineating patterns of error; or
- discriminating between what is necessary in a draft and what in the end serves little purpose.

Metacognition requires that writers think about their mental processes. Metacognitively aware writers are able, in William Blake's' words, to "look thro it, & not with it" (qtd. in Berthoff 1978, 232). In other words, they engage in "thinking about thinking" (Berthoff 1978, 13). The need for metacognition assumes special importance when writers find themselves required to work in unfamiliar contexts or with forms with which they are unfamiliar. In those cases, metacognition allows writers to assess which skill and knowledge sets apply in these novel situations and which do not. In the end, while cognition remains critical to effective writing, it is metacognition that endows writers with a certain control over their work, regardless of the situation in which they operate.

Popular conceptions of what it means to write assume that knowledge of a subject (e.g., the history of the Civil War) is enough to produce a successful written report on that subject, or that knowledge of the rules of language, grammar, and mechanics is sufficient to produce an effective piece of written communication. In fact, cognition, while essential to thoughtful performance, cannot guarantee success, given the challenges of writing across disciplines, for varied audiences, and in diverse genres. It must be accompanied by metacognition.

5.3

HABITUATED PRACTICE CAN LEAD TO ENTRENCHMENT

Chris M. Anson

When writers' contexts are constrained and they are subjected to repeated practice of the same genres, using the same processes for the same rhetorical purposes and addressing the same audiences, their conceptual framework for writing may become entrenched, "solidified," or "sedimented." When this happens, they may try to apply that framework in a new or unfamiliar writing situation, resulting in a mismatch between what they produce and the expectations or norms of their new community (see 2.1, "Writing Represents the World, Events, Ideas, and Feelings," and 3.3, "Writing Is Informed by Prior Experience").

Repeated practice of the same mental task or activity can lead to what psychologists call *automaticity* or *unconscious competence*, the application of a process or the retrieval of information that doesn't require conscious attention (Van Nieuwerburgh and Passmore 2012). For example, among experienced drivers, the process of shifting gears becomes so habituated through repeated practice that it usually reaches a stage of automaticity, allowing drivers to do it while performing other tasks such as talking to a passenger and gauging the distance of the car from a stoplight. Although writing is far more complex than gear shifting, the principle of automaticity also applies. A veteran police officer who has written many hundreds of incident reports may apply habituated practices, such as being as highly objective as possible, in other situations that call for a different approach, such as sharing subjective impressions or using an elegant, elaborated style.

In writing, the misapplication of habituated practices often occurs among novice writers, such as those who are trained throughout high school to write five-paragraph-style essays for standardized tests (Anson 2008). Placed in a new situation where the audience, purpose, genre, and other aspects of writing may be very different from those required in five-paragraph themes, such writers may resort to their habituated practice and fail to meet the expectations of their new rhetorical community. Habituation also explains the struggles more proficient writers experience when they have practiced certain genres for years and then try to deploy their abilities in new settings. For example, even prolific academic writers who are highly skilled at producing research reports and articles may struggle to write in new or unfamiliar settings. A significant body of literature has accumulated around the problems associated with scientists who are unable to "translate" their complex knowledge and research findings for public audiences. Such translation requires consciously breaking with entrenched practices and being rhetorically flexible enough to think about how a text will be understood by a broader range of readers.

To counter the effects of habituation, some writing experts advocate a pedagogical approach that emphasizes rhetorical dexterity and an ability to confront new writing situations with a high degree of metacognition or rhetorical awareness learned through exposure to writing studies (Downs and Wardle 2012). Such awareness is said to help writers study and reflect on what they must to do in their writing to succeed by the standards of the community. There is some scholarly debate, however, about the effectiveness of this kind of pedagogy. Using theories of situated cognition, some writing experts argue that in spite of a high level of metacognitive awareness, writers will always have difficulty moving across disparate rhetorical communities and must always, to some degree, "learn anew" in unfamiliar settings (Russell 1995).

5.4

REFLECTION IS CRITICAL FOR WRITERS' DEVELOPMENT
Kara Taczak

Writers develop and improve with practice, time, and—among other things—reflecting throughout the process. Reflection is a mode of inquiry: a deliberate way of systematically recalling writing experiences to reframe the current writing situation. It allows writers to recognize what they are doing in that particular moment (cognition), as well as to consider why they made the rhetorical choices they did (metacognition) (see 5.1, "Writing Is an Expression of Embodied Cognition"). The combination of cognition and metacognition, accessed through reflection, helps writers begin assessing themselves as writers, recognizing and building on their prior knowledge about writing. This deliberate type of reflection centers on writers' ability to theorize and question areas such as their processes, practices, beliefs, attitudes, and understandings about writing, along with the ability to consider why they made the rhetorical choices they did (see Driscoll 2011; Sommers 2011; Yancey 1998). This ability to theorize and question is especially important for writers engaging in new or especially challenging tasks because it helps writers relocate the knowledge and practices acquired from one writing site to another (i.e., a writer might learn genre awareness in a first-year writing course and later relocate the awareness about genres in helping to create a business memo for an advertising course).

Reflection can be troublesome because for some writers, reflection isn't an integral part of their processes and practices. This may be because (1) writers believe reflection needs to happen after the fact rather than seeing it as a critical, rhetorical act within the process; (2) writers assume reflection happens naturally and without prompting; (3) writers think reflection *only* means considering how they *feel* about their writing; (4) some writers may never have been asked to reflect on their writing and thus may simply not think of doing so; and (5) some writers may not be developmentally ready to reflect. All of these suggest that reflection itself can be challenging; thus, such experiences with and misconceptions about reflection can result in writers who do not use reflection as an active and engaged part of their writing processes and who don't understand that reflection can benefit their development and success as writers.

Importantly, and as demonstrated by the other threshold concepts, many factors help ensure students' success with writing; however, almost any of these factors can depend upon writers' ability to use effective reflection as part of their writing processes. For example, writers who are more attuned to conscious reflection make "deeper choices" (2.0, "Writing Speaks to Situations through Recognizable Forms"); writers' identities are connected to various parts of their lives, including their histories, processes, and prior experiences, and using reflection allows them to tap into these as a way to become better writers (see 3.2, "Writers' Histories, Processes, and Identities Vary"; 3.3, "Writing Is Informed by Prior Experience"; and 3.4, "Disciplinary and Professional Identities Are Constructed Through Writing"); revision, which includes some amount of failure, becomes particularly helpful when writers reflect and learn from these experiences (see 4.1, "Text Is an Object Outside of Oneself that Can Be Improved and Developed")."; 4.2, "Failure Can Be an Important Part of Writing Development"; 4.3, "Learning to Write Effectively Requires Different Kinds of Practice, Time, and Effort"; and 4.4, "Revision Is Central to Developing Writing"). Reflection has the unique ability to connect across the various threshold concepts because it offers writers the ability to be active agents of change, making meaningful contributions to any rhetorical exchange (see 5.1, "Writing Is an Expression of Embodied Cognition"; 5.2, "Metacognition Is Not Cognition").

Reflection allows writers to recall, reframe, and relocate knowledge and practices; therefore, it must be worked at in order to be most effectively learned and practiced.

References

Alcorn, Marshall. 2002. *Changing the Subject in English Class: Discourse and the Constructions of Desire*. Carbondale: Southern Illinois University Press.

Angeli, Elizabeth. 2015. "Three Types of Memory in Emergency Medical Services Communication." *Written Communication* 32 (1): 3–38.

Anson, Chris M. 2008. "Closed Systems and Standardized Writing Tests." *College Composition and Communication* 60 (1): 113–28.

Barber, Chris, Paul Smith, James Cross, John E. Hunter, and Richard McMaster. 2006. "Crime Scene Investigation as Distributed Cognition." In *Distributed Cognition*, ed. Stevan Harnad and Itiel E. Dror, special issue of *Pragmatics and Cognition* 14 (2): 357–85.

Bazerman, Charles. 2012. "Writing, Cognition, and Affect from the Perspectives of Sociocultural and Historic Studies of Writing." In *Past, Present, and Future Contributions of Cognitive Writing Research to Cognitive Psychology*, ed. Virginia W. Berninger, 89–104. New York: Psychology Press.

Bereiter, Carl, and Marlene Scardamalia. 1987. *The Psychology of Written Composition*. Hillsdale, NJ: Erlbaum.

Berninger, Virginia W., and T. Richards. 2012. "The Writing Brain: Coordinating Sensory/Motor, Language, and Cognitive Systems in Working Memory Architecture." In *Past, Present, and Future Contributions of Cognitive Writing Research to Cognitive Psychology*, edited by Virginia Berninger, 537–563. New York: Psychology Press.

Berninger, Virginia W., and William D. Winn. 2006. "Implications of Advancements in Brain Research and Technology for Writing Development, Writing Instruction, and Educational Evolution." In *Handbook of Writing Research*, edited by Charles A. MacArthur, Steve Graham, and Jill Fitzgerald, 96–114. New York: Guilford.

Berthoff, Ann E. 1978. *Forming, Thinking, Writing: The Composing Imagination*. Rochelle Park, NJ: Hayden.

Berthoff, Ann E. 1981. *The Making of Meaning: Metaphors, Models, and Maxims for Writing Teachers*. Upper Montclair, NJ: Boynton/Cook.

Bizzell, Patricia. 1982. "Cognition, Convention, and Certainty: What We Know and What We Need to Know About Writing." *Pre/Text* 3 (3): 213–43.

Bloom, Lynn Z. 1981. "Why Graduate Students Can't Write: Implications of Research on Writing Anxiety for Graduate Education." *JAC: Journal of Advanced Composition* 2.1 (2): 103–18.

Bridwell, Lillian S. 1980. "Revising Strategies in Twelfth Grade Students' Transactional Writing." *Research in the Teaching of English* 14:197–222.

Britton, James, Tony Burgess, Nancy Martin, Alex McLeod, and Harold Rosen. 1975. *The Development of Writing Abilities(11–18)*. London: MacMillan.

Cooper, Marilyn M. 2011. "Rhetorical Agency as Emergent and Enacted." *College Composition and Communication* 62 (3): 420–49.

Downs, Douglas, and Elizabeth Wardle. 2012. "Teaching about Writing, Righting Misconceptions: (Re)Envisioning 'First-Year Composition' as 'Introduction to Writing Studies.'" *College Composition and Communication* 58 (4): 552–84.

Driscoll, Dana Lynn. 2011. "Connected, Disconnected, or Uncertain: Student Attitudes about Future Writing Contexts and Perceptions of Transfer from First Year Writing to the Disciplines." *Across the Disciplines* 8 (2). http://wac.colostate.edu/atd/articles/driscoll2011/index.cfm.

Elbow, Peter. 1981. *Writing with Power: Techniques for Mastering the Writing Process*. New York: Oxford University Press.

Flower, Linda, and John R. Hayes. 1981. "A Cognitive Process Theory of Writing." *College Composition and Communication* 32 (4): 365–87. http://dx.doi.org/10.2307/356600.

Gardner, Howard. 2008. *Frames of Mind: The Theory of Multiple Intelligences*. New York: Basic Books.

James, Karin H., and Laura Engelhardt. 2012. "The Effects of Handwriting Experience on Functional Brain Development in Pre-Literate Children." *Trends in Neuroscience and Education* 1 (1): 32–42. http://dx.doi.org/10.1016/j.tine.2012.08.001.

Kellogg, Ronald T. 2008. "Training Writing Skills: A Cognitive Developmental Perspective." *Journal of Writing Research* 1 (1): 1–26.

Lu, Min Zhan. 1999. "Importing 'Science': Neutralizing Basic Writing." In *Representing the "Other": Basic Writing and the Teaching of Basic Writing*, edited by Bruce Horner and Min Zhan Lu, 56–104. Urbana, IL: National Council of Teachers of English.

MacKay, Wendy E. 1999. "Is Paper Safe? The Role of Paper Flight Strips in Air Traffic Control." *ACM Transactions in Computer-Human Interaction (TOCHI)* 6 (4): 311–40.

Moffett, James. 1968. *Teaching the Universe of Discourse.* Upper Montclair, NJ: Boynton/Cook.

Perl, Sondra. 1979. "The Composing Processes of Unskilled College Writers." *Research in the Teaching of English* 13 (4): 317–36.

Quinlan, Thomas, Maaike Loncke, Mariëlle Leijten, and Luuk Van Waes. 2012. "Coordinating the Cognitive Processes of Writing: The Role of the Monitor." *Written Communication* 29 (3): 345–68. http://dx.doi.org/10.1177/0741088312451112.

Richards, Todd L., Virginia W. Berninger, Pat Stock, Leah Altemeier, Pamala Trivedi, and Kenneth R. Maravilla. 2011. "Differences between Good and Poor Child Writers on fMRI Contrasts for Writing Newly Taught and Highly Practiced Letter Forms." *Reading and Writing* 24 (5): 493–516. http://dx.doi.org/10.1007/s11145-009-9217-3.

Rose, Mike, ed. 1985. *When a Writer Can't Write: Studies in Writer's Block and Other Composing-Process Problems.* New York: Guilford.

Russell, David. 1995. "Activity Theory and Its Implications for Writing Instruction." In *Reconceiving Writing, Rethinking Writing Instruction*, edited by Joseph Petraglia, 51–77. Mahwah, NJ: Erlbaum.

Soliday, Mary. 2002. *The Politics of Remediation: Institutional and Student Needs in Higher Education.* Pittsburgh: University of Pittsburgh Press.

Sommers, Jeff. 2011. "Reflection Revisited: The Class Collage." *Journal of Basic Writing* 30 (1): 99–129.

Sommers, Nancy. 1980. "Revision Strategies of Student Writers and Experienced Adult Writers." *College Composition and Communication* 31 (4): 378–88. http://dx.doi.org/10.2307/356588.

Van Nieuwerburgh, Christian, and Jonathan Passmore. 2012. "Creating Coaching Cultures for Learning." In *Coaching in Education: Getting Better Results for Students, Educators, and Parents*, edited by Christian van Nieuwerburgh, 153–72. London: Karnac.

Vygotsky, Lev S. 1986. *Thought and Language.* Cambridge: MIT Press.

Yancey, Kathleen Blake. 1998. *Reflection in the Writing Classroom.* Logan: Utah State University Press.

PART 2

Using Threshold Concepts

INTRODUCTION
Using Threshold Concepts

Linda Adler-Kassner and Elizabeth Wardle

Part 1 of *Naming What We Know* took up the task of finding a set of foundational concepts on which a group of disciplinary experts in writing studies could agree. Part 2 of the book considers what writing faculty or, in some instances, faculty who use writing in their teaching, can do or have done with that set of threshold concepts. How can naming and considering threshold concepts explicitly help us in the many tasks in which this range of faculty engages? Naming threshold concepts, after all, should not be a navel-gazing exercise. Instead, it is a pressing prerequisite to being able to work more effectively with our various stakeholders, from students to colleagues in other disciplines to administrators to lawmakers.

These chapters demonstrate the broad scope of our field's work, from general education courses to writing majors and doctoral programs, all of which must be assessed, and from writing centers to writing-across-the-curriculum programs and other outreach efforts.

These varied sites of expert practice, of teaching and learning, demonstrate the dual importance of our field's threshold concepts, as we discussed in the "Metaconcept: Writing Is an Activity and a Subject of Study": the threshold concepts of writing studies are relevant not only for learners hoping to join our discipline but to anyone who writes or provides feedback on student writing. Although we chafe at being designated a "service" discipline, our work exists simultaneously within and beyond our disciplinary boundaries as we study writing within multiple contexts. Moreover, the results of our research are relevant and valuable to many sorts of people; although we may not conduct research with the primary intent of being a service to others, much of what we learn may, in fact, usefully *provide* such a service to others—if we can find ways to share it.

The chapters in part 2 of *Naming What We Know* explicitly take up the threshold concepts from part 1 in an effort to demonstrate how those concepts either have informed or could inform particular sites of work, or how those concepts shed light on difficulties in certain sites of work. The first set of chapters in part 2 focus on the use of threshold concepts in courses and programs. In the opening chapter, Heidi Estrem takes up the question of learning outcomes, asking readers to consider the relationship between learning outcomes and threshold concepts and considering the benefits of each. In their chapter on first-year composition, Doug Downs and Liane Robertson describe the ways threshold concepts can provide the content for a course that has historically been understood as contentless or remedial. They demonstrate how the threshold concepts from part 1 can be grouped around four sites of troublesome knowledge about writing that students from all majors can benefit from interrogating. Similarly, Blake Scott and Elizabeth Wardle examine the ways department members can benefit from explicitly attempting to name shared threshold concepts as they design undergraduate programs and attempt to create a set of student learning outcomes. Like Estrem, they note some ways threshold concepts can encourage the hard and messy work of learning rather than shutting it down or confining it, as learning outcomes sometimes can. Kara Taczak and Kathleen Blake Yancey continue the conversation about learning by examining how learning happens within a writing studies doctoral program. They note that learning in doctoral programs is not linear and that it happens not only in the delivered curriculum designed by faculty but also in the lived and experienced curriculum, adding another layer of complexity to the conversation about when and how learning thresholds are crossed.

The second set of chapters in part 2 consider the role of writing threshold concepts outside the classroom and particular writing programs. How is writing assessed, and how should it be assessed, given our field's foundational knowledge about writing? Peggy O'Neill urges readers to not only consider that question but also to recognize that anyone who designs a writing assessment must also become familiar with threshold concepts from the field of educational assessment. Rebecca S. Nowacek and Bradley Hughes similarly note that other threshold concepts, beyond those outlined in part 1, come into play for writing center consultants who are working with students from a variety of disciplines and are themselves representative of those disciplines. They also note that threshold concepts can inform a tutor training program in useful ways. Linda Adler-Kassner and John Majewski, followed by Chris Anson, push us to consider how our field's threshold concepts inform our work with colleagues across the disciplines. How can we use our explicitly named and understood concepts to help us better communicate what we know in conversations with those faculty? And how can we use the frame of threshold concepts to ask our colleagues to name what *they* know about writing and to consider how their conceptions of writing (even if unstated) inform their teaching practices?

We offer the chapters in part 2 as a way to push forward the conversation about how our field's threshold concepts can be explicitly named and can aid us in the work we are undertaking, to improve writing and the teaching and learning of writing in its myriad forms and contexts.

Using Threshold Concepts in Program and Curriculum Design

6

THRESHOLD CONCEPTS AND STUDENT LEARNING OUTCOMES

Heidi Estrem

One of the premises of this edited collection is that descriptions of writing matter, and matter deeply. Writing—for reasons articulated throughout this collection—is particularly vulnerable to uneven or problematic portrayals. In higher education, it has become common practice to characterize student learning about writing via identified learning outcomes that students are to meet by the end of a course or program; more recently, entire undergraduate degree experiences are described through an outcomes framework. For example, postsecondary educational reform efforts like the American Association of Colleges and Universities' Liberal Education, America's Promise (LEAP) Initiative structure the undergraduate degree experience around identified "essential learning outcomes," one of which is "written and oral communication" ("LEAP" 2013). Outcomes offer a way to articulate more clearly what shared values for learning might be and how courses support those values; further, they provide an entry point for meaningful assessment. As Jeremy Penn explains, educational outcomes, when employed within a university context and through extensive faculty and student engagement, can "exhibit learning and achievements that are unique to each of our institutions" and "[facilitate] a dialogue about what we expect students to learn in our institutions" (Penn 2011, 12). Working to describe what students should learn as undergraduates is, of course, a worthy goal. The challenge is to ensure writing development is depicted in meaningful ways.

Generalized, outcomes-based depictions of student learning about writing hold two immediate challenges: (1) they locate evidence of learning at the *end* of key experiences—certainly one valuable place to begin understanding learning, but not the only place; and (2) they

DOI: 10.7330/9780874219906.c006

often depict writing as only a skill (albeit an "intellectual" or at least "practical" one) (AAC&U 2013). While outcomes-based depictions hold a certain kind of currency and explanatory power in educational reform efforts and will likely continue to do so, a threshold concepts approach provides a differently meaningful framework for intervening in commonplace understandings about writing. Threshold concepts offer a mechanism for faculty to articulate the content of their courses, identify student learning throughout the course experience, and create shared values for writing in a way that a focus on end products—on outcomes—cannot.

This chapter thus explores the implications of using a threshold-concepts approach to articulate shared understandings of student learning about writing. It does so in the interest of speaking back to an outcomes-based framework for undergraduate education. I first briefly examine some of the challenges that outcomes-based depictions of student learning raise, particularly when they are used to describe writing development. Then, to ground an exploration of how threshold concepts for writing might offer different possibilities for depicting undergraduate student learning, I examine a particular location where shared, university-wide student learning outcomes for writing have been newly ascribed to particular courses through a restructuring of undergraduate education at Boise State University. Specifically, I draw on interviews with faculty who teach what are called *communication in the disciplines courses* here, courses housed in departments, taught by departmental faculty, and also now linked to a new, university-wide Writing Undergraduate Learning Outcome. The interview data contribute to the broader case that threshold concepts might provide a generative lens through which to both understand student learning about writing *and* to begin developing a shared knowledge base of *learning about writing* that spans disciplines and contexts, thus enriching outcomes-based depictions of student learning.

MAPPING STUDENT LEARNING VIA OUTCOMES: NEW POSSIBILITIES, NEW CHALLENGES

Before describing the potential a threshold concepts approach offers (particularly for writing instruction), it is worth briefly considering the powerful frame outcomes-based education has become within higher education. In addition to being employed for campus-wide, undergraduate-degree reform efforts, outcomes-based frameworks are increasingly encouraged, if not required, by disciplinary accreditation bodies and other external stakeholders, who see outcomes as a way to understand and assess student learning across courses. Reform-based initiatives like AAC&U's LEAP project use outcomes to create "a guiding vision and national benchmarks for college student learning" (AAC&U 2013), for instance. Regional accreditation bodies like the Northwest Commission on Colleges and Universities (NWCCU) require each college and university under their jurisdiction to state student learning outcomes at the course, program, and degree level (Northwest Commission on Colleges and Universities 2010). In addition, accreditation programs for specific degrees, like engineering's Accreditation Board for Engineering and Technology (2010), also require student learning outcomes to be defined and assessed throughout the curriculum. They are nearly ubiquitous for good reasons: they make expectations for student learning more visible; they foster curricular connections and cohesiveness; and they offer productive possibilities for assessment.

As a faculty member, I have seen firsthand how productive it can be to rearticulate course content as *objectives* or *outcomes* that can be identified to students and to which course materials are explicitly linked. On our campus, our reform of undergraduate education engaged faculty and other stakeholders in lively, interdisciplinary discussions that eventually resulted in the creation of university-wide learning outcomes. Working together to articulate what our shared values for student learning were was productive and fulfilling (see Boise State University 2013). Outcomes-based approaches can be enormously useful tools for curricular development in higher education, then, particularly when no prior curricular framework existed.

Outcomes-based approaches also offer a way to tie assessment to a specific, meaningful goal. As Amy Driscoll and Swarup Wood explain, outcomes-based education is inextricably linked with assessment because it seeks to "[foster] continuous attention to student learning and [promote] institutional accountability based on student learning" (Driscoll and Wood 2007, 4). On our campus, our new university-level outcomes provide a new and clear mechanism for collecting and assessing student work. One rationale for the University Learning Outcomes refers to richer assessment:

> Active and authentic assessment of student learning is guided by the ULOs. Connections between student assessment in courses to the broader institutional outcomes also provides a way to contextualize students' learning in broader contexts: each of our outcomes has a rubric which describes the behaviors and levels of proficiency we expect from our

students. This allows faculty to determine when, where, and to what extent students are demonstrating the kinds of learning that will transfer from one class to another and from Boise State to the world 'beyond the blue' [beyond our campus, a reference to this university's blue football field]. (Boise State University 2013b).

These macrolevel outcomes assessments, then, give universities and programs ways to document student learning across courses. These assessments can address the interests of stakeholders from outside the academy who are looking for some way to understand learning development over time. An outcomes-based curriculum can thus provide a useful entry point for students, faculty, and administrators to help shape and learn from assessment while also responding to these external parties' interest in documenting and understanding student growth.

At the same time, the oversimplification of outcomes-based depictions of student learning raises challenges, particularly for writing instruction. Because they *are* assessable in some way beyond the context of the course, outcomes can quite seamlessly become competencies, which can be used in turn to give college credit for student learning in ways beyond the course credit hour. In an era of significantly declining funding, higher education in general and state institutions in particular face additional pressures to certify student learning by means other than actual college classes. Even at traditional universities, which are still largely driven by the Carnegie credit hour, there is an increased expectation that faculty will provide ways to give credit for student learning beyond course credit hours (see Kamanetz 2013 for a recent report on the rise of programs and entire universities that certify learning through outcomes assessments).

The expectation that learning can be assessed solely through outcomes is a particular pressure faced by introductory university courses like those that teach writing and other "intellectual skills." Describing our first-year writing courses at Boise State via outcomes (something we have had in place for years) has, in fact, led to very real local pressures to certify learning based on those outcomes; I have been asked by an administrator why our first-year writing courses, which seek to orient students to writing as an area of study and practice within our university context, need to be taught on our campus and by our program faculty. Since we have outcomes for the courses, the logic goes, then we should be able to assess whether students (regardless of age, location, or context) have met those outcomes. So while outcomes-based depictions of student learning can be productive, they make student learning vulnerable to this kind of decontextualization.

Even within our field, we have been complicit in moves to document student learning about writing at specific stopping points along a trajectory. We have generated productive and rich documents—those I have used extensively and admire, like the Framework for Success in Postsecondary Writing and the CWPA Outcomes for First-Year Writing—that have put us in a bind by representing writing as a trajectory from one place—one location—to the next. In fact, the CWPA Outcomes Statement played a central role in our on-campus educational reform discussions related to our university-wide learning outcome for writing, now called the Writing Undergraduate Learning Outcome. There were several times I was deeply grateful for the existence of the Outcomes Statement, for it spoke to national understandings of writing that complemented my (and my colleagues') own arguments about how best to depict writing development. However, our field's focus on signposts (frameworks, benchmarks, outcomes) also leaves us entangled in a model that conceives of learning as a straight line (from framework at the beginning to outcome at the end) when we know learning is much more like scrambling across rocky terrain: learners make progress, slip back, try again, get a little higher, slip back again.

So, as useful as outcomes are, they can't account for the messy, hard, uneven work of learning. They can provide useful snapshots of end points, of what students are *able to do* at different curricular moments. What a threshold concepts approach has the potential to do, if we can create professional development to engage faculty and students with this way of thinking about learning, is provide students with a purposeful cross-curricular writing curriculum that reflects two critical ideas: (1) that threshold concepts for writing (and perhaps other kinds of learning) *across* courses and disciplines may exist; and (2) that when these threshold concepts are made more explicit, students may be more likely to at least recognize, and perhaps even access, aspects of those concepts or the threshold capabilities that lead to them.

MAKING WRITING VISIBLE ACROSS THE
UNDERGRADUATE EXPERIENCE

To examine this potential, I will next focus on Boise State's current undergraduate context, the place of writing within it, and how a threshold concepts framework might foster richer understandings and more intentional descriptions of student learning about writing. Until 2012, our campus had no meaningful depictions of student learning at the undergraduate level. Each department, of course, depicted programs of study for their majors, while our general education program (introductory courses) was significantly underdescribed. Instead, it presented students with a smorgasbord of introductory courses in several categories simply called *areas* with no descriptors at all—Area 1, Area 2, and so on. First-year writing courses (English 101 and 102) were not in these introductory areas but were literally a sidebar in the catalog, a requirement separate from the rest of general education. The implication was that these introductory gen ed courses provided some kind of introduction to disciplinary learning across campus—but what kind, exactly, wasn't at all clear. In addition, writing instruction wasn't located in any particular disciplinary area but was a skill to be developed outside of other contexts for student learning and only in one place: English 101 and 102. Of course, this message is in direct contradiction to some of the central threshold concepts described in part 1 of this book: that Writing is a Social and Rhetorical Activity (1.0) and that All Writers Have More to Learn (4.0) as they work with writing in specific contexts. Therefore, taking this first campus-wide step to developing learning outcomes for writing that span the undergraduate experience—even having conversations about what students should learn and experience—was tremendously valuable. Our outcomes are now described as creating the "'glue' that "holds together the academic and social learning across courses, disciplines, academic classes and general University experiences," in addition to "represent[ing] the general knowledge and skills that business and community leaders as well as graduate schools expect from our graduates" (Boise State University 2013a, 2013b).

The development of University Learning Outcomes also gave new visibility to writing, which is now reflected in what has become known on campus as "*the* Writing ULO" (my emphasis). This outcome states only that students will be able to "write effectively in multiple contexts, for a variety of audiences" (Boise State University, 2013b):

Table 6.1 Boise State University undergraduate learning outcomes

University Learning Outcomes	Cluster Name
1. Write effectively in multiple contexts, for a variety of audiences.	Writing
2. Communicate effectively in speech, both as speaker and listener.	Oral Communication
3. Engage in effective critical inquiry by defining problems, gathering and evaluating evidence, and determining the adequacy of argumentative discourse.	Critical Inquiry

continued on next page

Table 6.1—Continued

University Learning Outcomes	Cluster Name
4. Think creatively about complex problems in order to produce, evaluate, and implement innovative possible solutions, often as one member of a team.	Innovation and Teamwork
5. Analyze ethical issues in personal, professional, and civic life and produce reasoned evaluations of competing value systems and ethical claims.	Ethics
6. Apply knowledge of cultural differences to matters of local, regional, national, and international importance, including political, economic, and environmental issues.	Diversity and Internationalization
7. Disciplinary Lens: Mathematics. Apply knowledge and the methods of reasoning characteristic of mathematics, statistics, and other formal systems to solve complex problems.	Mathematics (DLM)
8. Disciplinary Lens: Natural, Physical, and Applied Sciences. Apply knowledge and methods characteristic of scientific inquiry to think critically about and solve theoretical and practical problems about physical structures and processes.	Natural, Physical, and Engineering Sciences (DLN)
9. Disciplinary Lens: Visual and Performing Arts. Apply knowledge and methods characteristic of the visual and performing arts to explain and appreciate the significance of aesthetic products and creative activities.	Visual and Performing Arts (DLV)
10. Disciplinary Lens: Literature and Humanities. Apply knowledge and the methods of inquiry characteristic of literature and other humanities disciplines to interpret and produce texts expressive of the human condition.	Literature and Humanities (DLL)
11. Disciplinary Lens: Social Sciences. Apply knowledge and the methods of inquiry characteristic of the social sciences to explain and evaluate human behavior and institutions.	Social Sciences (DLS)

The new institution-wide writing University Learning Outcome is operationalized through four specific kinds of courses. Two are positioned in what historically would have been identified as general education: first-year writing (English 101 and 102) and a new 200-level interdisciplinary Intellectual Foundations course. Then, two additional courses—housed in departments and taught by disciplinary faculty across campus—are identified with the Writing ULO: newly reconfigured communication in the disciplines (CID) courses, housed within each discipline across campus, and finishing foundations courses, capstone courses in each discipline across campus. The communication in the disciplines courses must include both the Writing ULO and the Oral Communication ULO; finishing foundations courses can include either the Writing ULO or the Oral Communication ULO (see fig. 6.1).

In this new structure, writing instruction is no longer depicted as one set of first-year courses separate even from general education. Instead, writing is explicitly mapped into the student experience in specified

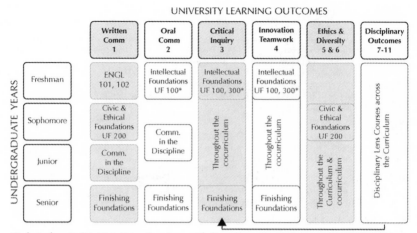

*Students who enter Boise State University as "core certified" or with an AA or AS degree enroll in UF 300, which meets the learning outcomes as above.

Figure 6.1. Undergraduate learning outcomes over time (Boise State University 2013b).

courses and through the university learning outcomes. This refiguring represents a substantial improvement from its significant underrepresentation in the previous general education plan. Yet this new depiction of writing via outcomes is also a macrolevel description in real need of deepening if it is to be of value to faculty across campus. If our shared campus vision of writing remains at the outcome level, writing remains a decontextualized skill (albeit one given attention in specific courses). But a threshold concepts framework offers a particularly powerful way to begin documenting what student learning looks like and to develop a shared, cross-disciplinary vocabulary that might support meaningful student writing development over time.

ENRICHING DEPICTIONS OF STUDENT LEARNING ABOUT WRITING WITHIN THE WRITING ULO

While Meyer and Land note that threshold concepts might be easier to identify "within disciplinary contexts where there is a relatively greater degree of consensus on what constitutes a body of knowledge," I found that this process can work just as well in reverse: the threshold concepts framework is particularly powerful in helping faculty *begin to generate a shared body of knowledge* (Meyer and Land 2003, 9). Within our new learning-outcomes framework, the communication in the disciplines (CID) courses are both discipline specific (housed in departments, taught by departmental faculty) *and* explicitly linked to the Writing Undergraduate Learning Outcome. In these courses, then, writing is taught not as an isolated skill but as disciplinary practice, an embodiment of "how people 'think' within a discipline" (Meyer and Land 2003, 1). The CID courses are thus a particularly rich site for considering (1) what the threshold concepts for writing *at the introduction to the discipline* might be; (2) how they illuminate or complicate the Writing University Learning Outcome; and (3) how their depiction might begin to foster particular kinds of identification and alliance, both vertically along the Writing Undergraduate Learning Outcome trajectory (how might threshold concepts for writing connect from English 101 and 102, UF 200, CID, and Finishing Foundations courses?) *and* horizontally, among faculty who teach communication in the disciplines courses across campus (how might these courses with substantially different content and focus foster student writing development in appropriate ways?).

Threshold concepts for initial disciplinary writing as evident in the CID courses emerged from interviews with faculty teaching CID courses across majors and course contexts. These threshold concepts were: (1) writing is an act of disciplinary identity; (2) disciplinary writing requires rhetorical flexibility and increasing meta-awareness, or discernment; and (3) disciplinary writing is not necessarily mastered in one particular course. These threshold concepts as identified at the midway point of CID courses offer us the potential to now build a more complex picture of the student learning that might enrich the as-of-now brief description used for the Writing ULO (see table 6.1).

The first threshold concept for writing within CID courses that emerged from the interview data focused on how writing is not just about transcribing thought but about enacting a discipline. In their CID courses, faculty witness how students begin to shift in identity through their writing—professionally and personally (see 2.3, "Writing Is a Way of Enacting Disciplinarity"; 3.1, "Writing Is Linked to Identity"; and 3.4, "Disciplinary and Professional Identities Are Constructed Through Writing"). Students struggle to see writing as a more complex act of communication rather than a kind of display—and it is this deeper understanding faculty see as critical. Al Heathrow[1] draws on a metaphor to describe this critical shift in understanding: "A big thing that I talk about quite a bit in talking about writing in the health sciences is that you very rarely quote. You just don't. Especially if you're reviewing studies you focus on the findings and it's almost just a stylistic thing. It looks tacky. I mean the analogy I give is like wearing cutoffs to a cocktail party. You just don't do it. Part of it is just understanding the conventions of the discipline and you just don't do it." Heathrow's comments can elucidate the struggle students sometimes have understanding that even citation conventions can "tell us something about the discipline's values and practices while also recreating them by enacting them" (see 2.3, "Writing Is a Way of Enacting Disciplinarity").

In a different way, Brian Tollefson, an English education professor, also notes how students must move from a passive perspective to actively identifying with their chosen profession in texts they write. He notes how aspiring teachers often assume they'll be delivering prepackaged material and they don't realize, even in the current educational climate, how much they'll be responsible for. He says, "A lot of them come in [to the CID course] thinking, 'Well there's a recipe book that you follow, isn't there?' That's what they think. [I tell them,] 'No, you're writing a book yourself.'" So first a shift in psychological orientation is needed: future teachers must begin to accept their identity as teachers. Then they realize, eventually, that they will be able to "write the book" themselves—and that that act of writing is an act of embracing a teaching identity. Indeed, at the thresholds of their teaching professions, these writers begin to realize how they are "socialized, changed, through their writing in new environments"; they also begin to see how "these changes can have deep implications" (see 3.0, "Writing Enacts and Creates Identities and Ideologies").

Another consistent threshold concept for learning about writing within CID courses is developing meta-awareness and greater discernment about writing situations within the discipline (see 4.0, "All Writers Have More to Learn," and 5.0, "Writing Is [Also Always] a Cognitive Activity"). These concepts are articulated in one way by Camilla Bennett, a kinesiology professor, describing how she helps students see where writing is at work in their careers ahead:

> We look at the various responsibilities, and communication and advocacy is one of our responsibilities. So then how does the communication tie in? What are the kinds of jobs? So they all have to go and interview somebody to see, 'Oh, so how is communication used?' So we look at the various settings where health educators work, so how does a work-site health educator communicate versus somebody in a health care setting versus in a public health setting?

She contends, then, that students need a strong sense of rhetorical flexibility if they are to be successful writers within the discipline.

Other faculty describe the idea of meta-awareness as a kind of rhetorical attunement; they saw students struggling to develop what Sawyer Glover, from philosophy, described as a different level of "accuracy" and what Evan Mattison, from psychology, named "precision": the growing ability to see perhaps-subtle but important textual distinctions (see 4.0, "All Writers Have More to Learn"). Ralph Sylvester, a civil-engineering professor, notes that for many students, "writing is one category [of generic school writing] for them. And that's it. And some students, frankly, don't move away from that mindset no matter what we do." His frustration also speaks to what faculty in Linda Adler-Kassner and John Majewski's study noted: disciplinary practices that seem "obvious" to experts—that technical reports are completely different from research-based essays, for example—are not so obvious to students. Sawyer Glover describes the novice moves students make as writers in philosophy. They are learning how to summarize what theorists say, but that's no longer enough. He tells students, "Then I want you to say something new and interesting. . . . There's this notion of accuracy which we struggle to convey." He describes how students engage with philosophical theorists by just pointing out something they *disagree* with, and he wants them to push for *why*. This is difficult work; he says,

> I think people are still struggling to recognize that or to get comfortable with that demand and [struggling] to work out when it's okay to sort of gloss the hand wave a bit to motivate and when precision is required. So I think part of what's making it difficult for them to do, it's like it's hard to—something like the following. It's hard to improve your dance skills if you can't hear the beat.

Helping students recognize that a "beat" exists is a matter of tuning that attention to discourse differences that aren't immediately evident for those new to the discipline. Glover is depicting a kind of meta-awareness—an attunement to ways of writing one's self into those contextualized practices.

In this depiction of student writers learning to hear the beat, we see threshold concepts overlapping and interacting. Learning to do a disciplinary dance well is both about identity—about understanding how to navigate *as* a philosopher, in this case—and about the ongoing reorientation to the "beat" of the discipline's language, orientations, beliefs, and values. As students struggle to tune their ear to a different beat within written work, they begin to engage in a meta-awareness about disciplinary writing. Important for faculty, recognizing that All Writers Have More to Learn (see 4.0), while also understanding the roles of meta-cognition and reflection (see 5.2, "Metacognition Is Not Cognition," and 5.4, "Reflection Is Critical for Writers' Development") helps illuminate why and how the Writing ULO is distributed throughout the university experience. Further, it helps faculty consider how they might help raise students' attunement to important textual differences within their disciplines that are often familiar enough to be invisible to expert writers like themselves.

The final threshold concept for writing that emerged from these interviews is this idea: learning to write within a discipline is an extended process that will not be mastered within one course. In their chapter, Adler-Kassner and Majewski describe how their interviews led faculty to consider the ways in which student learning "can be supported through deliberately sequenced learning opportunities" (187). Simply discussing the CID courses both in terms of threshold concepts and with the vertical writing strand in mind led faculty to recognize the possibilities for student development over time; we began to see the vertical writing strand as a meaningful context in itself. At the same time, faculty also often understood how uneven the progression in writing strategies might be for students. First, there are inevitable challenges related to how students encounter courses. As Al Heathrow (health sciences) was describing the placement of his department's CID course in the curriculum, he noted, "We're focusing on junior level [for the CID course] but that said . . . it's probably not a bridge to nowhere but that's got to be a really long bridge [between first-year writing, CID, and later writing-focused courses]." Then, there are the realities of how learning occurs for individual students. When discussing student learning within the one CID course he teaches in engineering, Ralph Sylvester describes how uneven it can be: the semester's work includes intensive and extensive lab reports, and he notes that "by the end of the semester . . . there is some backsliding. They kind of—it's like they're exhausted and they don't even think about it anymore." Sylvester's conception of student learning here is useful: he sees that progress is not an even uphill climb but a messy, troublesome process, and his course is one location in that journey for students. Pointing to the unstable and complex journey this kind of new understanding about writing needs, Evan Mattison notes, "It takes a while for them to really absorb that, and they may not, even by the end of the semester." With these conversations about the threshold concepts not of their disciplines but of *writing in the CID course*, about a course both part of their disciplines and responsive to the new Writing Undergraduate Learning Outcome, these faculty are able to begin conceptualizing students' journey along the vertical writing strand, from first-year writing to CID and later finishing-foundations courses, as a context in which they now teach. These conversations make visible how writing is not perfectible (see 4.0, "All Writers Have More to Learn"). A threshold concepts approach, then, helps illuminate new and overlapping contexts for courses labeled *communication in the disciplines* at Boise

State. These courses can now begin to be identified (1) along the trajectory of courses aligned under the Writing Undergraduate Learning Outcome; (2) with other communication-in-the-disciplines courses across campus, where these collected depictions of student learning about writing overlap in thought-provoking ways; and (3) within their disciplines, as they had always (and previously, only) been aligned.

One immediate benefit of holding interviews with communication in the disciplines (CID) faculty was our shared realization that any meaningful connection of courses within the vertical writing strand, from English 101 and 102 and into CID courses, was going to be challenging. While our courses were newly networked through the Writing ULO, students encounter them years apart, the point Al Heathrow made in discussing that "really long bridge." If we were going to build any bridge at all, we needed to understand what the meaningful possibilities for connection might be; the CID threshold concepts offer one avenue for continuing conversations.

Second, focusing on what student learning really looks like *in the struggle, in that uneven climb across rocky terrain*, enabled these faculty to begin seeing their courses not only as one in a vertical series of courses aligned under the Writing ULO but also as a CID course, a kind of threshold experience we are now providing more systematically across campus. The threshold concepts framework enabled faculty to see the *content* of teaching (disciplinary) writing, a shared knowledge base we might build across campus. Instead of focusing only on what students are able to do by the end of a course, as a productive outcomes-based discussion would have enabled us to do, a threshold concepts–grounded discussion—and the explicit embrace of struggle, difficulty, and uneven uptake—led these faculty to depictions of what student learning looks like throughout a course. When we collectively begin to understand (or remind ourselves) that learning is uneven and complicated, that understanding can inform the neat story the Writing ULO seems to tell.

CONCLUSION: KEEPING STUDENT LEARNING IN THE PICTURE

While these initial depictions of threshold concepts for writing at a particular curricular moment are only "partially articulated notion[s] of thresholds," they offer depictions of student learning that are, as Patrick Carmichael found, "more wide ranging and exploratory than the conventional professional development" might evoke (Carmichael 2012, 39). Describing how students experience learning about writing through these interviews also pushes at the threshold aspect of the threshold concepts framework: working to articulate student learning throughout an undergraduate experience highlights the "protracted," uneven journey that learning really is (Meyer and Land 2006, 3). As such, the description of threshold concepts for *writing* can provide a meaningful entry point for describing the rich student learning that lies between course names and beneath "The Writing ULO" on a chart.

Perhaps serendipitously, these faculty depictions of threshold concepts of writing map quite nicely onto our field's threshold concepts for writing, as depicted in part 1 of this book. These shared understandings, once articulated, then make visible how encountering "learning thresholds," as Ray Land recently described them, might occur within a vertical writing curriculum (Rehm 2013). For example, it's quite possible to see how the first-year writing curriculum, which seeks to help students interrogate genre, purpose, and audience in specific rhetorical situations (see 2.0, "Writing Speaks to Situations through Recognizable Forms"), could then lead to CID faculty developing approaches within those courses that help students in turn interrogate disciplinary rhetorical contexts and develop strategies for moving among them. In addition, the ways in which the CID faculty describe the importance of understanding disciplinary writing as an act of identification with that discipline usefully echo the work of first-year writing: in English 101, our curriculum asks students to interrogate their assumptions about who and what a writer is (see 3.0, "Writing Enacts and Creates Identities and Ideologies," and 2.3, "Writing Is a Way of Enacting Disciplinarity"). Working together to analyze threshold concepts for writing as identified by faculty at different points in the curriculum (English 101/102, UF 200, CID, FF) could, in turn, provide a meaningful campus-wide depiction of student learning over time. In other words, TCs can be employed as a way to *develop* the "shared knowledge base" around a cross- and interdisciplinary attribute like writing.

As we begin to map out productive ways to both facilitate student learning and then assess student learning across the undergraduate experience via the Foundational Studies Program, these faculty depictions of learning about writing provide an additional perspective to bring to discussions of enhancing connections between courses and meaningful assessment—key areas where faculty have begun raising questions now as the new program is enacted. Assessing student uptake of threshold concepts across CID courses, for example, or along the Writing Undergraduate Learning Outcome trajectory could both create a useful picture of student learning and account for learning contexts in a way that outcomes-based assessments might not.

Threshold concepts provide an alternative perspective on the neat vision set forth by the use of learning outcomes alone, reminding us that the actual learning happens between these signposts and outcomes. If we agree that our courses are not only content to describe and skills to certify, then working with faculty to articulate what threshold concepts for learning might be at various points along a curriculum offers a two-fold benefit. First and most importantly, describing threshold concepts for writing offers new opportunities for cross-course connections and intentional sequencing of key concepts across spans of time and student development. Second, threshold concepts provide another way to communicate to external audiences (on campus and beyond) how and why student learning is debased—and the college experience devalued—when it is broken down into discrete skills. Threshold concepts articulate the messiness of student learning in a way outcomes alone won't. They help faculty, students, and, potentially, external stakeholders focus on the "long tunnels"[2] of learning difficult and critical concepts now visible through a structure like the vertical writing curriculum. They now provide a map of student learning that gets closer to acknowledging, more honestly, the uncertain and uneven work of learning about writing that has the potential to be supported and developed more meaningfully across the curriculum.

Notes

1. All names are pseudonyms
2. Thanks to John Majewski for this additional metaphor.

References

American Association of Colleges and Universities (AAC&U). 2013. "Liberal Education and America's Promise (LEAP)." http://www.aacu.org/leap/.

Accreditation Board for Engineering and Technology. 2010. "Assessment: Defining Student Outcomes." http://www.abet.org/defining-student-outcomes/.

Boise State University. 2013a. "Foundational Studies Program." http://academics.boise state.edu/fsp/.

Boise State University. 2013b. "University Learning Outcomes." http://academics.boise state.edu/fsp/university-learning-outcomes/.

Carmichael, Patrick. 2012. "Tribes, Territories, and Threshold Concepts: Educational Materialisms at Work in Higher Education." *Educational Philosophy and Theory* 44 (1): 31–42.

Driscoll, Amy, and Swarup Wood. 2007. *Developing Outcomes-Based Assessment for Learner-Centered Education.* Sterling, VA: Stylus.

Kamanetz, Anya. "Are you Competent? Prove it." *New York Times*, October 29, 2013. http://www.nytimes.com/2013/11/03/education/edlife/degrees-based-on-what-you-can-do-not-how-long-you-went.html?pagewanted=all.

Meyer, Jan H. F., and Ray Land. 2003. "Threshold Concepts and Troublesome Knowledge: Linkages to Ways of Thinking and Practising." ETL Project Occasional Report 4. http://www.etl.tla.ed.ac.uk/docs/ETLreport4.pdf.

Meyer, Jan H. F., and Ray Land. 2006. "Threshold Concepts and Troublesome Knowledge: An Introduction." In *Overcoming Barriers to Student Learning: Threshold Concepts and Troublesome Knowledge*, edited by Jan H. F. Meyer and Ray Land, 3–18. New York: Routledge.

Northwest Commission on Colleges and Universities. 2010. "Standard Two, Resources and Capacity." http://www.nwccu.org/.

Penn, Jeremy. 2011. *Assessing Complex General Education Student Learning Outcomes.* Hoboken, NJ: Wiley.

Rehm, James. 2013. "Before and after Students Get It." *Teaching Talk* (blog). https://teachingcommons.stanford.edu/teaching-talk/and-after-students-get-it-threshold -concepts.

7
THRESHOLD CONCEPTS IN FIRST-YEAR COMPOSITION

Doug Downs and Liane Robertson

INTRODUCTION

First-year composition (FYC) is "a space, a moment, and an experience—in which students might reconsider writing apart from previous schooling and work, within the context of inquiry-based higher education" (Downs 2013, 50). It should be, in other words, a curricular space with two goals, one for students and one for the course itself: (1) for students to examine and ideally reconsider prior knowledge about writing in light of new experiences and knowledge offered by their FYC course(s), and (2) for the course itself to serve as a general education course, teaching transferable knowledge of and about writing so that what is taught and learned can be adapted to new contexts of writing. This mission is incredibly challenging given the nature of writing as a radically contextual and situated activity, one that varies dramatically from instance to instance and site to site.

When we examine first-year composition with an eye toward teaching threshold concepts of and about writing, we find that these goals for FYC—helping students examine prior knowledge and teaching for transfer—dovetail with a pedagogy that makes threshold concepts the declarative content of the course. Threshold concepts connect with reexamining prior knowledge because, as Meyer and Land (2006) suggest, early knowledge of writing is likely to be built on incomplete and inaccurate ideas about writing—misconceptions of the nature of the activity and misguided expectations as to how writing ought to work and go. To say that FYC will focus on threshold concepts, then, is to say that it will, in part, focus on misconceptions and work toward richer conceptualizations of writing. Threshold concepts connect as well with the

DOI: 10.7330/9780874219906.c007

mission of teaching for transfer because the threshold concepts of writing are general principles that apply across a wide range of writing situations, even as those situations vary widely. Unlike narrow procedural (how-to) knowledge, which varies from task to task, threshold concepts apply broadly to almost every writing situation. A general education writing course is helped tremendously in its mission of teaching transferable knowledge about a situated activity when threshold concepts are the declarative content taught in the course.

Although we are relatively new to the language of threshold concepts and have only recently begun explicitly designing our FYC courses with them in mind, we have been implicitly making threshold concepts the declarative content of our FYC courses for some time. In this chapter, we first provide examples from our own courses to explore groups of threshold concepts that help FYC accomplish the two purposes we outline above (i.e., addressing misconceptions of writing and teaching for transfer). We then use this discussion of specific threshold concepts to help us develop grounded pedagogical examples in the second part of the chapter. There, we explore threshold concepts as a conceptual framework for FYC, theorizing about the reasons threshold concepts make effective content for FYC and unpacking the claims we've made in this introduction. In the final section of the chapter, we consider how threshold concepts can shape student learning outcomes and serve as course content. Ultimately, we contend that designing a first-year composition course around threshold concepts is feasible and that threshold concepts are a key to helping FYC achieve the dual missions of addressing misconceptions in students' writing knowledge and of teaching for learning transfer to later, different writing situations.

WHICH TO TEACH? CHOOSING THRESHOLD CONCEPTS FOR FYC

Writing is an exercise in, as Ann Berthoff (1987) famously puts it, *allatonceness*. No element of the writing process is ultimately separable from the other parts. The same is true of writing's threshold concepts. In part 1 of this book, individual concepts are bundled under overarching thematic concepts, but each concept is thick with cross-references to other concepts because they are interdependent and intertwined. In composing this chapter, we have also recognized that our FYC courses concern themselves with a large number of individual threshold concepts, and we have bundled them under four overarching categories. Here, we detail these categories and the individual threshold concepts that connect to them.

Our experiences have suggested that four areas present particular challenges when we attempt to address FYC's twin missions (addressing misconceptions and teaching for transfer): writing as human interaction (rhetoric); textuality; epistemology (ways of knowing and the nature of knowledge); and writing process. Students' misconceptions about writing most often relate to one of these categories. Thus, we believe these four areas are important to emphasize in FYC. Here we discuss each of these areas and attempt to connect them to the threshold concepts defined in part 1 of this book.

Human Interaction (Rhetoric)

Seasoned writers usually treat writing as rhetorical human interaction in which readers and writers interact to shape writing and meaning. Novice writers are much less likely to recognize the interactional nature of writing. To them, writing is strictly about getting sentences right rather than interacting with or being responsible to readers. Building an understanding of writing as a rhetorical activity, as human interaction, seems an essential threshold concept for FYC.

In the category of human interaction, we include threshold concepts that identify and explore the relationships writing invites and requires between humans: writer, audience, and context; and writing as collaboration. As discussed in the first section of part 1, human interaction positions writing as a social and rhetorical activity (1.0). It addresses, invokes, and/or creates audiences (see 1.2, "Writing Addresses, Invokes, and/or Creates Audiences")—directly or indirectly, actively or passively. Writing also mediates activities (see 1.5, "Writing Mediates Activity"), which reminds us that rhetorical theory stresses the situated nature of writing—that writing is constrained by the situation-specific exigence of particular people (readers, users, writers) who need a text to accomplish a particular goal. Writing speaks to situations using genres enacted by writers and readers with specific purposes and audiences in mind (see 2.2, "Genres Are Enacted by Writers and Readers"). These threshold concepts seem fundamental to building students' understandings of rhetoric and the nature of writing as rhetorical. So do two other threshold concepts implied by rhetorical theory but not explicitly named here: writing is contingent (based on contingent guidelines and conventions rather than on universal rules), and writing is always collaborative—because readers/users are writers constructing meaning in conjunction with their understandings or perceptions of audience(s) (again, see 1.2).

It is this set of threshold concepts, then, that is in play when we focus course content on human interaction and rhetoric.

Textuality

New college students often hold misconceptions about another important threshold concept associated with texts: that meaning is constructed by readers, not wholly contained within the text itself. Yet there are few more essential conceptual shifts than this one, as gaining an understanding of meaning as constructed fundamentally alters both writers' and readers' relationships to texts.

Under the heading of *textuality*, then, are threshold concepts that relate to the nature of texts and how they integrate the relationships between writers and texts. Two central threshold concepts in this category are Words Get Their Meaning from Other Words (1.4) and Texts Get Their Meaning from Other Texts (2.6). We also emphasize that texts *do* things (get things accomplished), or in Andrea Lunsford's words, Writing Is Performative (2.5). In addition, it's important for students to learn that texts are objects *apart from* writers and can be improved and developed (see 4.1, "Text Is an Object Outside of One's Self that Can Be Improved and Developed"). We are also concerned with overturning the misconception that form and content are separable; writing integrates them as *arranged material*. Similarly, writing does not equal grammar or formula—in other words, texts cannot be reduced to syntax and formal concerns (see 2.2, "Genre Is Enacted by Writers and Readers"). The concerns that shape texts are greater than replicating accepted language conventions, and thus composing writing requires more than attention to formal concerns. To write is to invent content, not just to arrange sentences.

Epistemology (Ways of Knowing)

In asking students to understand textuality differently, we are also asking them to consider the nature of knowledge itself: writing is more than transmitting existing information, it is instead a means of *creating new knowledge*. Considering knowledge in this way requires tackling a series of threshold concepts related to epistemology.

Students will need to learn that Writing is a Knowledge-Making Activity (1.1). That knowledge is socially constructed is itself a threshold concept (related closely to the threshold concept that textual meaning is constructed as well), as is the notion that writing and reflection iteratively construct knowledge. Therefore, writing creates new meanings rather than transmitting information unaltered—writing is not simply a conduit. The concept that Reflection Is Critical for Writers' Development (5.4) also seems critical here. Another related threshold concept involves recognizing that all writing is creative because all writing produces something new; this threshold concept can conflict with students' expectations that "informative" or "researched" writing is distinct from "creative" writing.

Beyond the nature of writing itself as epistemic, students need to encounter threshold concepts related to how writing is learned. Writing must be learned, so writers are often aided by learning *about writing* (see 4.0, "All Writers Have More to Learn"). Students' prior experiences and knowledge influence their writing (see 3.3, "Writing Is Informed by Prior Experience") and can sometimes act as barriers to developing new knowledge about writing (Driscoll and Wells 2012; Robertson, Taczak, and Yancey 2012). For FYC students, learning about writing in ways that enable them to develop a conceptual framework *about* writing (Beaufort 2007) will be helpful as they face new writing situations. Through metacognition and cognition, they are better able to construct their own knowledge about writing, which they can repurpose for each situation in which writing is produced, particularly in challenging or new writing situations.

Process

The fourth area in which we encounter deeply problematic misconceptions of writing among FYC students is connected to the composing and inscription (Prior 2004) involved in the production and reproduction of text, which we shorthand as *process*. We want to note here that we are not referring simply to drafting, writing, revising, and editing, but instead to a more complicated question: how do FYC students believe texts come into being, and what threshold concepts will change their thinking?

A number of threshold concepts on process align with FYC. Because Texts Get Their Meaning from Other Texts (2.6), we teach that invention is intertextual, not purely inspirational, and we try to help students understand revision as development of new ideas, not just "editing" (see 4.4, "Revision Is Central to Developing Writing"). Students often still need to encounter the threshold concepts that writing is not natural (see 1.6, "Writing Is Not Natural") but rather unavoidably a technological activity (see 1.9, "Writing Is a Technology through Which Writers Create and Recreate Meaning"). In addition, FYC students rarely initially understand how writing is an ongoing and iterative process only ever completed for now. The cutting edge of networked, electronic writing environments is illustrating more and more that texts *themselves* (not just the act of writing) are processes too—never completed, perpetually in circulation and development by multiple writers and readers.

As we consider our FYC courses and how we think about building them around threshold concepts, these four areas—the rhetorical nature of writing as human interaction, the nature of textuality, epistemology, and writing process—seem to us to have been critical in achieving the two goals for FYC courses we described in the introduction: addressing students' misconceptions and teaching knowledge that will be applicable in later writing situations.

THRESHOLD CONCEPTS AS A CONCEPTUAL FRAMEWORK FOR FYC

Why do threshold concepts—and these in particular—seem so effective for framing FYC courses? To answer this question, we will unpack the importance of three claims we have thus far simply asserted: that writing conceptions and theories are important to the activity of writing; that prior knowledge plays an important role in writing courses; and that there is value in making threshold concepts FYC's declarative content. We will come back to a more thorough discussion about why threshold concepts are an effective organizing framework for FYC in our closing discussion of curricular strategies for implementing threshold concepts in FYC.

Threshold Concepts and Personal Theories of Writing

We have to this point asserted that a writer's conceptions of writing—what they understand the nature of writing to be and their expectations for how writing ought to work—ought to be a central focus of first-year composition, and that the power of threshold concepts in shaping students' conceptions of writing makes a curriculum organized around threshold concepts desirable. Much in our argument hangs on the premise of the importance of these conceptions of writing.

Every writer has a set of knowledges and beliefs about writing, some explicit and some tacit, that make up their personal theory of writing. The conceptions that make up this personal theory are developed through education, experience, observation, and cultural narratives of writing; few writers will ever explicitly articulate their theory, but they will live by it. By *theory*, we mean a systematic narrative of lived experience and observed phenomena that both accounts for (makes sense of) past experience and makes predictions about future experience. The better—the more completely, consistently, and elegantly—a theory accounts for past experience and the more accurate its predictions about future experience, the stronger or more robust it is, and thus the more useful it is. The writer's personal theory of writing—their conceptions of what happens when they write, what ought to be happening, why that does or does not happen—shapes both their actions while writing and their interpretations of the results of their writing activities. This theory of writing and the set of conceptions that make it up are how a writer—in our case, an FYC student—understands "the game" of writing.

The role these conceptions and theories play in writing is therefore of great importance in writing instruction. Take, for example, the conception of *giftedness*, as studied by Palmquist and Young (1992). Does a writer imagine writing ability as an unteachable talent or "gift," or as teachable and learnable regardless of initial talent? A student's belief in this regard will change their experience of a writing course. As conceptions bundle into theories, the influence grows. For example, the conception that writing well requires a gift, Michael Palmquist and Richard Young found, often occurs alongside the conception that the purpose of writing is "to express your own feelings about something" (Palmquist and Young 1992, 156–57). These "romantic" notions of writing (Palmquist and Young 1992, 158–59) shape students' dispositions toward writing by interacting with writing apprehension: in the study, students with a strong belief in giftedness and low self-efficacy had high writing apprehension (Palmquist and Young 1992, 151). We see in such a study, then, interplay between conceptions of writing, the meshing together of conceptions to form—whether consciously or in effect—theories of writing, and the impact those theories can have on writing experiences and performance.

Threshold concepts, we find, provide a means of locating individual theories about writing within a framework that allows for transformation, the shift in values about writing that affords a reconceptualization *of* writing. The threshold concept of revision as development (within our area of process knowledge) is an easy example, as it takes little imagination to predict the difference in writing process between a student who believes revision is essentially a punishment for making mistakes and a student who believes revision is a desirable and essential part of writing.

Prior Knowledge

Theories of writing begin with one's first literacy experiences. Because a writer makes predictions about future writing experience based on prior knowledge of writing, to work on theories of writing is inevitably to bring prior knowledge of writing into play. Threshold concepts specify a particular role for and import of students' prior knowledge: when students find a threshold concept challenging, the challenge often relates to the types of writing they have engaged in and their prior knowledge. For example, many students seem to leave high school believing writing is formulaic, or writing in one context is universal for all contexts. Teaching threshold concepts exposes, and requires that students reconsider, prior knowledge that might be a barrier to learning to think in new ways about writing, and it asks students to think about writing conceptually rather than formulaically. Research on prior knowledge (Driscoll and Wells 2012; Reiff and Bawarshi 2011; Robertson, Taczak, and Yancey 2012) indicates that students' dispositions and experiences often get in the way of their ability to see writing differently in college, sometimes causing them to fail at assignments for which they apply inappropriate prior knowledge because they don't understand the expectations of that context—what Anne Beaufort (2007) calls "negative transfer."

When FYC is framed as an encounter with threshold concepts, prior knowledge that may be a barrier to new learning is understood as "the problem" to which teaching threshold concepts might be "the solution." While not all prior knowledge is problematic, the resistance to letting go of prior knowledge that prevents writers from seeing new possibilities is potentially limiting (Robertson, Taczak, and Yancey 2012). One of the defining features of threshold concepts is, in fact, the "troublesome knowledge" they create for a learner. A threshold concept is, in part, characterized by its difficulty to grasp, in terms of, or in light of, an individual's prior knowledge—troublesome knowledge manifested in "learning bottlenecks" that occur in such instances (Meyer and Land 2006). Teaching threshold concepts can help clear those bottlenecks by allowing the learner to loosen the prior knowledge that may have challenged their conceptual understanding. In the same way that a new paradigm is almost impossible to understand from inside an old one (see Polanyi 1994), threshold concepts can ease a learner into acceptance of troublesome knowledge that seems counterintuitive, alien, or incoherent (Meyer and Land 2006; Perkins 1999).

Threshold Concepts as Declarative Course Content

When threshold concepts are the subject matter that provides a theoretical framework for a writing course, they offer not only a raison d'etre and a mechanism for student learning but also the declarative content students study in the course and take to future writing situations. A wide array of research on transfer demonstrates the importance of mindfulness to transfer (Beaufort 1999; Carter 2007; Nowacek 2011; Perkins and Salomon 1992; Rounsaville 2008; Wardle 2007), and mindfulness is facilitated by declarative knowledge. Threshold concepts provide the framework into which students might transfer their prior knowledge: knowledge transfers in, is transformed or not, and then choices are made by students (with instructor guidance) through the framework of threshold concepts. And this framework extends to what to think about learning. If students understand that the threshold concepts they consider in FYC can transform their thinking about writing, they'll be open to threshold concepts in other contexts as they encounter them as learners. Having experienced the portal that threshold concepts might enable in FYC, and having experienced troublesome knowledge that has been or is being worked through, students will more easily recognize threshold concepts elsewhere or be confident that troublesome knowledge will lead to more learning.

ROLES FOR THRESHOLD CONCEPTS IN WRITING CLASSROOMS

Teaching threshold concepts, then, can help us achieve FYC's dual mission of helping students reconceive writing and transfer their learning to new contexts. And while threshold concepts remain a new way for us to think, in this final section of the chapter we draw on a great deal of experience gained using threshold concepts in our classrooms *in effect* to look specifically at three aspects of our classrooms: learning outcomes, principles for teaching threshold concepts, and materials with which we teach them.

Learning Outcomes

In developing writing-about-writing pedagogies, Downs and Wardle (2007) argued that one shift in a WAW course is *goals*. FYC becomes less about how to write and more *about writing*—its nature and processes (see the metaconcept "Writing Is an Activity and a Subject of Study"). From this perspective, declarative knowledge is emphasized. Though procedural knowledge—the how—remains central to the writing of the course, first-year writing is no longer posited as a course in how to write at the college level, one of the most frequently stated goals in non-WAW FYC pedagogy, but instead becomes a course in learning to study writing and using writing as a means for facilitating that study. This shift from emphasis on procedural to declarative knowledge is in fact a shift in learning outcomes. This shift can also be understood as one toward a pedagogy shaped by threshold concepts: those we desire students to learn become declarative content in the course, with an accompanying shift in learning outcomes.

In Doug's program, for example, student learning outcomes are almost entirely grounded in threshold concepts:

1. Understand the nature of writing and your own experiences with writing differently than when you began.

The implicitly stated overall goal for the course is to encounter and learn a wide range of threshold concepts that unsettle prior knowledge. (Some of these are demonstrated in other outcomes in the list.)

2. Increase your ability to read rhetorical situations and make rhetorical choices consciously in your writing.

Here we directly engage the ideas about human interaction and rhetorical knowledge we describe above, which draw on many of the concepts in the first part of this book.

3. Know what questions to ask when entering new rhetorical situations in order to adjust your approach to writing to meet that situation.

Here we apply the threshold concept of rhetorical knowledge to a directly stated goal of transferability.

4. Be a more reflective (mindful, self-aware, thoughtful) writer.

Here we engage the threshold concept that both writing and the transfer of writing knowledge require mindful reflection (see 5.4, "Reflection Is Critical for Writers' Development").

5. Build your ability to collaborate in communities of writers and readers.

Again with human interaction, engaging the threshold concept that writing is always interactive and collaborative between readers and writers (see 2.2, "Genre Is Enacted by Writers and Readers," and 1.5, "Writing Mediates Activity").

6. Gain comfort with taking risks in new writing situations.

Here we engage the threshold concept that writing is contingent on situation and that old rules will not always apply in new situations (again echoing the rhetorical and activity-theory principles of threshold concepts related to "Writing Is a Social and Rhetorical Activity" [1.0] and "Writing Speaks to Situations through Recognizable Forms" [2.0]).

7. Increase your control of situation-appropriate conventions of writing.

Here is another statement of the threshold concept that writing is contingent, plus the concept that writing is not rule driven but rather convention and guideline driven, engaging the subject area of textuality.

8. Expand your research literacy.

Here we engage the subject area of epistemology (see 1.1, "Writing is a Knowledge-Making Activity").

Though these outcomes were written more than two years before Doug encountered the idea of threshold concepts, they show the implicit presence of threshold concepts in the course.

In Liane's FYC class, the use of writing concepts, key terms that help students develop a vocabulary for articulating their knowledge about writing and on which they continue to build beyond the course, inherently reflect the subject areas and particular threshold concepts for FYC we suggest here. For example, students learn the terms *audience, genre, rhetorical situation,* and *reflection* during the first few weeks and work toward understanding how to recognize these concepts in a range of writing situations, to theorize how the concepts work in each situation (see 1.1, "Writing Is a Knowledge-Making Activity"), and to reflect on their own knowledge and practice about writing as they learn (see 5.4, "Reflection Is Critical for Writers' Development"). This concept-based content is intended to transform student understanding of writing; in fact, it fits all the criteria by which we define a threshold concept. The concept-based content is intended to transform student understanding of writing; concepts act as "anchors" of writing knowledge students are developing, and this mirrors the role of a threshold concept, especially in the epistemology area. This writing-concepts based, teaching-for-transfer design (Yancey, Robertson, and Taczak 2014), like writing-about-writing approaches, has as its foundation the threshold concepts of FYC we have highlighted here. If these successful course models are based on threshold concepts, even if they include threshold concepts only as implicit content, then we can assume these threshold concepts resonate with students and instructors in FYC.

Principles for Teaching Threshold Concepts in FYC

A few recurrent principles systematize our FYC instruction in threshold concepts. First, because to learn threshold concepts is essentially to experience paradigm shifts, we can expect the same learning principles to apply: the need to build a series of experiences and data points that create strong dissonance with prior knowledge that is discarded as no longer useful, but which will at first be explainable only within the frameworks the prior knowledge provides. Only with a critical mass of dissonance-inducing learning and experiences will there come the "aha!" moment that constitutes crossing the threshold into the new concept. A critical incident is often the impetus for learning, especially when students perceive failure at something as an opportunity for learning, as is the case when a science experiment that fails can provide greater insight than one that goes smoothly (Robertson, Taczak, and Yancey 2012).

Second, learning within a threshold concepts framework is facilitated by (and usually requires) explicit, extensive reflection on what's being learned. The mindful process of interrogating one's knowledge and deliberately, thoughtfully trying to compare different ways of thinking is an essential oil for the learning process.

Third, it's important to expect that the learning in a threshold concept driven course is likely to occur either near its end or after the course is over because of the time required to build critical mass against any ineffectual prior knowledge and to reflect on new explanations for experiences that prior knowledge then fails to explain.

Three teaching approaches might prove useful in introducing threshold concepts to students: providing research-based explanations, using metaphors and analogies, and helping students experience the threshold concepts themselves. Explanations for experiences that seem counterintuitive to prior knowledge should be *research based,* meaning that readings grounded in accessible existing scholarship and primary (firsthand) research experiences are crucial to help students understand both how knowledge is made and how they might contribute to the discussion about subjects they are researching. New explanations are further assisted by *translational* work—metaphor, analogy, and other comparisons—and by concrete examples. When we're able to give abstract threshold concepts referents through the use of example, analogy, and metaphor—like equating revision-as-development to driving with headlights (each draft takes you as far as the headlights reach, and in "driving" that far with one draft, you can then see where to drive with the next one)—students are able to work with the new concepts more quickly and easily. Lastly, new explanations for failures in prior knowledge must be *experiential*—students need to be able to see for themselves and understand that since, for example, writing is not perfectible, there is no "right way" to write and therefore writing changes with each context. They need to see themselves as novice college writers (see 4.3, "Learning to Write Effectively Requires Different Kinds of Practice, Time, and Effort," and

4.1, "Text Is an Object Outside of One's Self that Can Be Improved and Developed") so they can write their way into the expertise (Sommers and Saltz 2004) of college writing; if not, they will remain resistant to sloughing off the prior knowledge they no longer want or need and reticent to allow new knowledge to seep in.

These three approaches for teaching new explanations—research based, translational, and experiential—create transparency so that troublesome threshold concepts are more accessible to students, a "pulling back of the curtain" to reveal the realities of the "wizard" behind it (in Oz-ian terms) (see also Nowacek 2011).

Curricular Materials

What, then, can an FYC curriculum look like when it's based on threshold concepts embedded in learning outcomes and responsive to the above pedagogical principles? We teach threshold concepts through specific combinations of course readings, writing assignments, and classroom activities including discussion and workshopping. We both attempt to provide students experiences that create dissonance with ineffectual prior knowledge and new explanations that help resolve that dissonance. However, there is often so much intellectual space to negotiate between the first and last day of the term that students can find the experiential learning of college a tough boundary to cross (in Reiff and Bawarshi's [2011] terms). In an attempt to help other teachers overcome that boundary, we offer examples of curricular arrangements that teach each of the four subject areas for threshold concepts noted as important for FYC courses.

Human Interaction (Rhetoric)

A number of readings in rhetorical theory and discourse/literary studies can provide a foundation for the discussion of human interaction in writing: Keith Grant-Davie (1997) and Lloyd Bitzer (1968) on rhetorical situation and James Corder (1985) on rhetoric as love, for example. Others readings can offer practical examples in which a writer has successfully navigated the rhetorical situation (i.e., *Letter From a Birmingham Jail*, by Martin Luther King Jr. [1963]) or considered its impact (i.e., Gloria Anzaldua's [1987] "How to Tame a Wild Tongue"). In-class work can include analyses of rhetorical situations, rhetorical summaries, close examinations of the elements within the rhetorical situation that might be at work in a piece (i.e., purpose, audience), and the study of examples of academic and everyday writing genres that address a rhetorical situation.

Textuality

A number of relevant readings in rhetoric, linguistics, discourse analysis, literacy studies, and activity theory are available to assist teachers in presenting ideas on textuality. Such readings might include James Porter (1986) on intertextuality, Haas and Flower (1988) on rhetorical reading, and David Russell (1995) or Russell and Yañez (2002) on activity theory or genre systems. Course work might focus on reading responses, workshopping of drafts, and other activities that illustrate the provisionality and constructedness of meaning (i.e., a reading self-protocol).

Epistemology (Ways of Knowing)

Epistemology might be explored through readings like Donald Murray's (1991) "All Writing is Autobiography," chapters from John Swales's (1990) book on genre analysis, James Gee (1989) on discourses, Margaret Kantz (1990) on "using textual sources persuasively," Walter Fisher (1984) on narrative knowing, the National Research Council's (2000) *How People Learn*, Michael Carter's (2007) "Ways of Knowing," or Kathleen Blake Yancey's (1998) *Reflection in the Writing Classroom*. In the classroom, reflection can be used not just as a process tool as it is often seen but also as a tool for learning—as leading to metacognition, as helping create a framework of knowledge, and as a vehicle by which students might transfer these ways of knowing to new situations. Research also supports ways of knowing, especially any research project framed as *generating new knowledge via primary research.*

Process

Process should be practiced as well as studied theoretically through readings that might include Paul Prior's (2004) piece on process (composition and inscription), Carol Berkenkotter and Donald Murray's study of Murray's writing processes (Berkenkotter and Murray 1983), Nancy Sommers (1980) on revision, and Yancey (1998) on reflection as part of the revision process. Assignments to illustrate process as both declarative and procedural might include process analyses, self-observations, invention activities, revision exercises, and reflection that is reiterative and sustained throughout an entire semester so it becomes embedded in process.

CONCLUSION

Threshold concepts for FYC are not overly ambitious, nor are they too theoretical for first-year students, as some instructors might think. But they do represent a different way of approaching the design and experience of FYC curricula, a difference we embrace. Transfer research demonstrates the need for students to develop a framework of knowledge (Beaufort, 1999; 2007) they can bring to new writing contexts that have varying, often unclear, expectations of successful writing. Threshold concepts can provide that framework to which students can transfer revised or reimagined prior knowledge, from which they can transfer new or reconceptualized knowledge to a wide range of writing situations, and with which they can understand that the nature of learning (especially that which they'll see throughout college) is inquiry based and troublesome yet potentially transformative, thus opening themselves to greater potential for that learning to occur. When students understand the end goal is learning how to learn to write (Bergmann and Zepernick 2007) for any future context, rather than learning the right way to write, they will be more successful at writing in all contexts. Threshold concepts as an approach to FYC offer both students and instructors the opportunity to experience the troublesomeness of knowledge about writing and the teaching of writing, as well as the transformation learning through threshold concepts affords.

References

Anzaldua, Gloria. 1987. "How to Tame a Wild Tongue." In *Borderlands/La Frontera: The New Mestiza*, by Gloria Anzaldua, 2947–2955. San Francisco: Aunt Lute Books.

Beaufort, Anne. 1999. *Writing in the Real World: Making the Transition from School to Work.* New York: Teachers College.

Beaufort, Anne. 2007. *College Writing and Beyond: A New Framework for University Writing Instruction.* Logan: Utah State University Press.

Bergmann, Linda S., and Janet Zepernick. 2007. "Disciplinarity and Transfer: Students' Perceptions of Learning to Write." *WPA: Writing Program Administration* 31 (1–2): 124–49.

Berkenkotter, Carol, and Donald M. Murray. 1983. "Decisions and Revisions: The Planning Strategies of a Publishing Writer." *College Composition and Communication* 34 (2): 156–72. http://dx.doi.org/10.2307/357403.

Berthoff, Ann E. 1987. "Recognition, Representation, and Revision." In *A Sourcebook for Basic Writing Teachers*, edited by Theresa Enos, 545–56. New York: Random House.

Bitzer, Lloyd. 1968. "The Rhetorical Situation." *Philosophy & Rhetoric* 1 (1):1–14.

Carter, Michael. 2007. "Ways of Knowing, Doing, and Writing in the Disciplines." *College Composition and Communication* 58 (3): 385–418.

Corder, James. 1985. "Argument as Emergence, Rhetoric as Love." *Rhetoric Review* 4 (1): 16–32. http://dx.doi.org/10.1080/07350198509359100.

Downs, Doug. 2013. "What Is First-Year Composition?" In *A Rhetoric for Writing Program Administrators*, edited by Rita Malenczyk, 50–63. Anderson, SC: Parlor.

Downs, Doug, and Elizabeth Wardle. 2007. "Teaching About Writing, Righting Misconceptions: (Re)Envisioning FYC as Intro to Writing Studies." *College Composition and Communication* 58 (4):552–84.

Driscoll, Dana L., and Jennifer M. H. Wells. 2012. "Beyond Knowledge and Skills: Writing Transfer and the Role of Student Dispositions in and beyond the Writing Classroom." *Composition Forum* 26. http://compositionforum.com/issue/26/beyond-knowledge-skills.php.

Fisher, Walter. 1984. "Narration as a Human Communication Paradigm: The Case of Public Moral Argument." *Communication Monographs* 51 (1): 1–22. http://dx.doi.org/10.1080/03637758409390180.

Gee, James Paul. 1989. "Literacy, Discourse, and Linguistics: Introduction." *Journal of Education* 171 (1):5–17.

Grant-Davie, Keith. 1997. "Rhetorical Situations and Their Constituents." *Rhetoric Review* 15 (2): 264–79. http://dx.doi.org/10.1080/07350199709359219.

Haas, Christina, and Linda Flower. 1988. "Rhetorical Reading Strategies and the Construction of Meaning." *College Composition and Communication* 39 (2): 167–83. http://dx.doi.org/10.2307/358026.

Kantz, Margaret. 1990. "Helping Students Use Textual Sources Persuasively." *College English* 52 (1): 74–91. http://dx.doi.org/10.2307/377413.

King Jr., Martin Luther. 1963. *Letter from a Birmingham Jail.* Philadelphia, PA: American Friends Service Committee.

Meyer, Jan H. F., and Ray Land. 2006. "Threshold Concepts and Troublesome Knowledge: An Introduction." In *Overcoming Barriers to Student Understanding: Threshold Concepts and Troublesome Knowledge*, edited by Jan H. F. Meyer and Ray Land, 3–18. London: Routledge.

Murray, Donald. 1991. "All Writing Is Autobiography." *College Composition and Communication* 42 (1): 66–74. http://dx.doi.org/10.2307/357540.

National Research Council. 2000. "How Experts Differ from Novices." In *How People Learn: Brain, Mind, Experience, and School: Expanded Edition*, ed. John Bransford, Ann Brown, and Rodney R. Cocking, 31–50. Washington, DC: National Academies.

Nowacek, Rebecca. 2011. *Agents of Integration: Understanding Transfer as a Rhetorical Act.* Carbondale: Southern Illinois University Press.

Palmquist, Michael, and Richard Young. 1992. "The Notion of Giftedness and Student Expectations about Writing." *Written Communication* 9 (1): 137–68. http://dx.doi.org/10.1177/0741088392009001004.

Perkins, David. 1999. "The Many Faces of Constructivism." *Educational Leadership* 57 (3): 6–11.

Perkins, David, and Gavriel Salomon. 1992. "Transfer of Learning." In *International Encyclopedia of Education*, 2nd ed., ed. Penelope Peterson, Eva Baker, and Barry McGraw, 2–13. Oxford: Pergamon.

Polanyi, Michael. 1994. "Scientific Controversy." In *Professing the New Rhetoric: A Sourcebook*, ed. Theresa Enos and Stuart Brown, 194–203. Chicago: University of Chicago Press.

Porter, James E. 1986. "Intertextuality and the Discourse Community." *Rhetoric Review* 5 (1): 34–47. http://dx.doi.org/10.1080/07350198609359131.

Prior, Paul. 2004. "Tracing Process: How Texts Come into Being." In *What Writing Does and How It Does It*, edited by Charles Bazerman and Paul Prior, 167–200. Hillsdale, NJ: Erlbaum.

Reiff, Mary Jo, and Anis Bawarshi. 2011. "Tracing Discursive Resources: How Students Use Prior Genre Knowledge to Negotiate New Writing Contexts in First-Year Composition." *Written Communication* 28 (3): 312–37. http://dx.doi.org/10.1177/0741088311410183.

Robertson, Liane, Kara Taczak, and Kathleen Blake Yancey. 2012. "Notes toward a Theory of Prior Knowledge and Its Role in College Composers' Transfer of Knowledge and Practice." *Composition Forum* 26. http://compositionforum.com/issue/26/prior-knowledge-transfer.php.

Rounsaville, Angela. 2008. "From Incomes to Outcomes: FYW Students' Prior Genre Knowledge, Meta-Cognition, and the Question of Transfer." *WPA: Writing Program Administration* 32 (1): 97–112.

Russell, David. 1995. "Activity Theory and Its Implications for Writing Instruction." In *Reconceiving Writing, Rethinking Writing Instruction*, edited by Joseph Petraglia, 51–77. Mahwah, NJ: Erlbaum.

Russell, David R., and Arturo Yañez. 2002. "Big Picture People Rarely Become Historians: Genre Systems and the Contradictions of General Education." In *Writing Selves/Writing Societies: Research from Activity Perspectives*, edited by Charles Bazerman and David R. Russell, 331–62. Fort Collins, CO: WAC Clearinghouse and Mind, Culture and Activity.

Sommers, Nancy. 1980. "Revision Strategies of Student Writers and Experienced Adult Writers." *College Composition and Communication* 31 (4): 378–88. http://dx.doi.org/10.2307/356588.

Sommers, Nancy, and Laura Saltz. 2004. "The Novice as Expert: Writing the Freshman Year." *College Composition and Communication* 56 (1): 124–49. http://dx.doi.org/10.2307/4140684.

Swales, John. 1990. *Genre Analysis*. Cambridge, UK: Cambridge University Press.

Wardle, Elizabeth. 2007. "Understanding 'Transfer' from FYC: Preliminary Results of a Longitudinal Study." *WPA: Writing Program Administration* 31 (1–2): 65–85.

Yancey, Kathleen Blake. 1998. *Reflection in the Writing Classroom*. Logan: Utah State University Press.

Yancey, Kathleen Blake, Liane Robertson, and Kara Taczak. 2014. *Writing across Contexts: Transfer, Composition, and Cultures of Writing*. Logan: Utah State University Press.

8

USING THRESHOLD CONCEPTS TO INFORM WRITING AND RHETORIC UNDERGRADUATE MAJORS

The UCF Experiment

J. Blake Scott and Elizabeth Wardle

The Department of Writing and Rhetoric at UCF was formed in July 2010 with an initial group of five tenured faculty members specializing in various areas of rhetoric and composition. By fall 2013 we had reached our goal of twelve tenured/tenure-earning faculty members and around twenty full-time non-tenure-earning instructors. When we separated from English in 2010 to become our own department, we brought with us an MA in rhetoric and composition, as well as a graduate certificate in professional writing. What we did not have was an undergraduate major or the array of courses that would be included in such a major. Thus, we have spent the last three years creating and revising courses and starting a minor and undergraduate certificate—all of which helped us work our way toward a major. Our major (BA) in writing and rhetoric was approved by the university's board of trustees in March 2014 and officially began in the summer of 2014.

Because of our status as a freestanding department, our strong cadre of rhetoric and composition specialists, and the encouragement of our dean's office to enact new curricular visions, we were able to build from our collective (and, to some degree, changing) sense of the knowledge, values, and boundaries of our field without having to cobble together programs from existing courses and curricular goals, as commonly happens when writing tracks or majors are created within English or other longstanding departments. We have had the opportunity and responsibility to consider and articulate what we know and value as a field and what parts of that knowledge are likely to be relevant for undergraduate

DOI: 10.7330/9780874219906.c008

students who would use our BA to engage in a variety of professions and civic activities.

Although we did not begin the process of creating the major by directly considering threshold concepts, looking back it is clear that some threshold concepts have guided our work along the way—not only in the curricula and courses we developed but also in how we undertook this development work. Though we accomplished a great deal without explicitly articulating our threshold concepts, we have come to believe that doing so could have been a helpful addition to our curriculum planning. Some of our faculty have recently begun to more strategically use threshold concepts as a helpful frame for clarifying, linking, and distinguishing among courses and other program elements. Using the lens of threshold concepts can continue to help our faculty plan and coordinate teaching and learning across the interrelated sites and trajectories of our students' experiences as they move through our proposed major.

As we will discuss in our case history of developing an undergraduate writing and rhetoric major at UCF, threshold concepts can help faculty members imagine pathways of learning through a somewhat flexible curricular structure and help clarify underlying assumptions about a program's curricular goals and emphases, revealing places to work toward agreed-upon understandings and practices. Such curricular planning can be imagined as flexible alignment rather than standardization; the nature of threshold concepts offers more flexibility than student learning outcomes while still enabling faculty members to define and articulate the emphases, boundaries, and interrelationships among a set of courses and experiences.

As the following chapter seeks to illustrate, working with threshold concepts implicitly and/or explicitly has been useful in our program-development work thus far in several ways.

First, *the nature of threshold concepts*—not goals, not learning outcomes, but foundational assumptions that inform learning across time—makes them *flexible* tools for imagining a progression of student learning across a curriculum rather than at one specific moment or in one short period of time.

Second, the *liminality* of threshold concepts is particularly useful in the context of program development. Threshold concepts are learned over time and across liminal, unstable spaces in which learners reconstitute what and how they know. This recognition enables us to have realistic expectations about what students can learn and when—and how difficult that learning may be. Our job as program faculty is to come to some agreement about what we want students to learn and how to scaffold and otherwise coordinate this learning across the entire curriculum, informed by our own difficulties in learning the field's knowledge. This curricular coordination should involve helping students build on foundational concepts and relate new knowledge and practices back to them, all the while recognizing that these foundational concepts must sometimes be relearned at different points.

Finally, asking faculty members to name their unstated assumptions as threshold concepts can be difficult but rewarding. Working out what we know together takes time and, as our case demonstrates, can involve some disagreement, but such work can ultimately generate a shared vision for and investment in a writing and rhetoric major. Working through differences is more possible when faculty members unpack and lay out their sometimes differing assumptions about what we know, which sets of knowledge should take priority, and how to teach this to students in our major.

In this chapter, we offer our department's experiences working toward a major in order to illustrate how threshold concepts can inform programmatic planning in ways that can be understood as both flexible and rigorous. Toward this end, we describe how threshold concepts informed our planning process, including our courses, course groups, and goals and outcomes. We did not explicitly identify and discuss threshold concepts in designing the first iteration of our proposed major, but such concepts still implicitly guided our work and are now coming to more explicitly guide it. Our attempts to compose a writing and rhetoric major illustrate how threshold concepts are more than declarative knowledge—they guide the ways we enact our knowledge.

THRESHOLD CONCEPTS AS IMPLICIT GUIDES IN PLANNING A MINOR AND MAJOR

We began developing plans for our minor and major in summer 2010 as soon as we became a new department (we had to design courses and implement the minor as preliminary steps in creating the major, so we discuss all of these initiatives here as efforts toward creating a major). We had brought a few courses with us from English but were encouraged by our dean's office to imagine our programs and courses from the ground up. With this charge, our tenure-line faculty members set about the task of collectively mapping the field of rhetoric and composition in order to determine what students in a minor and future major would need to learn, understand, and use. We began by identifying three overlapping strands of the field's scholarship: rhetorical studies, writing studies, and literacy and language studies, the latter including linguistics. We also categorized the field in another way—naming pedagogical, historical, and theoretical scholarship as important overlapping dimensions of the field's work.

From the beginning, then, we were working implicitly from the threshold concept that our field is a discipline with a body of knowledge (including scholarly, pedagogical, and professional knowledge); in other words, that *writing and rhetoric is a subject of study* (see the metaconcept "Writing Is an Activity and a Subject of Study"). Although all the tenure-line faculty in our department shared this understanding, we had somewhat different ideas about what this should look like institutionally (in a stand-alone department with programs designed to teach and support research in the discipline) and pedagogically (in faculty and student enactments of teaching and learning). In addition, we were keenly aware that other stakeholders at our university—including other departments and students—did not always share our understanding of this threshold concept, and some were not open to it at all.

We soon came to recognize that the areas and knowledge we could build into our programs depended on the field-specific expertise of, and the professional enactments of this expertise by, our faculty members, including new hires. While rhetoric and composition covers a variety of subfields and thus enacts many threshold concepts, our own faculty did not have the expertise to cover all of them. Because we had several faculty members with expertise in rhetorical studies and experience with teaching and enacting civic engagement, an emphasis on rhetoric as civic engagement seemed like one key area to include in our program. Another strength was professional writing, which in our program meant emphasizing the rhetorical dimensions of professional problem-solving contexts, especially those involving digital texts and networks. Although we had identified literacy and language studies as an important thread of our field, we didn't have enough faculty members with expertise in linguistics to make this a significant part of the curriculum.

We also had to determine and balance our knowledge, expertise, and interests as a faculty with those of the undergraduate students who would enroll in our programs. Most of the students in our minor and major would not pursue graduate study in rhetoric and composition. Although we wanted students in the minor to engage the field's research in some depth, we had to articulate curricular pathways for pragmatic training in professional and civic writing, the sites where threshold concepts might be enacted as well as studied. Concerns about student job preparation also led us to require an electronic writing portfolio. While we did not consciously frame the problem this way, we were grappling with questions about what threshold concepts would be appropriate for students at different levels and with different goals.

The minor in writing and rhetoric was implemented in fall 2011. It was originally structured around a core course called Rhetoric and Civic Engagement and at least one course in each of three curricular areas: rhetorical history and theory, professional and civic writing, and language and literacy. Over the 2011–2012 academic year, as enrollments in the minor steadily grew, we continued to develop our proposal for the major and plan corresponding revisions to the minor. As new faculty members joined our department, we were able to expand and reconstitute areas of the curriculum—primarily digital and multimedia writing and additional contexts of professional and civic writing (e.g., medical and nonprofit contexts). This process was guided implicitly by additional threshold concepts as our tenure-line faculty grew; for example, some of the newer courses were created from the assumption that students can best learn professional writing through practice across various professional and digital contexts.

Our curriculum committee, complete with new faculty members, revised the minor to be organized less around types of research in the field and more around different types of rhetorical contexts—including educational, professional, and civic—in and across which students might need training. In making these changes, we were implicitly guided by two related threshold concepts discussed in part 1 of this collection— that Writing Is a Social and Rhetorical Activity (1.0) and that Writing Speaks to Situations through Recognizable Forms (2.0)—along with the premise that *practice adapting writing in various types of contexts is an effective way to improve writing competencies,* a variation of the threshold concept that Learning to Write Effectively Requires Different Kinds of Time, Practice, and Effort (4.3).

Our take on writing rhetorically asked students to develop *techne,* or productive knowledge acquired through social, context-dependent, and contingent communicative exchanges with others (Atwill 1998, 172). Our core course, Rhetoric and Civic Engagement, shifted from an emphasis on studying rhetorical history and theory to practicing various rhetorical *techne* of civic engagement with various publics. Our enactment of the threshold concept that Writing Is a Social and Rhetorical Activity entailed more specific notions about rhetoric, such as the ways rhetoric is enacted through and across interconnected contexts. For example, our Writing for Social Change course asks students to consider how public writing must account for exigencies and constraints that work across contexts and shift over time. Such an approach is grounded in the following modification or extension of the part 1 threshold concept that *writing is a rhetorical activity: the rhetorical dimensions of writing are transcontextual* (see Edbauer 2005 for an excellent discussion of rhetoric's transcontextual and ecological dynamics).

Our creation of some new courses and revision of existing ones had to account for the ways these courses related to and differed from other courses offered by our department and by other departments. Threshold concepts implicitly undergirded this work of boundary demarcation, too. The premise that Writing Speaks to Situations through Recognizable Forms (see 2.0) is an idea that informed our departmental philosophy that faculty working in other disciplines are best equipped to teach the writing conventions of those disciplinary discourse communities (and our WAC program supports faculty from across the university in this endeavor). This premise informed our creation of two new courses, Writing *about* Health and Medicine and Writing *about* Science and Technology (emphasis added), with the primary intent of helping students adapt more technical disciplinary knowledge to various public and nonspecialist audiences.

Once the minor was underway, we began developing program-level student learning outcomes for our major. In this case, too, threshold concepts served as the unstated premises undergirding our student learning outcomes. Sometimes we were able to make headway without intense disagreement over these unstated beliefs. For example, one program outcome states that students will "recognize and exemplify rhetorical features—including genres, language conventions, and methods of delivery—employed in civic and professional discourse communities." This outcome depends on the more fundamental understanding that Writing Speaks to Situations through Recognizable Forms; while we never explicitly articulated this concept, we were able to work from without much contention.

At other times, however, we found it difficult to move forward; we recognize now that these difficulties were the result of disagreements over unstated and assumed threshold concepts—what they were or which ones were being privileged. For instance, we might have more readily arrived at specific outcomes regarding students' ethical awareness (that students will "contribute to the responsible management of texts produced in discourse communities of which they are members") had we begun with the threshold concepts regarding how writing conveys and enacts ideologies (3.0) and how writing entails making ethical choices (1.8). Not stopping to talk about our underlying beliefs about the relationship between ethics, ideology, and writing made it difficult for us to agree on related outcomes.

Developing working notions of shared threshold concepts prior to creating program outcomes might have served as a useful middle ground between our overall vision and goals for the program and the more specific competencies we wanted students to achieve. In turn, naming our shared understanding earlier and more fully might have helped us more easily determine the nature of the courses and other curricular elements in and across which students will learn and develop as writers.

Threshold concepts have also been useful in the ongoing process of explicitly articulating and demarcating some of the core and required elements of the major's curriculum, the process to which we will now turn. In order to follow the next part of our discussion, it might be useful to first look over Appendix A, which shows the major's curricular requirements.

THRESHOLD CONCEPTS IN THE CORE CURRICULUM OF THE MAJOR

Some of the same threshold concepts that implicitly guided our planning of the minor and the initial sketch of the major became more explicit as we approached the task of articulating the major's curricular components and movement for ourselves and other stakeholders. Based on our earlier departmental discussions of how we defined the major strands of work in the field, we designed the major to include three core courses: one focused on rhetorical studies, one on writing studies, and one on literacy studies. Each of these courses also emphasized a more unique aspect of the major's larger goals around teaching civic engagement, research methodology, and professional identity and literacy management. For instance, the rhetorical studies course emphasizes rhetorical *techne* (as opposed to, say, rhetorical theory and criticism) as a means of civic engagement.

Beyond the goal of introducing students to the knowledge of our field, however, we also needed other ways to define and explain the three core courses, and to this end we turned to two additional shared threshold concepts (articulated by us slightly differently than they appear in part 1 of this book): *writing is rhetorical and context specific* and *rhetoric enacts identities and value systems*. The following table lays out the ways these concepts enable us to usefully distinguish among the three core courses, something we plan to emphasize in our advising materials to students.

Table 8.1 Threshold concepts in the major's three core courses

TC Core Course	TC 1: Writing and rhetoric is a discipline with unique and useful knowledge.	TCs 2 and 3: Writing is a rhetorical activity that speaks to specific contexts through recognizable conventions.	TC 4: Writing and rhetoric enact identities and value systems.
Rhetoric and Civic Engagement	Rhetorical history, theory, and techne are part of our disciplinary knowledge.	Writing and rhetoric develop across, are embedded in, respond to, and help shape various civic and community-based contexts.	Civic identities and the values associated with them are enacted through rhetorical action.
Researching Writing and Literacy	Studies of writing and literacy practices, including educational ones, are part of our disciplinary knowledge.	Writing and literacy develop across, are embedded in, respond to, and help shape educational and disciplinary contexts.	Educational and disciplinary identities and values are enacted through research and writing processes.
Professional Lives and Literacy Practices	Professional literacy and writing practices are part of our disciplinary knowledge and its applications in business and organizational contexts.	Writing and literacy continue across, are embedded in, respond to, and help shape workplace and organizational contexts.	Professional identities and the values associated with them are enacted through organizational literacy practices.

As this table shows, our three core courses are defined in terms of the field's scholarship, contexts for writing and rhetoric, and identities enacted through writing and rhetoric. Further, the third column extends the threshold concept of writing as rhetorical by accounting for how it must accommodate but can also help shape the exigencies, constraints, and interactions around communicative exchanges and their contexts. As rhetorical action and exchange, writing can help create or call attention to *kairos*, for example (see Hawhee 2004 for a useful discussion of the "accommodation" and "creation" models of the rhetorical situation).

Working from our faculty's shared threshold concept that *rhetorical dexterity is gained through study, practice, and performance over time* and the recognition that this learning should be scaffolded across a range of contexts, our major's curricular structure builds on the three core courses in several ways. First, as shown in "Core Requirements: Advanced Level" of Appendix A, students must build on the knowledge they gain in the core courses through at least two additional courses in the category Extending Theories and Histories of Writing, Rhetoric, and Literacy; these courses provide students with additional opportunities to enhance their understandings of particular threshold concepts embedded in the core courses. The course Literacy and Technology, for example, builds on Professional Lives and Literacy Practices by exposing students to additional disciplinary knowledge about literacy, this time focused on how technology coconstructs notions and practices of literacy. This course, then, enacts a more specific version of the threshold concept that *writing and rhetoric constitute a disciplinary field of study*. To cite another example, the Visual and Material Rhetorics course extends notions of rhetorical action or performance learned in the core course Rhetoric and Civic Engagement by exploring how visual, material, and linguistic elements work together as symbolic action to produce rhetorical meaning and effects.

Along with courses extending students' understanding of key concepts of the field, the BA requires students to take at least three courses that emphasize different context-specific versions and applications of these concepts. The restricted elective categories Applications of Civic and Cultural Writing and Rhetoric and Applications of Professional and Digital Writing include courses that position students to apply and adapt their understandings of writing, rhetoric, and literacy in and across various types of professional, digital, civic, and cultural contexts, such as popular culture practices, community problem-solving efforts, publication in the digital networks of professional organizations, and transnational language use. Building on the threshold concepts that writing is rhetorical and writing is context dependent, the courses in these two application categories engage students with additional writing contexts and scholarship about these contexts. In Writing about Science and Technology, for example, students engage the field's research (Myers 1990; Poe et al. 2010; others) about how scientists learn to write and how they adapt arguments for various audiences; then students practice such rhetorical adaptation themselves.

Students' practice with writing in various contexts is further extended when they take the Writing Internship or another of three practicum courses. Like some of the application courses, the practicum courses ask students to enact threshold concepts—as both declarative and procedural knowledge—in real-world situations, at the same time encouraging students to develop metacognitive awareness about their enactments through reflective writing about their experiences. Because threshold concepts are largely liminal and require time and reinforcement, these practicum courses provide students with additional opportunities to recognize and internalize them. In asking students to write about the ways they are employing some of their coursework-based knowledge in new professional contexts, we hope students can begin to recognize some of the ways their writing and rhetorical competencies are usefully adaptable across contexts (another version of our shared threshold concept that *rhetoric is transcontextual*).

Beginning in the Rhetoric and Civic Engagement core course and throughout their work in the program, students develop their required writing ePortfolios. The ePortfolio functions as a space where students can learn to present and explain their work to professional audiences (e.g., potential employers and admissions committees), as spaces for their integrative learning and the rhetorical enactments of their writerly identities, and, important for this discussion, as spaces for them to illustrate and develop metacognition around their understanding and enactment of threshold concepts. We hope that the ePortfolio—the longitudinal development of which the program supports through a student guide, workshops, advising, and coursework assignments—enables students to build a deeper understanding and meta-awareness of their writing and rhetorical knowledge and competencies, to synthesize and explain the writing and rhetorical acts they have enacted in various contexts, and to relate these enactments to their writing identities. To facilitate students' integrative understanding of their competencies at work, we ask them to explain and reflect on how they have applied broader concepts in the ePortfolio's featured texts and projects. We've been experimenting with the ePortfolio with our minor and certificate, and some of those students have arranged their ePortfolio primarily around writing and rhetorical competencies, featuring relevant work across school, work, and/or civic contexts under each competency. Another way the ePortfolio can facilitate the integration of knowledge, including threshold concepts, is by providing a space for students to enact writerly identities. In the profile of a writer section, for example, students are encouraged to approach the ePortfolio less as a representation of their identity and more as an enactment of it, actively and explicitly fashioning their ethos. Students are also encouraged to consider how their educational, (pre)professional, and civic writerly identities can connect in their existing and future experience.

As they complete the program, students take a Writing and Rhetoric Capstone in which they integrate the threshold concepts and other disciplinary knowledge they have developed and enacted, examining how they have learned to transfer writing competencies and strategies across different contexts. Much of this work is accomplished through reflecting, integrating, and explaining in the ePortfolios, which might be understood as the capstone of their metacognitive enactment of threshold concepts. The capstone course asks students to develop their own theories of writing and rhetorical transfer by analyzing how they have adapted key competencies across contexts, an assignment that depends on students' internalization of threshold concepts about learning to write. The capstone course also asks students to reflect on their emerging professional and civic identities as they research and prepare for the next phase of their lives. At this point, if not earlier, students should have arrived at a reconstituted understanding of how writing and rhetoric enact identity and, consequently, should be able to imagine themselves as communicators with agency.

Although the curricular structure we've been describing does not require students to follow a strictly linear sequence, it does move them along the general trajectory shown in the figure on the next page. Through this movement, students are expected to gradually develop disciplinary knowledge, gain versatility and competencies in writing across rhetorical contexts, and learn to manage their various writing/rhetorical identities through writing and communication—all activities that depend on the threshold concepts introduced in the core courses. After being (re)exposed to threshold concepts in the core courses, students practice with, build on (e.g., through related core concepts), and try out more nuanced understandings of the concepts in additional coursework before moving on to further enact, internalize, reflect on, and articulate their own working understandings of the concepts. The increase in the size of the arrow in Figure 8.1 is meant to suggest the increased likelihood of students crossing the specific learning thresholds (around writing knowledge, contexts, and identities) we have been discussing.

It is impossible to predict when and how students will "cross" the thresholds toward which the major directs them. Students will likely cross these thresholds in different ways, as a result of different "triggers," and at different times. Threshold concepts, unlike course outcomes, can't be easily taught or assessed, and when and how they are learned depends a great deal on the individual learner's past experiences, identities, goals, and learning styles, among other factors. That said, we have strategically designed our major to provide students with multiple, scaffolded, and varied opportunities to encounter and be transformed by their understandings and enactments of threshold concepts. We think students can benefit from recognizing and consciously employing and reflecting on some of the specific threshold concepts we've named. However, we are less concerned that undergraduate students articulate threshold concepts in specific ways and more concerned with

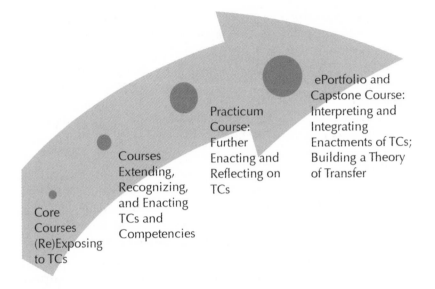

Figure 8.1. Curricular development of threshold concepts across the major.

their ability to utilize threshold concepts to make new connections and develop more rhetorical agency and dexterity.

DIFFICULTIES WITH THRESHOLD CONCEPTS: DEFINITIONAL TENSIONS AND INSTITUTIONAL CONSTRAINTS

We hope our own experiences in planning toward a BA illustrate the usefulness of considering the threshold concepts faculty share and want to forefront in a program's curriculum. In addition, we hope the addition of threshold concepts to the planning process will enable programs to think about learning as happening flexibly across time and not necessarily in a predictable, linear order, as Heidi Estrem discusses in chapter 6 of this collection. In other words, we think it would be worthwhile for other faculty who are planning a new writing and rhetoric major or even revising one to take the time to articulate, deliberate about, negotiate shared understandings of, and build around threshold concepts. But using threshold concepts to guide curricular planning is not a process without difficulty. Before concluding, we think it is important to discuss the difficulties we encountered in order to provide others with a more complete picture of what they might expect if they attempt to use threshold concepts for program development. Not all of our faculty see the same usefulness in threshold concepts that the two of us do, and the faculty as a larger group have sometimes found articulating and defining threshold concepts to be troublesome and/or even threatening.

First, we found naming threshold concepts to be a difficult task, something we did not necessarily expect given the apparent ease with which scholars agreed upon threshold concepts for part 1 of this book. Perhaps because of their expertise, our tenure-line faculty members were inclined to tease out nuanced and varied understandings of threshold concepts. Our attempts to agree on threshold concepts have thus far been fraught with fairly extensive disagreements about what we believe about writing and rhetoric and how to most usefully and precisely articulate those beliefs. For example, while they agreed that writing is a social and rhetorical activity, faculty argued over what *rhetorical* meant in this context, pointing to such factors as the embodied dimension of rhetorical action, the ecological nature of rhetorical movement, and various types of material, technological, and institutional constraints. It appears to us that the more deeply faculty members understood the research and theory of the field, the more complicated they found naming basic threshold concepts about which we could agree enough to introduce them to newcomers without the complexity that comes with greater knowledge over time.

Second, our faculty members have also disagreed about the very concept of threshold concepts—whether these are worth naming, and whether they *should* be named. In our limited department discussions, more than one faculty member has expressed concern that naming threshold concepts risks creating fixed and standardized goals for our major; more than one has warned that mapping threshold concepts onto specific courses may limit faculty members' pedagogical freedom to envision a shared course in a new or alternative way based on differing values or another strand of research from the field; and more than one has pointed out that determining which concepts get named is a matter fraught with power and politics and, of course, historical battles with winners and losers.

A third difficulty with discussing threshold concepts as a department is determining how to include the voices of the many non-tenure track (NTT) faculty members who do not come from any wing of writing, rhetoric, and/or literacy studies and who were hired to teach first-year composition with backgrounds in creative writing or literature. It seems clear from the conversations we've had that some faculty members from these disparate backgrounds may not, in fact, share the threshold concepts that those of use in the field might agree upon. Even when tenure-line faculty argue about the nuances of our threshold concepts, it is clear that there are basic matters upon which we agree because we have read and accept much of the same research and theory (even if we accept it critically). The same is not true for some of our non-tenure-earning instructors, a few of whom may not be familiar with the research at all, or even willing to accept there is research about writing with which they should be familiar. A few of our department's NTT instructors have wondered aloud whether the threshold concepts of rhetoric and composition constitute a type of dogma or creed to which faculty are expected to conform. These are difficult concerns even to discuss, much less resolve.

A fourth difficulty in imaging our new major around threshold concepts comes from external constraints. Achieving the status of a freestanding writing and rhetoric department did not mean we were free of any and all institutional constraints. Any course or program we designed and proposed had to clear hurdles created and/or guarded by individuals and groups with different values and concerns. While our concerns are very specific to Florida and our own institution, they exemplify the sorts of constraints any department might expect to face. The state of Florida, for example, recently implemented a new requirement that any proposed major must be approved at the preproposal stage by a statewide committee of academic vice presidents before it can even begin going through the usual stages and levels of approval. In part, this new requirement was implemented to prevent duplication of programs across the state, a concern of the current governor, who believes that duplication creates inefficiency. Thus, rather than simply designing a program based only in our own beliefs and expertise, we also had to ensure that the program we designed was different from other, already existing ones. Within our own university, issues of duplication and turf are equally, if not more difficult, to navigate. Our former colleagues in English demonstrated varying levels of concern that our proposed program would take students from those colleagues' existing programs—an understandable concern at a university that distributes funding primarily based on credit-hour production. Some English faculty are also concerned that we may be teaching courses that either duplicate their existing ones or enact course concepts they feel to be within their intellectual domain. So, for example, one group of faculty asked that we revise all our courses to remove the words *culture, literacy, digital,* and *technology.* Such requests, which we rejected, demonstrate potential constraints and roadblocks to simply creating a program that enacts our field's threshold concepts. Some threshold concepts may be shared across the boundaries of closely allied fields such as literary studies, thus prompting arguments regarding who has the responsibility or right to teach toward those concepts.

We want to stress here that difficulties are not necessarily negative. Rather, they provide both constraints and affordances. For example, debates about defining (or whether to even try to define) threshold concepts highlighted differences across our field and provided a cautionary message against presenting our field's knowledge monolithically. Taking the extra time to debate our core sets of knowledge helps ensure a diverse and thoughtful program vision. Even contention around the usefulness of using threshold concepts for curricular alignment can help us find ways to maintain a productive balance between articulating the emphases and boundaries of courses and enabling a continual (re) imaging of them and their interrelationships.

We've discussed some of the difficulties of using threshold concepts to design a BA in order to alert other departments to expect some challenges, both internally and externally, if they follow a similar path. Nonetheless, engaging in the task of naming threshold concepts holds interesting promise for considering what we know and how to introduce that knowledge to undergraduate students. The troublesome nature of defining and using threshold concepts can contribute to, rather than detract from, a strong program.

CONCLUSION: OUR CONTINUED TRANSFORMATION WITH THRESHOLD CONCEPTS

As we refine the foci of and relationships among courses, develop and share new pedagogical strategies around them, train additional faculty to teach them, explain them in student marketing and advising, and assess them, we predict that threshold concepts will be useful additions to the usual tools of course descriptions and student learning outcomes. For example, we might use threshold concepts in curriculum mapping for assessment planning, in explaining our program's goals to advisors in other units, and in helping faculty advise students around the required writing ePortfolio. In addition, the upper-division curriculum committee is continuing a collaborative process of further defining the emphases and boundaries of key courses, and threshold concepts will likely serve as one framework for doing so. We are also using threshold concepts in a new program for training NTT instructors in the field-specific knowledge needed to teach particular courses; in this case, threshold concepts productively complicate knowledge taught in first-year writing, the teaching context with which most NTT instructors are most familiar. After multiple faculty members have taught one of our new courses, we might return to earlier discussions of threshold concepts to determine whether and how we might, once again, revise course goals and share a broader repertoire of approaches and resources for teaching toward these goals. Additions to or changes in our faculty, and new developments in the field, will also create exigencies for returning to our vision and goals for the BA and its courses. Certainly, we can continue to work with a mission and vision, strategic goals, and program-level student learning outcomes, but we think threshold concepts offer a usefully flexible lens through which to define and distinguish our curricular components and the relationships among them and our field's ever-growing knowledge.

Naming threshold concepts within a department is no easy task. It is a troublesome endeavor, fraught with concerns that extend beyond knowledge and disciplinary training to matters of power and institutional politics. Yet the very troublesomeness associated with threshold concepts suggests that attempting to name them is a worthwhile endeavor. Even if we do not agree in some cases, being able to see *where* we disagree can be helpful. Perhaps these disagreements can explain contradictions we have felt but not understood and can suggest some paths forward. In our continued efforts, as in our planning of the writing and rhetoric major, we hope and expect that threshold concepts will continue to serve as flexible guides—less specific than student learning outcomes but more specific than a mission and vision—for generating and enacting a vision of what students should learn in and how they might emerge from a major in our field.

APPENDIX

UCF BA IN WRITING AND RHETORIC

OVERVIEW OF CURRICULAR REQUIREMENTS

The BA in Writing and Rhetoric provides students in-depth training in writing, rhetorical, and literacy studies, preparing them for active and ethical citizenship, graduate/professional school in communication-related disciplines, and/or a range of writing-focused jobs that involve the analysis, creation, editing, and coordination of texts.

CORE REQUIREMENTS: BASIC LEVEL	9 HOURS
• ENC 3331 Rhetoric and Civic Engagement	3 hours
• ENC 3502 Researching Writing and Literacy	3 hours
• ENG 3836 Professional Lives and Literacy Practices	3 hours

CORE REQUIREMENTS: ADVANCED LEVEL   6 HOURS
Extending Theory and Histories of Writing, Rhetoric, and Literacy

- ENC 3373 Cultural Rhetorics   3 hours
- ENC 4374 Gendered Rhetorics   3 hours
- ENC 4434 Visual and Material Rhetorics   3 hours
- ENC 3417 Literacy and Technology   3 hours
- ENC 3521 Writing across Difference   3 hours
- ENC 3315 Argumentative Writing   3 hours
- ENC 3503 Topics in Writing and Literacy Studies   3 hours

RESTRICTED ELECTIVES   18 HOURS
- Students must take at least 9 hours from the Applications courses (either category), 3 hours from Practicum category, and 6 hours of Advised Electives.

Applications of Civic and Cultural Writing and Rhetoric

- ENC 3311 Essay as Cultural Commentary   3 hours
- ENC 4353 Writing for Social Change   3 hours
- ENC 3375 Rhetoric in Popular Culture   3 hours
- ENC 4378 Writing in Global and Transnational Contexts   3 hours
- ENC 4354 Writing with Communities and Nonprofits   3 hours
- ENC 3372 Topics in Civic Rhetoric and Writing 3 hours

Applications of Professional and Digital Writing

- ENC 3250 Professional Writing   3 hours
- ENC 4212 Professional Editing   3 hours
- ENC 3351 Writing for Publication   3 hours
- ENG 3833 Marketing Your Writing   3 hours
- ENC 3453 Writing about Health and Medicine   3 hours
- ENC 3455 Writing about Science and Technology 3 hours
- ENC 4416 Writing in Digital Environments   3 hours
- ENC 3433 Multimedia Writing and Composition   3 hours
- ENC 3454 Topics in Professional and Digital Writing   3 hours

Writing Practicums

- ENC 4275 Theory and Practice of Tutoring Writing   3 hours
- ENC 3473 Writing in Disciplinary Cultures   3 hours
- ENC 4944 Writing Internship   3 hours

Advised Electives
- Can be met by upper-division Writing and Rhetoric courses not otherwise used to satisfy major requirements or by approved

upper-division (3000- or 4000-level) writing-intensive courses from other departments.

CAPSTONE REQUIREMENTS   3 HOURS

- ENC 4379 Writing and Rhetoric Capstone   3 hours
- Writing E-Portfolio (completed in ENC 4379 and approved by program director)

OTHER KEY REQUIREMENTS

- Proficiency equivalent to one year of college instruction in a foreign language taught by the Department of Modern Languages and Literatures or Judaic Studies. Standardized examinations for foreign languages may be used to meet the requirement. Students who are considering graduate school should complete two years of a foreign language.
- Students must complete a minor, certificate, or approved area of study (minimum 18 hours) outside of the department.

References

Atwill, Janet M. 1998. *Rhetoric Reclaimed: Aristotle and the Liberal Arts Tradition.* Ithaca, NY: Cornell University Press.

Edbauer, Jenny. 2005. "Unframing Models of Public Distribution: From Rhetorical Situation to Rhetorical Ecologies." *Rhetoric Society Quarterly* 35 (4): 5–24. http://dx.doi.org/10.1080/02773940509391320.

Hawhee, Debra. 2004. *Bodily Arts: Rhetoric and Athletics in Ancient Greece.* Austin: University of Texas Press.

Myers, Greg. 1990. *Writing Biology: Texts in the Social Construction of Scientific Knowledge.* Madison: University of Wisconsin Press.

Poe, Mya, Neal Lerner, and Jennifer Craig. 2010. *Learning to Communicate in Science and Engineering: Case Studies from MIT.* Cambridge: MIT Press.

9
THRESHOLD CONCEPTS IN RHETORIC AND COMPOSITION DOCTORAL EDUCATION
The Delivered, Lived, and Experienced Curricula

Kara Taczak and Kathleen Blake Yancey

What role do threshold concepts play in graduate school? In this chapter, we take up this question, beginning with what we see as one antecedent for threshold concepts, key terms, and in the process showing how threshold concepts build from key terms. We make this argument while also articulating the curriculum for doctoral study in rhetoric and composition in its three parts: the delivered curriculum, the lived curriculum, and the experienced curriculum. Given this context, we trace the ways faculty can use threshold concepts in doctoral curricula in writing studies through including them in curricula and through employing them collectively as an informal mechanism for review.

KEY TERMS AND THRESHOLD CONCEPTS: A QUICK INTRODUCTION

Historically, key terms have informed the field (if not defined it), but a claim like this can be difficult to support given the dynamic quality of key terms; they have changed over time. Erika Lindemann's work on the bibliographic categories whose key terms have organized and constructed composition, for instance, reveals how even a central, defining key term like *process* isn't stable. Lindemann (2002) notes that while the 1986 *CCCC Bibliography* included *process* in three of twelve categories (or 25%), that term completely disappeared in the 2001 MLA successor to the CCCC's bibliography. Paul Heilker and Peter Vandenberg's two edited collections on key terms tell the same story. Their first collection,

DOI: 10.7330/9780874219906.c009

published in 1996, included fifty-four terms, ranging from *academic discourse* and *audience* to *composing, critical thinking,* s*elf/subject,* and *writing center* (Heilker and Vandenberg 1996). Now, nearly twenty years later, Heilker and Vandenberg (2015) have published a second edition, with a set of thirty-six key terms; only four are duplicates—*ideology, literacy, multiculturalism,* and *research*—and none of those is *writing*.

Threshold concepts do more than key terms, of course. Key terms can demarcate a field and locate its historical origin: the key term of *process*, for instance, is often cited as a marker for the beginning of the field. But it does not make a claim about process; it has no predicate. Threshold concepts, in contrast, build claims from key terms. Thus, a term like *processes* may be important, but it does not make a claim; a threshold concept employing the concept of process—like people's writing histories, experiences, *processes,* and stances vary, and they are not the same as yours—does, and it's a claim that, as this volume suggests, provides a threshold into a specific field of study. Likewise, for over twenty years, we have thought of composition as having made the social turn, but threshold concept 1.0, Writing Is a Social and Rhetorical Activity makes a very different claim, one about compositionists' view of writing as always and inherently social; the social turn, in this threshold concept version of it, is a very specific statement about the nature of writing. Still other claims, like All Writing is Multimodal (2.4), rely on newer key terms like *multimodality*—it's worth noting the number of new jobs in the field in 2013 that ask for a specialty in multimodality (e.g., Westchester University; Oakland University)—but make claims not located in the past but in the present and future and in assumptions that are still contentious. In that sense, threshold concepts can speak both to consensus and to consensus-in-formation.

In sum, the field itself is dynamic, which means any claims we would make about key terms and threshold concepts would be contingent. Similarly, key terms in any doctoral program are likewise contingent: Florida State University's doctoral program in rhetoric and composition, here exemplifying a doctoral program in writing studies we both have participated in, is dynamic in the way the field is and at the same time dynamic in its own highly specific way. In addition, the dynamic quality of both individual programs and the larger field is animated by interactions across and among programs and between individual programs and the field. Moreover, because of the number of doctoral programs in rhetoric and composition (at least eighty-seven by last count) and because of their individual purposes and characters, it's very difficult to generalize about how key terms and threshold concepts may anchor or influence programs. Even regarding issues as seemingly straightforward as program titles and kinds of required courses, we see variation: the titles of both courses and programs vary—programs in the same field go by different names, including, for example, rhetoric and composition; writing studies; composition and cultural rhetoric—and at least one program (Michigan Tech) does not require any specific courses at all.

Despite the research and these considerations, however, *writing*—in terms of practice, theory, and/or research as well as the teaching of writing—is, we believe, at the center of the field, as the overarching threshold concept Writing Is an Activity and a Subject Of Study suggests; it's thus reasonable to think that writing—and threshold concepts surrounding writing—plays a role in the field's doctoral programs. More specifically, as this volume explains and illustrates, given that faculty can identify threshold concepts they believe locate the field, it's reasonable to expect we would also see threshold concepts informing doctoral education given the nature of such education: they introduce students to, and in some ways socialize them into, the field, whether explicitly or more implicitly. As a particular example of this claim, in this chapter we consider how threshold concepts are enacted in the Florida State's doctoral program in rhetoric and composition in three integrated doctoral curricula: delivered, lived, and experienced.

The *delivered form of the curriculum*, which we take up first, is defined by Yancey as the curriculum "we design. We see it in syllabi, where course goals are articulated. . . . We see it in assignments, where students deal with the specifics of the curriculum. We see it in readings, where students enter a specific discourse and specific ways of thinking" (Yancey 2004, 17). In the case of the FSU doctoral program in writing studies, we would expect to find threshold concepts in courses—in descriptions, syllabi, and assignments—as well as in nonclassroom sites like preliminary exams and the dissertation.

The second kind of curriculum, what Yancey calls "the lived curriculum," is the set of "prior courses and experiences and connections that contextualize the delivered curriculum" (Yancey 2004, 16) as well as the curriculum into which students will graduate: as our review of the FSU doctoral program in RC shows, its purpose is to prepare students through the delivered curriculum for the lived curriculum of the field.

But of course, students will make their own sense of the curriculum, and that's a third and final curriculum, the *experienced curriculum*, "what some call the de facto curriculum—that is, the curriculum that *students construct* in the context of the delivered curriculum we seek to share" (Yancey 2004, 58). This curriculum, then, is the enactment of the delivered curriculum by the students themselves.

In the rest of the chapter, then, we consider how, and in what ways, threshold concepts are woven into the doctoral program in rhetoric and composition at FSU, Yancey writing first from the perspective of a designer of the program and its delivered and lived curricula, and then Taczak writing from the perspective of a program participant and a shaper of the experienced curriculum. To forecast our claim: the FSU doctoral program locates writing as a mediating activity throughout both the delivered and the lived curricula, and it does so in the context of a culture of reflection. What's also particularly useful about threshold concepts, especially in the context of our three curricula, is how helpful they are in assisting us to see how elements of our program work together—or not.

THE DELIVERED AND LIVED CURRICULA:
KATHLEEN BLAKE YANCEY

The rhetoric and composition doctoral program at Florida State University includes five core courses—Rhetorical Theory, Composition Theory, Research Methods, Visual Rhetoric, and Digital Revolution and Convergence Culture; many optional courses (e.g., African American Literacies, Writing Assessment, Feminist Rhetoric); required one-credit reading courses (e.g., Rhetorical Invention, Literacies, Genre); and required postpreliminary exam meetings until graduation. Overall, the program goal is to offer a solid foundation with options students can tap as their interests dictate, a goal made visible through the record of the program's development since 2005, when I took up the task of rebuilding it. Hosted on the web and in our program files are syllabi, course descriptions, and the results of a program assessment faculty conducted in 2012, resources I draw upon here to characterize the program. As articulated in all these documents, students are the centerpiece of the program, which means the centerpiece, like the students, is capacious and diverse. Put another way, our students, much like the students at other programs, vary—for example, in the ways they write and the ways they understand writing—and as program faculty we value these differences. Our programmatic goal isn't so much to change those processes or to challenge understandings, but rather to help students approach writing as an object of study, often through practice, and to support students as they develop their own writing practices. In other words, through the delivered curriculum (in courses, preliminary exams, the dissertation) and through the lived curriculum (conference proposals, grant and award applications, and formal scholarship for journals) faculty hope to support students as they find and develop the approach, the techniques and strategies that best serve their scholarly and professional goals. In the specific terms of writing practices and the threshold concept that writing practices vary, such variation in our program thus means some students are slow to draft and need to plan copiously first, while other students write assemblage-like, in chunks they weave together, while still other students revise quickly and often: all of them need support.

More generally, my review of the FSU doctoral program and its artifacts suggests that all the threshold concepts informing this volume are at least minimally incorporated throughout it; a quick discussion of two TCs illustrates how threshold concepts animate and inform the program: (1) the metathreshold concept Writing Is a Subject of Study and an Activity, which governs the entire program; and (2) the threshold concept Learning to Write Effectively Requires Different Kinds of Practice, Time, and Effort (4.3). This second threshold concept regarding practice, as this volume suggests, is elaborated in part as "what we practice is who we are; if we want to be a writer, we need to write. And in the practice of writing, we develop writing capacities, among them the ability to adjust and adapt to different contexts, purposes, and audiences" (see 4.3). Much as this threshold concept suggests, all the courses in the program, beginning with our five required courses, include multiple occasions for writing, whether their intent is to support the development of writing itself, the development of an understanding of writing as a subject of study, or both. Each course builds in multiple opportunities for writing; collectively, they offer a wide range of opportunities for writing, as an examination of materials from course documents included in the program illustrates. In the required Rhetorical Theory course often taught by Kristie Fleckenstein, for example, students compose "6 short (2–3 page) response papers, regular posting[s] to the class discussion board . . . and 2 10–12 page papers" (Fleckenstein 2014). In the research methods course, which Michael Neal often teaches, students compose in multiple genres—journal analysis; research questions and rationale; brief review of research; brief research design; institutional review board application; coding and interpreting data; and research proposal (Neal 2011). In addition, as students write in these genres, they engage with other threshold concepts, among them Texts Get Their Meaning from Other Texts (2.6) and Writing Is a Way of Enacting Disciplinarity (2.3).

While the entire program enacts the threshold concepts named above, many other threshold concepts are also enacted across individual courses. In Visual Rhetoric and in Digital Revolution and Convergence Culture, three seem especially salient: the "unnaturalness" of writing; its relationship to technologies of all kinds; and the importance of reflection. In Visual Rhetoric, for instance, in addition to summarizing readings, creating blog postings, and completing a final project, students compose several smaller projects. In one project, for example, students are asked to "identify/find/create an image that 'documents' the year 2010." As part of the project, students are also asked to engage in reflection explaining their choices: "Include a one-pager where you discuss the process you used, the image you chose, and your rationale for including it." A second project in this course requires students to compose visually and reflect upon the process, paying explicit attention to the "role of the medium" in their composing:

> Creating Visual Rhetoric=compose your own visually rhetorical text using materials of your choice. In a one-pager, explain the logic of the text, the way(s) it is visually rhetorical, the context in which it participates (e.g., aesthetic, informative, public), the role of the medium, and the significance of the text for you, for the class, and for an external audience of your choice. (Yancey 2013)

Likewise, the Digital Revolution and Convergence Culture class assigns tasks specific to the content of the class that exemplify threshold concepts and that continue to define composition and composing. One smaller assignment asks that students create a map of circulation, "a representation showing how a given term has circulated across time and space and connections central to that circulation," which again includes "a one-page reflection on what you have learned about epistemology, how information is distributed/circulated, and what difference if any it makes to represent this learning visually and verbally." Clearly, multimodality is part of this assignment as well. A second smaller assignment brings together technology, multimodality, audience, the making of knowledge, and composing in a twenty-first-century context: in *Wikipedia*, create "an addition to a current entry (i.e., circulation itself) or a creation of a new entry," with a one-page reflection. What's interesting about this assignment, in part, is that the assignment is located inside the classroom as it also bridges to the lived curriculum, a place where the program faculty are not in control, and yet a place that has much to teach us all about composing. The program's preliminary exams (a.k.a. prelims, taken after the completion of coursework and preliminary to the writing of the dissertation), connecting the delivered and lived curricula, operate in much the same way: it's not uncommon for prelim questions to situate the student in a professional capacity—designing a class for TAs preparing to teach or answering a question in the context of an job interview—and thus to encourage students to think of the delivered curriculum of the reading list in the context of the lived curriculum to which they aspire. As important, the program provides multiple rhetorical situations through these courses—ones involving writing a research proposal in the methods course, a *Wikipedia* entry in Digital Revolution and Convergence Culture, and a rhetorically visual composition in Visual Rhetoric—through which students find that to be writers, they enact the threshold concept that "we need to write. And in the practice of writing, we develop writing capacities, among them the ability to adjust and adapt to different contexts, purposes, and audiences" (see 4.3, "Learning to Write Effectively Requires Different Kinds of Practice and Effort").

In contrast to the delivered curriculum, the lived curriculum is less predictable, largely because it operates in a context outside of the program and sometimes, as in the case of the *Wikipedia* assignment, outside of the academy. It's perhaps not surprising, then, that at least for the FSU writing studies doctoral program, the lived curriculum seems the place where students are more inclined to experience another threshold concept, that of failure. As Collin Brooke and Allison Carr explain in concept 4.2, "Failure Can Be an Important Part of Writing Development,"

> As students progress throughout their educational careers and the expectations for their writing evolve from year to year and sometimes course to course, there is no way we can expect them to be able to intuit these shifting conditions. They must have the opportunity to try, to fail, and to learn from those failures as a means of intellectual growth. (63)

This trajectory of the potential of failure is certainly accurate for a program: over several years, in the case of FSU, typically four, students may struggle with assignments, with prelims, and with the writing of a dissertation prospectus and the dissertation itself. During all these experiences, however, the faculty—the designers of the experiences, the coaches, and the judges—are committed to providing guidance from all three perspectives. In the case of conference proposals, of responses to CFPs, of manuscripts for publication, and of award and grant applications, faculty are coaches only. We do provide opportunities to prepare for such writing—for example, workshops on writing conference proposals—and we counsel students on an individual basis, but most if not all students in the program have experienced rejection or failure at some point as they have engaged in this lived curriculum of the field. Another responsibility faculty have, then, is twofold: helping students understand the "failure" in context, as part of a general process of learning, and often as a specific opportunity to revise and resubmit elsewhere.

In sum, the threshold concept that writing is a mediating activity permeates the FSU doctoral program throughout both the delivered and the lived curricula, and it does so in the context of a culture of reflection. This is, however, the view from these curricula. To see how the program functions as an experienced curriculum requires the view of someone who matriculated in and completed it.

THE EXPERIENCED CURRICULUM: KARA TACZAK

A Scene in the Experienced Curriculum

In late February of my first year of doctoral work, I sat shivering on a bench outside one of UC Santa Barbara's large auditoriums. For southern California, it was unusually damp and dreary. Having just presented at my second conference, I was reflecting on ways to improve my presentation style. Practice more. Read aloud. Print in bigger font. I felt like I floundered a bit throughout my session and was thankful only a handful of people showed up for it. Slightly depressed about my performance, my thoughts shifted toward the presentation I had seen a few hours earlier, given by my new mentor, Kathleen Blake Yancey. I reread her handout on *The Things We Carried*. Her presentation kept moving in and out of my thoughts, so flipping the page of my worn notebook, I began to jot another list down, hoping to generate a topic of interest for my dissertation. Hyperambitious and overly organized, I already felt behind.

I wrote:

Topics of interest.
Comfort. American Dream. Critical pedagogy.

All were topics I had dabbled with while an adjunct, before beginning doctoral work. I began again.

Genre (what does it take to create a new one? What direction are we headed in?). Transfer. Reflection (western vs. eastern; what else can we do with it in the classroom?). Visual rhetoric. Culture, specifically pop culture. FYC (what it takes to work)? What should be taught? What should students be learning?).

All these topics were of interest to me, and I wondered how I might take one or two of them and create a dissertation topic. What do they all mean to me, I wondered.

Satisfied for the moment with my two lists, I flipped through the other pages of my notebook, pausing to read through notes from months past, before stopping on one page that contained a small, yellow Post-it. The Post-it, given to me the previous semester, contained the message

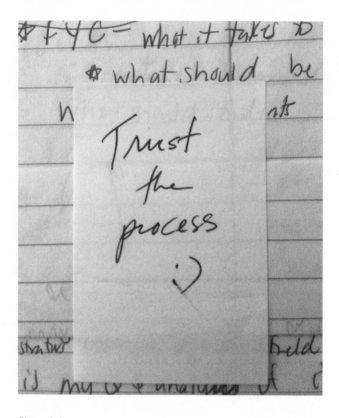

Figure 9.1.

that Kathi Yancey believed would help first-year grad students make it through the difficult experiences: "Trust the process" (see Figure 9.1).

I have known since I was fifteen when I was asked to write an essay on my future goals that I wanted to be an English professor. As with any journey in life, getting to this point required some detours—even living for a short time in the corporate world. However, a chance teaching job at the University of Akron pushed me back in the direction of becoming a professor. Like most adjuncts, I taught at multiple schools and thus taught a wide diversity of students ranging in age, walks of life, social class, and writing abilities. Especially as I began to teach more classes, I knew this was my opportunity to return to school, so I began to take actions to increase my chances for admission: taking graduate level classes in English to add to a master's degree in education; conducting a small research project at the University of Akron; serving on committees at a couple of the schools. Even though I was in theory taking the right actions, the first time I applied to PhD programs, I was accepted into only one of the four programs to which I applied, and that with little funding. Unwilling to give up, I worked even harder the next year to help ensure that I would not only get in but would be admitted to my top choice, Florida State. I took more English graduate classes; I designed and conducted a much larger research study; I coauthored and published my first article; I applied to the Research Network Forum at the Conference on College Composition and Communication and received a Professional Equity Project Grant; I retook the GRE. Without realizing it, in working at getting into grad school, I was enacting the threshold concept **Learning to Write Effectively Requires Different Kinds of Practice, Time, and Effort** (4.3). As Collin Brooke and Allison Carr explain, I was given the opportunity to "try, to fail, and learn from [that failure]" (63); the more focused writing I did the year after *not* getting into doctoral studies contributed to my acceptance at FSU.

As the above anecdote illustrates, the experienced curriculum does not follow a "straight line" but rather follows a recursive path—"doubling back on itself, leaping forward, and, at times, grinding to a halt" (Lay 2013, 37). The experienced curriculum and its underlying threshold concepts—some of which were discussed in the previous section—depend to a large extent on the student's previous experience. When and how a student approaches the threshold concepts and when and how they cross over the threshold depends a lot on where the student is coming from: prior experiences, knowledge, dispositions, and the like affect the how and the when. Once in a doctoral program, a student finds that working through the program, writing a dissertation, and graduating from that program and joining the field as a professional involve responding to (i.e., the when) and understanding (i.e., the how) at least some of the threshold concepts discussed in the first part of this chapter. Students' abilities to understand and come to terms with the different threshold concepts are, of course, uniquely contextualized by their individual prior knowledge (as my own example illustrates, above). The delivered and lived curricula allow students to begin to process and draw on prior knowledge in meaningful ways as they develop new knowledge and encounter the threshold concepts of the field as informed by the program. Thus, the delivered and lived curricula lead students to develop as writers, teachers, and scholars; in turn, the experienced curriculum, which is the individual construction of the other curricula, gives those other two curricula meaning. Students begin to make a place for themselves in the program and thus within all three curricula.

As outlined in the opening section of this chapter, many of the threshold concepts develop from key terms informing the field[1]. It's no surprise, then, that within doctoral programs, key terms show up in fairly conventional and explicit ways in courses (e.g., in course titles). There are also those terms such as *rhetorical situation* that show up across doctoral programs generally. Much of the delivered and lived curricula at Florida State center on such key terms, which assist students in learning important rhetorical concepts that they take up, repurpose, and extend in their own ways. For example, *rhetorical situation* is a key term introduced in one of the five required classes, Rhetorical Theory, which students typically complete within the first two semesters of doctoral work. Often a handful of students have heard of *rhetorical situation* before the class, but even those students, after taking the class, understand it in new ways and employ it in both scholarship and teaching. For example, some TAs use *rhetorical situation* as a key term in the first-year composition course they teach, including asking students to read and respond to Lloyd Bitzer's "The Rhetorical Situation," in effect inviting first-year students to experience the rhetorical situation in ways similar to the ways the graduate students experienced it in the Rhetorical Theory class.[2]

There are also key terms specific to each individual program: at Florida State, a key term central to the program is *circulation*, a term anchoring the Digital Revolution class. Interestingly, this key term, in the experienced curriculum, has informed many of the FSU grad students' theses and dissertations—including topics in both rhetoric and composition: Scott Gage's (2011) dissertation study of the circulation of postcards and their contribution to the formation of racist communities, *Creating the Cult: Image-Word in the Formation of a Supremacist Community,* for example, and Jennifer O'Malley's (2014) dissertation study of teacher enactment of the social in first-year composition, *The Social Dimension(s) of Writing: Locating Interaction and Circulation in the "Social Turn" Twenty Years Later.* Put another way, students' experienced curriculum has involved their repurposing key terms for the making of new knowledge. Terms unique to the Florida State program as well as those common within other programs can contribute to threshold concepts and create opportunities for students to define and redefine, create and design, and live and learn the delivered and lived curricula through their enactment of the experienced curriculum.

Similarly, students' experience of threshold concepts, like their experience of key terms, requires adaptation and can lead to new insights: controlling them brings the student (or learner) to new insights and connections. This is illustrated in the experienced curriculum for the threshold concept Writers' Histories, Processes, and Experiences Vary (3.2), an important threshold concept for any doctoral program. All of the histories, processes, and experiences students bring with them impact all dimensions of doctoral work, from courses to the relationships they develop to the job market. Moreover, because of the diversity of such prior activity (as evidenced, for example, in my own experience), most students will find that the experienced curriculum in general does not follow a straight line. At Florida State as elsewhere, this could mean a student changing dissertation topics or receiving a rejection for a conference proposal while at the same time publishing a first article or succeeding in one administrative position while struggling in teaching composition. The process students experience, contextualized by the prior, often zigs and zags.

Another threshold concept important for the FSU doctoral program, Writing Mediates Activity (1.5), begins in the delivered curriculum with courses and prelims and continues to govern students' experience of the doctoral program writ large. For example, students build upon their writing practices as they study and prepare for prelims. Do they read all of the texts and take notes along the way? Do they generate a detailed timeline of dates? Do they create notecards? Do they have a prelim journal? Do they take a practice prelim? Do they do all of the above? The strategies students themselves borrow, repurpose, and develop to prepare for prelims, part of the delivered curriculum, are a function of their experienced curriculum.

Another threshold concept important to the FSU program, Writing Is a Way of Enacting Disciplinarity (2.3), connects across the three curricula. This threshold concept plays out as students take more classes, as they write more projects, and as they propose conference sessions. One especially difficult moment in this sequence for many (though not all) arrives with writing the dissertation prospectus, which doctoral students often find to be an exhausting and frustrating genre. In part, the prospectus is frustrating because students have finally arrived at the moment when they can focus on their own research, so they may expect the process to be easier than it usually turns out to be. In part, it's frustrating because students think the experience will be similar to writing an MA thesis prospectus, but the doctoral prospectus is more unlike than like that earlier genre. In part, it's frustrating because students can be intimidated by composing a project that feels equivalent to a book, a project that grants the writer potential ownership but has few parameters and even fewer limits. Not least, the prospectus is frustrating because it is, in effect, a new genre for doctoral students; that genre provides a site for a research project that has yet to be fully articulated and that will require multiple drafts to become articulated. There is no way to predict how many drafts are needed. The experienced curriculum of the prospectus, then, is fraught, demonstrating the difficulty of learning to write in ways that enact the discipline a doctoral student hopes to join. And more new disciplinary genres follow this one: the dissertation itself and multiple high-stakes job documents—letters of application; CVs; teaching philosophy statements; administrative philosophy statements; dissertation abstracts; and research agenda statements—that facilitate students' search for academic positions. Writing in these rhetorical situations, each one a disciplinary exercise, students adapt and repurpose their prior writing practices. Likewise, it's through this combination of curricula—the delivered curriculum of coursework and dissertation, the experienced curriculum of the dissertation topic, and both used as material for conference presentations and letters of application that are the lived curriculum—that students learn and mature in ways that will help them as they cross the threshold into an academic position.

Throughout this process, threshold concepts overlap and connect, following the recursive path Lay describes. Along the way, students confront and deal with different threshold concepts, helping define who they are as writers. The classes, the teaching, the instruction received, and the field itself all participate in setting the stage for students' experienced curriculum. Doctoral students must engage in this trajectory and learn for themselves, as I did, to "trust the process."

CONCLUSION

At FSU, the overarching threshold concept that Writing Is an Activity and a Subject of Study provides a touchstone for the program; other threshold concepts, as we see in this chapter, are interwoven throughout the three curricula. Likewise, a review of this kind helps us, even if after the fact, to see how many threshold concepts—speaking to writing practices, to genres, to failure—appear in both delivered and lived curricula of a doctoral program in rhetoric and composition, both at the course level and at the program level. Moreover, putting the experienced curriculum into dialogue with these two curricula gives us a fuller sense of how threshold concepts function in a given program; how difficult it can be to learn and practice those concepts; and how very threshold the concepts are for doctoral students seeking entry into the field.

Much as we have engaged threshold concepts in thinking about the FSU doctoral program, we think using them as a lens for thinking about a program and its components—in the lived curriculum as well as in the delivered—can be helpful in other ways as well. Using threshold concepts—in whole or in part—we can review programs to see how they function, much as we have done in this chapter. And because threshold concepts are active and experienced, we would expect students to repurpose what they have learned about them: were there no evidence of this, we could consider what changes to make and how to make them. Likewise, we might decide that the lived curriculum, connected to the field, plays too small a role in a program: students might not be attending conferences, attempting to publish, or applying for grants. We might also find that we haven't provided for failure, that we don't incorporate students' prior writing practices, that across courses the rhetorical genres and situations are unhelpfully redundant, and/or that we don't provide writing opportunities connected to disciplinarity. We might find that too many threshold concepts are included in one course; we might find that certain threshold concepts are more salient than others at different points in a doctoral trajectory. We might also, as a heuristic exercise, compare our incorporation of threshold concepts with that of other programs; and we might review our program in light of disciplinary trends like those plotted by Derek Mueller (2012).

What we can see is that in the case of FSU and its three curricula, threshold concepts occur throughout the program; and what we can also see is that there is much left to learn about how they can support graduate students seeking to cross through our disciplinary threshold.

Notes

1. As we explain, key terms and threshold concepts are both important, though different. Our experience with the FSU doctoral program suggests that key terms are located in threshold concepts and that key terms may lead to such concepts.

2. See, for example, Yancey, Robertson, and Taczak's (2014) *Writing across Contexts: Transfer, Composition, and Sites of Writing* for a discussion of how rhetorical situation can animate FYC.

References

Fleckenstein, Kristie. 2014. Course Description: Rhetorical Theory.

Gage, Scott. 2011. "Creating the Cult: Image-Word in the Formation of a Supremacist Community." PhD diss., Florida State University, Tallahassee.

Heilker, Paul, and Peter Vandenberg, eds. 1996. *Keywords in Composition Studies.* Portsmouth, NH: Heinemann Educational Books.

Heilker, Paul, and Peter Vandenberg, eds. 2015. *Keywords in Writing Studies*. Logan: Utah State University Press.

Lay, Ethna Dempsey. 2013. "Making the Teacher." *College Composition and Communication* 65 (1): 37–39.

Lindemann, Erika. 2002. "Early Bibliographic Work in Composition Studies." *Profession* 2002 (1): 151–57. http://dx.doi.org/10.1632/074069502X85149.

Mueller, Derek. 2012. "Grasping Rhetoric and Composition by Its Long Tail: What Graphs Can Tell Us about the Field's Changing Shape." *College Composition and Communication* 64 (1): 195–223.

Neal, Michael. 2011. Syllabus: Research Methods.

O'Malley, Jennifer. 2014. "The Social Dimension(s) of Writing: Locating Interaction and Circulation in the 'Social Turn' Twenty Years Later." PhD Diss., Florida State University, Tallahassee.

Yancey, Kathleen Blake. 2004. *Teaching Literature as Reflective Practice*. Urbana, IL: National Council of Teachers of English.

Yancey, Kathleen Blake. 2013. Syllabus: Digital Revolution and Convergence Culture.

Yancey, Kathleen Blake, Liane Robertson, and Kara Taczak. 2014. *Writing across Contexts: Transfer, Composition, and Sites of Writing*. Logan: Utah State University Press.

Enacting Threshold Concepts of Writing across the University

10
THRESHOLD CONCEPTS AT THE CROSSROADS
Writing Instruction and Assessment

Peggy O'Neill

Writing assessment includes both the products and processes of writing. As Tony Scott and Asao Inoue explain, it "encompasses a range of activities, from responding with revision in mind to evaluation or grading of final products to large-scale programmatic assessments" (see 1.7, "Assessing Writing Shapes Contexts and Instruction"). While Scott and Inoue focus on the judging of the writer's text by someone else, assessment also "is an essential component of learning to write" (see 4.4, "Revision Is Central to Developing Writing"): "Through the prewriting, drafting, revision, editing, and publishing of a text, writers assess various components of the rhetorical situation as well as a variety of texts (their own and, frequently, others'). They must assess options and make decisions based on those assessments" (O'Neill, 4.5). This aspect of assessment is clearly linked to threshold concepts associated with metacognition (see 5.2, "Metacognition Is Not Cognition") and reflection (see 5.4, "Reflection Is Critical for Writers' Development").

Assessment is also linked to values and power. Through our assessment of texts, we convey what we value as readers. These values are closely linked to conventions about language and power relationships. Scott and Inoue (see 1.7, "Assessing Writing Shapes Contexts and Instruction") quote Stephen Gould and F. Allan Hanson to point out that "how teachers or others assess student writing, what products those assessment processes produce (e.g., grades, comments on papers, decisions about students, responses to peers' drafts, etc.), and the consequences of those products all can *create* the very competencies any writing assessment says it measures (Gould 1981; Hanson 1993)." Scott and Inoue continue, noting that writing assessment also

DOI: 10.7330/9780874219906.c010

"shapes relationships and power between teachers, students and institutions" (see 1.7, "Assessing Writing Shapes Contexts and Instruction"). Acknowledging the inherent power of writing assessment, whether it is in the classroom as part of the learning process or beyond the classroom as part of large-scale evaluation programs, is especially critical in writing studies because (as articulated in other threshold concepts) writing is closely linked to identity and ideology; it mediates activity and creates meaning; it represents the world and events; and it expresses ideas and feelings. Therefore, the assessment of writing influences our understanding of the world, of ourselves, and of our communication with each other.

While writing studies' threshold concepts are central to understanding writing assessment, they are not sufficient to such understanding because writing assessment lies at the intersection of threshold concepts specific to writing studies and those specific to educational assessment. Understanding writing assessment therefore requires understanding both sets of concepts and how they interact. Writing studies professionals who design and administer assessments must learn to understand critical concepts of validity and reliability associated with psychometrics since these concepts are widely used across disciplines and assessment contexts and have established power in the discourse of education and assessment. Conversely, assessment specialists, who may be responsible for designing and evaluating assessments across a variety of disciplines and contexts, must understand the threshold concepts associated with writing (articulated in part 1) if they are working in writing assessment. Both sets of concepts are required to create assessments that produce valid results and to use those results effectively and responsibly. However, assessment experts are all too often unfamiliar with writing theory and practice. Thus, if writing studies scholars, teachers, and administrators hope to influence assessment mandates and practices driven by those from outside writing studies, we bear the burden of learning assessment's threshold concepts. Sometimes writing professionals need to challenge decisions or proposals made by assessment experts when those decisions or proposals do not enact accurate conceptions of writing or support effective teaching and learning of writing. To do this well, we must be able to both understand and use the language of educational measurement. Toward this end, in this chapter I explain some of the key threshold concepts associated with educational measurement and the ways they are used in writing assessments, both large scale and classroom based.

VALIDITY AND RELIABILITY: KEY THRESHOLD CONCEPTS
FOR WRITING ASSESSMENT FROM PSYCHOMETRICS

Psychometrics is the discipline concerned with the theory and practice of psychological and educational evaluation, testing, and assessment. Threshold concepts essential to the field are addressed in the *Standards for Educational and Psychological Testing*, which is jointly authored by the primary professional organizations of the field: the American Educational Research Association, the American Psychological Association, and the National Council on Measurement in Education (1999). Another important text is *Educational Measurement* (Brennan 2006), a volume that includes chapters on the key concepts and issues in educational assessment authored by the leading scholars in the field. Published by the American Council on Education and the National Council on Measurement in Education, it is now in its fourth edition. Psychometric scholars and practitioners, as represented in these key texts, agree that validity and reliability are the two primary threshold concepts of the field; however, validity is "the most fundamental consideration in developing and evaluating tests" (AERA, APA, and NCME 1999, 9).[1]

Educational measurement "uses limited samples of observations to draw general and abstract conclusions about persons or other units" (Kane 2006, 17). These limited samples are the tests, exams, and assessments. The *Standards* defines an assessment as "any systematic method of obtaining information from tests and other sources, used to draw inferences about characteristics of people, objects, or programs" (AERA, APA, and NCME 1999, 172). While some professionals make distinctions between terms such as *test* and *assessment*, others don't because, as George Madaus argues, the process is the same regardless of the term:

> But strip away the linguistic veneer and, regardless of what noun we choose—assessment, exhibitions, examinations, portfolios, or just plain tests—all types of evaluation rest on the same basic technology. That is we elicit a small sample of behavior from a larger domain of interest . . . to make inferences about a person's probable performance relative to the domain. Then, on these inferences, we classify, describe, or make decisions about individuals or institutions. (Madaus 1994, 77)

Keeping this definition in mind is useful when working with assessment professionals because they might be thinking of assessment more narrowly than the way Madaus explains it. Being able to push back and explain why a particular sampling method, such as a portfolio, is more appropriate, or being able to argue that an impromptu essay exam does not adequately represent the domain of interest (writing ability), or doesn't allow us to draw accurate inferences about future performance,

can be important in ensuring that the writing concepts are not subordinate to the psychometric ones.

Validity, which "refers to the degree to which evidence supports the
use and interpretation of an assessment's results," does not reside in the
test but in the results and how they are used (AERA, APA, and NCME
1999, 9). But validity is not absolute; it exists along a continuum. Tests
themselves are not valid or invalid; rather, how the results are used and
interpreted are more or less valid. One test may produce valid results in
a particular context but not in another. For example, if a writing program uses a standardized placement test available from a national testing company to place students into the first-year composition curriculum, it needs to consider the results of that test within the context of its
own curriculum and students by gathering evidence to answer key questions: How is writing represented in the test? Does the task adequately
represent the skills and tasks needed to succeed in the composition
course? Does it elicit a sample that adequately represents the students'
skills and abilities? Are all students appropriately placed in the different
courses? Do different populations perform differently on the test? How
do students perform in the courses they place into? Is the scoring procedure appropriate? What is the long-term consequence of the placement
decision? Once evidence is gathered from the investigation, it must be
evaluated to determine if it is an adequate test.

Validation is the process of gathering evidence to answer these types
of questions. It "requires a clear statement of the proposed interpretations and uses" and an evaluation of the "rationale, or argument, for
the claims being made" (Kane 2006, 17). Validation for a new, proposed
test "implies an advocacy role, in the building of a case for the validity of
a proposed interpretation" (Kane 2006, 18). For assessment programs
already in place, validation "implies a more or less objective appraisal of
the evidence, pro and con" (Kane 2006, 17). As Michael T. Kane (2006)
explains, the more mature the testing program is, the more the evaluation
should consider both the positive and negative aspects of it. Validity, then,
is an argument that "must link concepts, evidence, social and personal
consequences, and values" (Cronbach 1988, 4; see also Messick 1989). In
building the validation argument, one must gather evidence in response
to this overarching question: "To what degree—if at all—on the basis of
evidence and rationales, should the test scores be interpreted and used in
the manner proposed?" (Messick 1989, 5). The argument should clarify
that the benefits of the interpretation and use of the assessment results
outweigh the costs because "ultimately, the purpose of educational assessment is to improve teaching and learning" (Moss 1994, 10).

The different kinds of questions in the above placement example are used to gather different types of evidence, all of which contribute to the validation argument. Theorists consider validity an emerging concept; that is, its meaning is not static but is still debated and developing. The current consensus, as articulated in the *Standards* (AERA, APA, and NCME 1999) and *Educational Measurement* (Brennan 2006), considers validity a unitary concept. This means that there are not distinct types of validity but rather different facets, or dimensions, to validity with different types of evidence that need to be considered in constructing a validity argument. Because of these different aspects, terms such as *construct, consequence, face,* or *consequential* are used to modify validity. Each of these terms considers a different facet of the assessment although facets are interconnected. Construct validity refers to the domain, skill, or ability being tested. But defining the construct and ensuring that it is what is being sampled in the test can be challenging because, as the concepts detailed in part 1 of this collection show, writing is complex. In validating a writing assessment, an argument would be needed to support the construct of writing represented in the test. Closely linked to construct is the dimension of content: is the content of the test actually measuring what it says it is measuring? For example, if something is considered a writing assessment but it consists of multiple-choice items about grammar and mechanics, test designers may have to justify the construct of writing—that is, the concept of writing—as well as the content of the test.

Linked to construct and content dimensions is face validity, which is how the assessment appears. Although face validity is sometimes dismissed by assessment scholars, it can contribute to how the test is perceived and even how test takers approach it. In writing assessment, the use of impromptu essay exams was often justified because test takers had to write extended responses. That is, essay exams had face validity because they required people to write and, therefore, were de facto tests of writing. In the 1980s and 1990s as portfolios became more widespread, the validity of the use of single-sample impromptu tests was challenged because writing scholar-teachers argued that it misrepresented the construct of writing and in many cases misrepresented the content of the writing curriculum.

Recently, consequential validity has been receiving more attention, although measurement scholars were discussing it in the 1980s (e.g., Cronbach 1988; Messick 1989). This dimension refers to both the intended and unintended outcomes of the assessment. For example, if a writing test is designed to determine if students have met the goals of the course to prepare them for the next educational level (what we sometimes call an *exit test* or *proficiency exam*), one would examine what, if any, impact the test is having on the course curriculum and teaching and learning. What happens to the students who pass—or don't pass— the test? Are students who pass the test prepared for the next level? Is the assessment influencing the teaching and learning in ways that were intended? Are some populations of students disproportionately passing or failing the test? What happens to students after the test? To respond to these types of questions, evidence must be gathered and evaluated in terms of the costs and benefits.

This kind of validation inquiry is "never finished," and because tests "influence who gets what in society, fresh challenges follow shifts in social power and philosophy" (Cronbach 1988, 5). This ongoing process requires us to examine the uses and interpretations of test results as social, political, and educational contexts shift and change. "Ideally, validators will prepare as debaters do," grasping both pro and con sides of the arguments (Cronbach 1988, 3). For writing programs, this means, for example, that writing administrators and assessors must continuously collect evidence about the use, interpretation, consequences, and other aspects of a writing assessment. We cannot design an assessment, such as a placement test, and claim it has been validated. The placement exam designed twenty years ago may no longer adequately sort students into the curriculum, it may no longer represent the kinds of writing tasks students do, or it may have consequences to students that can no longer be justified. The mass-marketed, standardized test purchased from a vendor may not produce valid results for a particular program given the curriculum, the student demographics and needs, and the consequences it has for student learning. Whether we use a nationally normed computer-scored exam or a locally designed assessment, we need to continue to validate the placement results, collecting information and analyzing it as part of a holistic argument that weighs all the evidence, both empirical and theoretical, both pro and con.

While validity is the most fundamental threshold concept in assessment, reliability is also an important one. The typical adage is that reliability is necessary but not sufficient for validity. In other words, an assessment must be reliable—and there are multiple dimensions of reliability—but reliability alone is not enough to claim validity. Reliability, according to the *Standards*, is "the degree to which test scores for a group of test takers are consistent over repeated applications of a measurement procedure and hence are inferred to be repeatable for an individual test taker" and includes the "degree to which scores are free of errors of measurement for a given group" (AERA, APA, and NMCE 1999, 180). Reliability, then, involves consistency—consistency in the test taker's performance, in the scoring, in the results, and in the interpretation of those results. The consistency allows for generalizability. As Madaus (1994) and Kane (2006) explain, a test or assessment is a sampling we use to make inferences and draw conclusions. We are generalizing from the test results to make decisions about future performance, general competence, or some other abstract concept. To make valid judgments, we must be confident that the results are consistent. The focus on scores and measures of errors means that reliability tends to be embedded in complex statistical concepts and formulas. It is usually reported in terms of calculations and coefficients.

This statistical element often leaves many of us in writing studies feeling as if we are out of our depth, so we tend to rely on the measurement experts more readily. However, in making a judgment about reliability, we must weigh all of the evidence—theoretical and empirical—much as we do in validation (Moss 1994; Parkes 2007). We should think of it in terms of a continuum—again, much like validity—instead of an absolute: "There should be a reliability argument that, consistent with a theory base (Nichols and Smith, 1998), relies on evidence to make an argument about the consistency of judgments" (Parkes 2007, 5). Tests should not be considered reliable or not, but rather evidence in support of reliability must be considered as part of a larger context. This also means we should include all facets of reliability (e.g., instrument reliability, which considers what would happen if "the same assessment were to be done again in the same way, with the same distribution of students, the same method of assessment, and the same general kinds of topics" [Cherry and Meyer 1993, 118]) and not simply hone in on one. However, in spite of its many dimensions, in writing assessment, reliability often has been reduced to interrater reliability, that is, the agreement between two raters. Yet even interrater reliability often has been misunderstood, misused, or misrepresented (Cherry and Meyer 1993; Hayes and Hatch 1999; O'Neill 2011). By deepening our understanding of the threshold concept of reliability and the way it contributes to a validity argument, writing studies professionals are able to create assessments that satisfy educational measurement expectations and still represent writing as a complex, contextual, meaning-making activity, as the threshold concepts of writing studies described in part 1 articulate.

Writing assessment scholars who have been able to work at this intersection of writing studies and educational measurement have developed program-wide assessments informed by both sets of threshold concepts, though they have not explicitly used the language of threshold concepts to discuss them. For example, William L. Smith (1992; 1993) looked at the many different components of reliability in developing his method of using expert teachers to read students' writing and place students into the appropriate composition courses. He found that this process was more reliable than using the standard practice of holistic scoring. Before he reached this conclusion, however, he conducted a series of studies that looked at all aspects of the placement test, going well beyond interrater reliability as he constructed a validation argument. Likewise, Richard Haswell (2001) and his colleagues at Washington State University designed an innovative two-tier scoring system for a junior portfolio. They conducted a robust series of studies as they developed and validated their writing-assessment system (Haswell 1998; 2001). Bob Broad (2003) created Dynamic Criteria Mapping from his research into a communal portfolio system. Like the assessment systems developed by Haswell and Smith, he used theoretical and empirical evidence to justify it in terms of validity and reliability (see also Broad, Adler-Kassner, Alford, et al. 2009). In these examples, the authors understood key concepts in both psychometrics and writing studies, which allowed them to develop new methods for assessing writing that not only produced valid and reliable results but also contributed to the theory and practice of writing assessment as a discipline. The assessments they developed endorsed the contextual, complex notion of writing and teaching writing articulated in the threshold concepts in part 1, using validity and reliability to improve teaching and learning.

CLASSROOM-BASED AND LARGE-SCALE WRITING ASSESSMENT

Validity and reliability are most often associated with large-scale assessments conducted beyond the classroom, so many writing teachers do not necessarily see the relevance of understanding these concepts. Yet, it is important for classroom instructors to understand them because there is not a complete separation between classroom-based and large-scale assessment. Some classroom-based practices for assessing writing—such as the use of portfolios, including a reflective or self-evaluative text along with a primary text, using a text as the basis for the writing task, or building in extended time for drafting and revising—coincide with practices used in large-scale assessments, especially those developed by local programs. But more often, the assessment practices used in standardized large-scale tests—such as a timed, impromptu exam using a single sample of student writing—conflict not only with classroom practices but with the threshold concepts associated with writing and learning to write. Because large-scale writing assessment has incredible power in educational policy, and educational policy influences classroom practice, as evidenced by the testing programs of the last several decades as well as the Common Core assessments, the conflict can mean instructors teach to the test in ways that undermine student learning. In large-scale assessments, psychometric concepts, and the technical apparatus that goes along with them, tend to dominate. If writing teachers, scholars, and administrators want to ensure the theories and practices essential to writing studies (articulated in the threshold concepts in part 1) are not subordinated or distorted by the privileging of those of educational measurement, we need to understand measurement concepts and how they relate to what we do in our writing classrooms.

This link between the classroom and large-scale assessments is clearly apparent in the use of portfolios as a program-wide exit proficiency assessment (O'Neill, Moore, and Huot 2009). The portfolios are produced in the classroom and evaluated by the instructor throughout the term. Students receive feedback, perhaps even grades, on the components of the portfolio and maybe even the portfolio as a whole. The instructor typically assigns the students' grades for the course. However, the portfolio also may be evaluated by other instructors in the program. Sometimes evaluation is done in small groups, sometimes through a sampling approach, or sometimes by a team of evaluators. The results of a program-wide portfolio assessment may be used to evaluate individual students, as with a proficiency exam, and/or they might be used as part of the writing program assessment. Instructors can also be evaluated by their students' performance on the portfolio or may modify their teaching practices because of it. In any case, the portfolio functions as a central focus: in the classroom it is an essential means of teaching and assessment; beyond the classroom, it serves as the primary instrument for large-scale writing assessment.

While the link between classroom assessment and large-scale assessment is obvious in this example, it can be just as important with other types of writing assessment. For example, if a student must pass a rising exam, whether designed by the writing program or imposed from outside (such as a state-mandated junior writing exam), the expectation is that the writing classes the students have taken (and passed) have prepared them for the exam (whether on not this, in fact, is true). Instructors can be required to teach to the test although the test may not be part of the course or may not be used to influence the students' grades in the course. This situation creates an incongruity between the test and the curriculum with the students and instructors caught in the middle.

If professionals from both writing and assessment communities do not recognize the significance of both sets of threshold concepts, there may be a potential mismatch between what students experience through a writing assessment—and the trickle down from that to teaching and learning and the students' educational progress—and the threshold concepts of writing studies. This mismatch is not just a theoretical disagreement; students can experience real consequences to their learning and educational progress, as was the case for students that Eleanor Agnew and Margaret McLaughlin (Agnew and McLaughlin 1999; 2001; McLaughlin and Agnew 1999) studied. Agnew and McLaughlin conducted a longitudinal, qualitative study of sixty-one students placed into basic writing at their university and found that state-mandated writing tests had distinctly different effects on black students than on white students. The university-system-mandated exam that placed students into the writing curriculum placed African American students disproportionately into basic writing. Once in basic writing, the African American students were more likely than white students to fail the exit exam, to drop out or be put on academic probation, and to fail the Georgia State Regents' Exam, a state-mandated literacy test. Agnew and McLaughlin found that the race of the students was a significant factor in how teachers viewed the students and their writing, how they evaluated the students' writing, and assumptions teachers made about the students' attitudes, actions, and abilities. Their research, which considers a whole system of assessment and instruction, documented the deleterious effects of the assessment of African American students' writing both in the classroom and in the large-scale testing system. Multimodal empirical research such as this, that goes beyond statistical analysis of raters' performance and scores and that grounds the inquiry in writing theory and practice (which are identified as threshold concepts in part 1), should be considered in creating validity and reliability arguments and evaluating writing assessments.

The links between teaching, learning, and assessment, which Agnew and McLaughlin explored, are critical components in the validation process; in understanding the role of assessment in teaching and learning to write, the threshold concepts from both writing and educational measurement are crucial. We need to consider process-based, ongoing, low-stakes formative assessment, which is typical in many writing classrooms, as well as product-based, high-stakes, summative assessment, focused on the texts that result from the writers' processes, which is typical beyond the classroom. The difference is not necessarily in the type of information collected, the information produced, or the activity students perform. Rather, it is in how the results are used. Are they used to help students learn and develop as writers (formative), or are the results used to demonstrate students' competencies at a particular moment in time (summative)?

Doug Downs identifies formative assessment as part of the process of writing in threshold concept 4.4, Revision Is Central to Developing Writing, when he notes that "to create the best possible writing, writers work *iteratively*, composing in a number of versions, with time between each for reflection, reader feedback, and/or collaborator development." The feedback and reflection mentioned by Downs are forms of assessment, as explained in threshold concepts Assessing Writing Shapes Contexts and Instruction (1.7), and Assessment Is an Essential Component of Learning to Write (4.5). Summative assessments, which aim to demonstrate the learning that has occurred and come at the end of a specified time or activity (such as a final grade on a paper, a score on a program-wide portfolio, or a course grade) are also addressed in the threshold concepts 1.7 and 4.5. Although these two types of assessment are typically seen as distinct and even oppositional, they are not mutually exclusive. For example, in a course a student may receive a grade on a writing assignment (a summative assessment) but with the expectation that this grade is also a formative experience in that the writer continues learning based on the feedback (which includes the grade).

When assignments in a class build on each other across the term, even formal assessments are aimed at helping the writer develop skills for future tasks. Students' grades and performances, for instance, are used to make decisions about students' preparation for more advanced classes or their ability to function in other contexts beyond the classroom. Regardless of whether a writing assessment is being used in a formative or summative way, or whether it occurs inside a course or beyond it, the threshold concepts of writing outlined in part 1, as well as the psychometric concepts of validity and reliability, should inform the framework for designing the assessments and evaluating their results. Writing assessments, whether in the classroom or beyond, must acknowledge that Writing Is a Social and Rhetorical Activity (1.0); that Writing Speaks to Situations and Contexts through Recognizable Forms (2.0); that Writing Enacts and Creates Identities and Ideologies (3.0); and that writing is a learned and cognitive activity (reflected in concepts 4.0 and 5.0).

If we think of the classroom in terms of validity and reliability, we might consider how our assignments support this understanding of writing and how Assessing Writing Shapes Contexts and Instruction (1.7). If our assessment in the classroom doesn't match this robust understanding of writing, we are not creating assessments that produce valid results. For example, evaluation criteria for assignments should represent—and value—this complex understanding of writing and not overprivilege—or underprivilege—one or two aspects. As classroom instructors, we can conduct our own informal validation inquiry: Do we really balance the different aspects of writing in our evaluation or do we overemphasize one, such as correctness? Do our comments frame writing as a meaning-making activity? Are we teaching forms as situationally embedded activities or more as a static, generic template? Do we acknowledge the link to identity and the role of prior experience in students' writing? How do we balance what we know about writing and developing writers with the expectations of our program and institution? Using assessment, in both formative and summative ways, to produce valid results is not easy, but it requires asking these kinds of questions within our own classrooms to ensure we are grounding our assessment in the threshold concepts.

Once we move beyond the classroom, into large-scale assessment, these kinds of issues become even more critical because technical concerns about validity and reliability are emphasized. If we aren't able to ground our classroom practice in threshold concepts, which link assessments to what we know about teaching and learning to write, we will have a more difficult time arguing for appropriate assessments in large-scale situations. The disconnect between classroom-based and large-scale assessment can happen in writing programs when tests are imposed by administrators or policymakers who do not understand, or do not value, the threshold concepts associated with writing. Although the writing instructors may know the test is not consistent with the theories and practices supported by the threshold concepts, they may be powerless to advocate for a change unless they understand validity and reliability. While other factors can contribute to a sense of powerlessness, such as structural or bureaucratic policies, understanding concepts of validity and reliability can help situate assessment results in more useful ways, or at least provide pushback or alternatives to mandated writing assessments.

For example, in many writing programs, decisions about placement methods are not made by the writing program but by an external entity. In the public institutions in Idaho, for instance, all programs were required to use the same placement method (standardized test scores) and all were dissatisfied with the results—they didn't think the tests were adequately placing students into the first-year composition sequence at their particular institutions. When placement isn't adequate, there are consequences to student learning, curriculum, and instruction. By using their knowledge about writing, and developing a better understanding of validity, the writing program administrators in Idaho were able to argue for a pilot study that allowed programs to customize their placement program (Estrem, Shepherd, and Duman 2014). The goal was to improve teaching and learning by creating a placement assessment that produced more valid results. From the results of the pilot, different institutions developed different placement procedures that fit their particular needs so students were more effectively placed into the composition sequence.

This kind of approach to writing assessment—demonstrated by others such as Smith, Haswell, and Broad—happens when professionals work at the crossroads of writing studies and educational measurement to create assessment practices that produce valid results and that are persuasive to decision makers outside of our own field. With the pressure to demonstrate learning at the postsecondary level increasing, it is more necessary than ever for writing studies professionals to deepen their understanding of the critical measurement concepts of validity and reliability so we can use assessment to improve teaching and learning.

Note

1. A revised version of the *Standards* was published in 2014 during the production of this volume. While specific quotations and references in this chapter are not aligned with the new edition, the general arguments hold.

References

Agnew, Eleanor, and Margaret McLaughlin. 1999. "Basic Writing Class of '93 Five Years Later: How the Academic Paths of Blacks and Whites Diverged." *Journal of Basic Writing* 18 (1): 40–54.
Agnew, Eleanor, and Margaret McLaughlin. 2001. "Those Crazy Gates and How They Swing: Tracking the System That Tracks African-American Students." In *Mainstreaming Basic Writers: Politics and Pedagogies of Access*, edited by Gerri McNenny and Sallyanne H. Fitzgerald, 85–100. Mahwah, NJ: Erlbaum.
AERA, APA, and NCME. 1999. *Standards for Educational and Psychological Testing.* Washington, DC: American Educational Research Association.
Brennan, Robert L., ed. 2006. *Educational Measurement.* ACE/Oryx Press Series in Higher Education. 4th ed. Westport, CT: Praeger.
Broad, Bob. 2003. *What We Really Value: Beyond Rubrics in Teaching and Assessing Writing.* Logan: Utah State University Press.

Broad, Bob, Linda Adler-Kassner, Barry Alford, Jane Detweiler, Heidi Estrem, Susanmarie Harrington, Maureen McBride, Eric Stalions, and Scott Weeden. 2009. *Organic Writing Assessment: Dynamic Criteria Mapping in Action.* Logan: Utah State University Press.

Cherry, Roger, and Paul Meyer. 1993. "Reliability Issues in Holistic Assessment." In *Validating Holistic Scoring: Theoretical and Empirical Foundations,* edited by Michael M. Willamson and Brian Huot, 109–41. Cresskill, NJ: Hampton.

Cronbach, Lee J. 1988. "Five Perspectives on Validity Argument." In *Test Validity,* edited by Howard Wainer and Henry Braun, 3–17. Hillsdale: Erlbaum.

Estrem, Heidi, Dawn Shepherd, and Lloyd Duman. 2014. "Relentless Engagement with State Education Policy Reform: Collaborating to Change the Writing Placement Conversation." *WPA Journal* 38 (1): 88–128.

Gould, Stephen J. 1981. *The Mismeasure of Man.* New York: W. W. Norton.

Hanson, F. Allan. 1993. *Testing Testing: Social Consequences of the Examined Life.* Berkeley: University of California Press.

Haswell, Richard H. 1998. "Multiple Inquiry into the Validation of Writing Tests." *Assessing Writing* 5 (1): 89–109. http://dx.doi.org/10.1016/S1075-2935(99)80007-5.

Haswell, Richard, ed. 2001. *Perspectives on Writing Theory, Research and Practice.* Vol. 5. Beyond Outcomes: Assessment and Instruction within a University Writing Program. Westport, CT: Ablex.

Hayes, John R., and Jill A. Hatch. 1999. "Issues in Measuring Reliability: Correlation versus Percentage of Agreement." *Written Communication* 16 (3): 354–67. http://dx.doi .org/10.1177/0741088399016003004.

Kane, Michael T. 2006. "Validation." In *Educational Measurement.* ACE/Oryx Press Series in Higher Education. 4th ed. Edited by R. L. Brennan, 17–64. Westport, CT: ACE Praeger Series in Higher Education.

Madaus, George F. 1994. "A Technical and Historical Consideration of Equity Issues Associated with Proposals to Change the Nation's Testing Policy." *Harvard Educational Review* 64 (1):76–94.

McLaughlin, Margaret A., and Eleanor Agnew. 1999. "Teacher Attitudes Toward African American Language Patterns: A Close Look at Attrition Rates." In *Attending to the Margins: Writing, Researching, and Teaching on the Front Lines,* edited by Michelle Hall Kells and Valerie Balester, 114–30. Portsmouth, NH: Boynton/Cook.

Messick, Samuel. 1989. "Meaning and Value in Test Validation: The Science and Ethics of Assessment." *Educational Researcher* 18 (2): 5–11. http://dx.doi.org/10.3102/00131 89X018002005.

Moss, Pamela A. 1994. "Can There Be Validity Without Reliability?" *Educational Researcher* 23 (2): 5–12. http://dx.doi.org/10.3102/0013189X023002005.

Nichols, P. O., and P. L. Smith. 1998. "Contextualizing the Interpretation of Reliability Data." *Educational Measurement Issues and Practice* 17 (3): 24–36.

O'Neill, Peggy. 2011. "Reframing Reliability in College Writing Assessment." *Journal of Writing Assessment* 4 (1). http://journalofwritingassessment.org/article. php?article=54.

O'Neill, Peggy, Cindy Moore, and Brian Huot. 2009. *A Guide to College Writing Assessment.* Logan: Utah State University Press.

Parkes, Jay. 2007. "Reliability as Argument." *Educational Measurement: Issues and Practice* 26 (4): 2–10. http://dx.doi.org/10.1111/j.1745-3992.2007.00103.x.

Smith, William L. 1992. "The Importance of Teacher Knowledge in College Composition Placement Testing." In *Reading Empirical Research Studies: The Rhetoric of Research,* edited by John R. Hayes, 289–316. Norwood, NJ: Ablex.

Smith, William L. 1993. "Assessing the Reliability and Adequacy of Using Holistic Scoring of Essays as a College Composition Placement Technique." In *Validating Holistic Scoring: Theoretical and Empirical Foundations,* edited by Michael M. Williamson and Brian Huot, 142–205. Cresskill, NJ: Hampton.

11
THRESHOLD CONCEPTS IN THE WRITING CENTER
Scaffolding the Development of Tutor Expertise

Rebecca S. Nowacek and Bradley Hughes

In writing centers, the question of how to cultivate expertise in writing and writing instruction takes on an urgency that stems from one of the great strengths and defining features of writing centers: their extensive use of undergraduate and graduate students as writing consultants or tutors. The tutors in our writing centers at Marquette University and the University of Wisconsin-Madison, as in many writing centers, are on staff for relatively short periods of time—some for three years or more, but many others for only a handful of semesters. Helping these tutors cultivate a sense of expertise that can prepare them to be simultaneously confident enough to work with writers from a wide range of disciplines and levels of experience and humble enough to remain open to constantly learning is a delightful challenge for writing center directors.

The framework of threshold concepts, we believe, can help writing center professionals do that work more effectively. To be clear, we have designed tutor education for years (and in Brad's case, for decades) without explicitly drawing on the threshold concepts framework to inform our work. Nevertheless, as we look at the approaches we've taken, we can see our understandings of threshold concepts have implicitly informed our tutor-education programs and approaches to mentoring. We believe that the conscious use of the framework provided by the threshold concepts of writing identified in this volume cannot only help writing center directors to articulate (and therefore clarify and sometimes revise) priorities for the structure of tutor-education programs, it can also help tutors themselves conceptualize their own work with writers and with faculty. Moreover, viewing the work of tutor education through the lens of threshold concepts in writing development challenges writing center

DOI: 10.7330/9780874219906.c011

scholars to ask whether there are additional, writing center-specific threshold concepts. We begin that project, and conclude this chapter, by proposing one such writing center-specific threshold concept.

WHAT'S AT STAKE: AN EXPANSIVE VISION OF THE WRITING CENTER

To highlight why educating tutors is so challenging and how threshold concepts can guide that work, we begin by foregrounding the range of writing center work and by suggesting the many ways strong, cross-curricular writing centers rely on and illuminate all five of the threshold concepts about writing articulated in part 1 of this volume. Perhaps the most broadly shared understanding of writing centers is that of a space in which writers and tutors talk about the process of writing and about drafts in progress. What is perhaps less visible to individuals who have not spent extended periods of time within strong cross-curricular writing centers is the incredible variety of that talk. Within our two writing centers, for instance, writers—including undergraduates, graduate students, faculty, staff, and community members—meet with tutors to discuss research proposals, statements of purpose, experimental research reports, personal statements, new media projects, research posters, academic essays, literature reviews, critiques, manifestos, policy analyses, job letters, resumes, and CVs. These conversations take place in person across our campuses, within dedicated writing centers and writing studios, learning commons, campus libraries, and coffee shops; they take place online, through written feedback, Skype, and Google doc consultations; they take place beyond our campuses in public libraries and community centers.

Furthermore, our writing centers offer much more than individual tutoring. We offer many workshops on common genres of academic writing. Our centers include both established and proto-WAC programs, offering consultations and workshops for faculty on teaching with writing and co-teaching custom units on writing within courses across the curriculum. We have writing fellows programs that blend WAC and writing centers. We mentor student-tutors in carefully designed initial and ongoing tutor education and mentor them as they conduct original research about academic writing and about talk around writing. And as Jackie Grutsch McKinney (2013) persuasively documents, our writing centers are hardly unique in this regard. Although the writing centers we direct cannot represent the full variety of writing center structures and missions, they do embody many of the most common ambitions of and challenges faced by cross-curricular writing centers.

Within all of these complex forms of writing center instruction, the five threshold concepts from part 1 of this collection clearly play a central role. By bringing writers together with readers to discuss papers in progress, writing centers make visible the fact that Writing is a Social and Rhetorical Activity (see concept 1.0). Within writing center collaborations, writers test out their evolving ideas and arguments with interested, encouraging, and critical readers—and through the tutor's reactions, writers can learn to talk about their writing rhetorically, to think more explicitly about their purposes in writing and about their audiences, to care more about their writing, and to value collaborative talk as part of the writing process (Bruffee 1984; Geller et al. 2007; Harris 1995; Hobson 1992; Lunsford 1991; North 1984). The understanding that writing must be learned and All Writers Have More to Learn (see concept 4.0) illuminates one of the key justifications for creating writing center programs and explains why writers can benefit so much from writing centers. Writing centers can and must be on the lookout for opportunities to teach, as Stephen North describes it, "at the conjunction of timing and motivation" (443). For some writers (and for many tutors), ongoing engagement in writing center conversations about writing illuminates how Reflection is Critical for Writers' Development (see 5.4).

Writers who come to a writing center vary considerably in their understanding of how Writing Speaks to Situations Through Recognizable Forms (see 2.0). As part of their preparation, then, tutors must learn the importance of genre knowledge so they can tap into the knowledge and models student-writers bring, and so tutors can learn to think in terms of genres as they work with student-writers. Finally, because Writing Enacts and Creates Identities and Ideologies (see 3.0), writing centers are hardly neutral sites of literacy instruction or assistance, and many recent publications explore the complex ways writing and identity converge in writing center work (e.g., Denny 2010; Grimm 1999). The writing assignments student-writers bring to writing centers, the literacy expectations of particular instructors and of universities, the identities of students, the spoken and unspoken literacy and educational goals that motivate students, the literacy orientations and politics of tutors and directors, the identities of tutors, the tacit and explicit missions of centers, the complex politics of writing center funding and status—these all inflect writing center work in powerful ways. In their mission and methods, some writing centers aim to be liberatory, to celebrate individual voices of students (Warnock and Warnock 1984), while others anchor their methods and identity in social construction (Ede 1989) and in collaborative learning (Bruffee 1984), and other centers aim to be change agents, making, for example, social justice and anti-racist work central to their missions (Condon 2007; Geller et al. 2007; Greenfield and Rowan 2012; Grimm 2012; Villanueva 2006).

THRESHOLD CONCEPTS IN FORMAL TUTOR-EDUCATION PROGRAMS

The notion of threshold concepts implies that writing tutors will be better equipped for their work if they learn to see with and through the threshold concepts of writing. If that is the case, how should a tutor-education program sequence the work of grappling with those threshold concepts? Are some threshold concepts more central to writing center work than others? Asking these TC-inspired questions has helped Rebecca better understand three dimensions of the tutor-education program at Marquette: choosing what to prioritize during the initial tutor-education course and what to defer until ongoing tutor education, making clearer decisions about hiring processes, and revising the content of the tutor-education course. (Here we shift into Rebecca's first person narrative.)

Potential undergraduate tutors at Marquette enroll in a four-credit course, spend fifteen hours shadowing an experienced tutor, and participate in a weekly staff meeting with tutors already on staff. Students choose whether to apply to become a writing tutor, and hiring decisions are made only after the course is complete. Despite this luxury of time, I still struggle with problems of coverage, inevitably wanting to stuff the course to the rafters with readings and experiences that will signal to potential tutors our center's many values and commitments (promoting writing and learning in the disciplines and working as an agent of social change, among others). Over the past five years, my choices about how to focus the initial course have been guided by the tutor-education program I inherited and by my recognition of a paradox that must be addressed by our tutor-education program.

Tutors are, at heart, conversational partners for writers: the mission of our writing center assumes Writing Is a Knowledge-Making Activity (see 1.1); that Learning to Write Effectively Requires Different Kinds of Practice, Time, and Effort (see 4.3); and that writing often requires revision (see 4.4, "Revision is Central to Developing Writing"). And yet, many of the students eager to become tutors have experienced academic success without regularly (or, in some cases, ever) having to significantly revise their own writing and therefore have relatively little experience undertaking significant revision based on a conversation with someone else. Reexamining this mismatch between institutional mission and individual experience through the lens of threshold concepts has helped me to more consciously determine the primary goal of the initial tutor-education course at Marquette: to help potential tutors engage in and reflect on processes of revision in ways many of these writers have not previously.

Coming to view the understandings of writing and revision at the heart of our writing center mission *as liminal threshold concepts*, as views that require not just cognitive understanding but sometimes profound reorientations of worldviews and even identities, strengthens my conviction that it is important to frontload a focus on writing as a knowledge-building process that requires practice and revision. To put it another way, if you give me a list of potential writing center values and ask me what I care about most, I find it exceedingly difficult to choose. If I begin from the premise that many of these values are grounded in beliefs that require significant cognitive and emotional reorientations and that I cannot reasonably expect everyone on my staff to fully come to terms with all of them immediately, I can more easily identify which beliefs are the necessary building blocks for the rest of our work. In the case of Marquette's writing center, the threshold concepts framework illuminates the value of giving potential tutors an *extended* opportunity to grapple with a view of writing and revising as a knowledge-making activity while introducing other threshold concepts more briefly, knowing they can be further explored during long-term professional development.

This insight also enables me to make more transparent the relationship between the initial course and our eventual process of selecting tutors. Certainly I don't need—or want—a staff of clones; threshold concepts should not become a mechanism of absolute standardization. And I am mindful of the fact that tutors frequently report that their views of writing are transformed through the deep engagement and repeated exposure made possible by their work in the writing center (Hughes, Gillespie, and Kail 2010). Nevertheless, given the mission of Marquette's writing center and the transformative but liminal nature of threshold concepts, I recognize that if even after a semester of reading, research, and discussion a potential tutor does not deeply engage with the view of writing as a knowledge-making activity that often requires significant revision, this individual is likely not a good fit for our writing center.

Other threshold concepts, although they may not prove crucial for selecting tutors, may still remain valuable resources for the work of tutoring. To the degree that I can reconcile myself to the idea that tutors may come to see through and with these other threshold concepts to greater or lesser degrees, at earlier or later stages of their work as tutors, I can come to terms with deferring extended engagement with these concepts (even those concepts I care deeply about) to the context of ongoing tutor education. For instance, as a rhetorical genre theorist with an interest in writing in the disciplines, I believe genre knowledge of the sort identified in concept 2 is a crucial resource for developing tutor expertise (Nowacek 2011). But given our writing center's mission and the experiences of our potential tutors, I now see more clearly the advantage of sequencing staff meetings about various genres to build up that knowledge over a longer period of time. After all, if tutors continually resist the premise that writing can be a knowledge-building activity that often requires revision, they may be considerably less likely to bring any genre knowledge they may have to bear productively in conversations with writers.

I am also convinced that the threshold concepts framework can become an important part of the tutor-education course itself. In the most recent iteration of the course syllabus, I included readings that not only address the various threshold concepts of writing (which have always, in various proportions, been present) but also explicitly introduced the very notion of threshold concepts. Early in the course we discussed threshold concepts as troublesome, transformative, and liminal; at midterm and finals, I invited students to articulate in text and pictures the degrees to which they saw (or didn't see) writing through the threshold concepts and to reflect on the sources of their own resistance to some of these concepts. I have saved all of these reflective writings and sketches and, as part of our ongoing reflective practices, we will continue to revisit these questions in an effort to review and consolidate our learning and to chart any changes in our understanding. I have also invited students to propose additional, tutoring-specific threshold concepts to share with future tutors—an invitation that initially puzzled the tutors on our staff but, even after one semester, has generated increasingly detailed and engaged conversations among experienced tutors.

We know that other directors at other centers, energized by different missions and different priorities, will make different decisions about what to emphasize in tutor education and when to emphasize it. The threshold concepts framework does not—and should not—eliminate the need to think critically about tutor-education programs each time we design and lead them. But in most any case, we are convinced that using threshold concepts as foundational knowledge for tutors can help tutors and directors remember what's central to our field and to our practice, helping us to make those difficult decisions about scaffolding tutor education.

USING THRESHOLD CONCEPTS TO COACH TUTORS TO WORK WITH WRITERS

In addition to helping tutors better understand and contextualize their own views of writing, bringing threshold concepts into writing center tutor education may offer tutors a means of better understanding their interactions with writers. To take one example, recognizing threshold concepts as threshold concepts—as understandings of writing that are consistently troublesome and counterintuitive for many individuals but that can change over time—may offer tutors a powerful framework through which to interpret (and perhaps reinterpret) some of the more frustrating conferences every tutor inevitably experiences.

Some conferences are a joy—intellectually stimulating and interpersonally rewarding. Such conferences often take place with writers who come through the door with already advanced understandings of writing. Even if they can't explicitly articulate the threshold concepts, with a bit of prompting these writers are willing to explore the conventions of their disciplines, ready to unpack the ideological challenges implicit in their work, open to brainstorming a wider range of options and collaboratively assessing the advantages and disadvantages of those options. Some of these writers feel relatively confident and optimistic about their work; others struggle mightily. Some writers return to build long-term relationships with a tutor; others are never seen again. Despite these variations, tutors often describe conversations with writers who actively participate in conversations and seem open to ideas for revision as being among the most enjoyable aspects of their work in the writing center.

Other conferences are less immediately rewarding. In such conferences, writers may be reticent to engage in conversation, offering only brief responses to tutor questions. Other times, writers may resist exploring possible avenues for revision, growing visibly frustrated, even hostile. It's easy for tutors to dismiss these conferences as failures and, whether intentionally or unintentionally, neglect to invite these writers to return. Indeed, Rita Malenczyk's analysis of writing center conference records demonstrates that tutors often describe conferences with writers who are "reluctant to work on their own, to engage in a dialogue, and perhaps in need of more help than the tutor can provide in one session"

(Malenczyk 2013, 88) in terms that tacitly but clearly code the conference as unsuccessful.

The threshold concepts framework can help tutors reinterpret these frustrating conferences by illuminating possible explanations for writers' resistance. In some cases, the causes may be dispositional (perhaps the writer is shy or nervous), cultural (perhaps the writer brings different expectations of how to interact with authority figures), or situational (perhaps the paper is due in an hour). But in other cases, writer and tutor may be conceptualizing writing in fundamentally different ways. For instance, it's not unusual for writers to arrive with a draft and ask tutors to "check it" for "grammar and flow." Such requests are often motivated by a view of writing that assumes that ideas present themselves to "inspired" writers, that words are a transparent medium for capturing those ideas on paper, and that, if appropriately tweaked, the words on paper can be made to meet the standards of Good Writing. On the one hand, we are deeply reluctant to portray such writers as entirely naïve or simply in need of being "enlightened" by our wisdom; writing center work can and should be reciprocal, and WAC scholarship has rightly challenged "missionary" metaphors (Haviland et al. 1999; Jablonski 2006). But if we can be wary of the least generous implications of the threshold concepts model, one of its great advantages is that it can help tutors view their conferences not in terms of the idiosyncratic "deficits" of individual writers (or particular demographics of writers) but in terms of processes of learning that challenge *many* individuals at *many* different stages of their academic careers.

Taking this view might help tutors remain more flexible and patient, better able to see the potential value of incremental progress or planting the seed of a threshold concept a writer can grapple with over a long period of time. Such a view might also ameliorate a sense of burnout among tutors who fear frustrating conferences are inevitably a sign of their own shortcomings. Finally, tutors who are more flexible and able to see the big picture of learning about writing may be more likely to create a welcoming space for writers in the early stages of engagement with the threshold concepts of writing, writers who may have a great deal to gain from sustained engagement with the threshold concepts through conversations in the writing center. Thus, the lens of liminal threshold concepts might offer tutors a way of interrogating the nature of resistance and considering the potential social justice implications of unexamined tutor frustration.

USING THRESHOLD CONCEPTS TO PREPARE
TUTORS FOR INTERACTIONS WITH FACULTY

Writing center tutors and directors interact not only with student-writers but also with faculty in disciplines across a university, in some of the same ways and facing some of the same challenges WAC professionals do (Haviland et al. 1999; Jablonski 2006; see Anson, this volume, for an extensive exploration of the challenges WAC leaders face as they collaborate with faculty across the curriculum). In the writing center at the University of Wisconsin-Madison, for example, a team drawn from our doctoral-level tutors, along with members of the center's professional staff, spend part of their time working with faculty in many disciplines through our outreach program, co-planning and co-teaching with faculty brief units on writing tailored to students and assignments within a particular course. In addition, all of the undergraduate writing fellows on our staff work collaboratively with faculty as well as with student-writers in courses across the disciplines. And even when there is no direct communication between faculty across the university and writing center tutors, faculty and their approaches to student writing are, in fact, omnipresent in writing centers. In their conversations with student-writers, tutors are trying to help students understand the expectations of faculty who design the writing assignments that bring students to the center, and they are often coaching students in how to have effective conversations with their faculty readers.

For tutors learning to work with faculty around writing assignments, among the many challenges they face, three seem key. First, tutors often understandably but mistakenly assume faculty have advanced understandings of how writing works and of how writers develop—and they assume faculty share the same vocabulary and concepts for talking about writing that tutor education gives tutors access to. Second, to tutors, each collaboration with faculty can seem *sui generis*, with unpredictable variables. And third, interactions between tutors or fellows and faculty inevitably involve power differentials that complicate tutors' abilities and willingness to share knowledge and to make suggestions with faculty. Tutors working in our writing center's outreach program at UW-Madison, for example, are sometimes frustrated when faculty are unwilling to give up enough class time for instruction tailored to a particular writing assignment, and writing fellows in our program are sometimes confused or frustrated by a professor's vague genre expectations in an assignment. Tutors discover that although some faculty understand that all writers have more to learn about writing and that writing is a situated practice within a particular discipline, others seem to believe that problems in student writing are necessarily the result of inferior previous education or lack of effort from students.

These situations and the beliefs underlying them may look all too familiar to experienced writing center directors and WAC professionals; to tutors just beginning to work with faculty, however, it is often a revelation that faculty across the curriculum vary in their understandings of the threshold concepts about writing. Here's where the framework of threshold concepts can come in. Writing center directors can use them to help tutors develop schema for listening analytically for faculty beliefs about writing and also to help tutors learn to accept and to expect realistic progress on perhaps only a single concept at a time.

We can coach tutors to interact with faculty—and to help the student-writers whom tutors are coaching to interact with faculty—in productive ways. The principles and methods we coach tutors to follow in our outreach instruction at UW-Madison, for example, are designed not only to benefit student-writers but also to invite faculty to see the benefits of and learn more about contemporary writing studies and pedagogy. We insist on meeting in person for extended discussions to plan the instruction, just as we do when we talk with faculty about having writing fellows from our staff work with students in a particular course (Hall and Hughes 2011). We want to ask questions and listen carefully to a faculty member's goals for writing and to their approaches to student writing. In our outreach instruction, our tutors are reinforcing or introducing key concepts about writing and about writing instruction—when we try to tap into a professor's knowledge about the disciplinary genre students are writing in, when we tailor instruction to particular assignments and genres, when we ask the course instructor to provide samples from actual student writing, when we try to build in actual student talk about writing in progress.

When colleagues in various departments and the staff in the writing center are already on the same wavelength about some threshold concepts or are ready to learn more, these methods can work well and the results can truly be impressive. The UW-Madison Writing Center's collaboration with a colleague in nuclear engineering offers a good example. This professor initially contacted our writing center for help planning writing assignments for a sequence of courses for juniors in a new undergraduate research track within that major. This colleague already understood that writing and research are intertwined, that advanced writing skills within a major must be learned, and that faculty have an opportunity and obligation to design intentional learning activities around writing within a discipline—but did not know how to help students understand the rhetorical work genres within that discipline do or how to tap into the social dimensions of learning to write. Working together with our center, this colleague planned an impressive sequence of scaffolded assignments to help first-semester juniors learn to read and understand primary scientific literature. In the second-semester course, students wrote a sequenced literature review and worked on writing proposals for their senior theses. This professor invited our staff to co-lead an in-class session of peer review—instruction and practice that helped juniors start to see themselves as valuable professional reviewers. Through this collaboration, our colleague's understanding of threshold concepts deepened, as did our writing center staff's understanding of how these concepts play out in this particular field of engineering. The learning around threshold concepts with colleagues in different disciplines can truly be reciprocal.

EXPERT OUTSIDERS: A THRESHOLD CONCEPT OF TUTORING?

The process of reflecting on how the threshold concepts of writing are made visible in the writing center has led us to ask whether there are additional *writing center-specific* threshold concepts. And, indeed, as we consider the nature of expertise within writing centers, we are convinced there are. To be successful working with writers and faculty from many different disciplines and levels, tutors must come to understand a concept that initially is very difficult to accept, one that seems counterintuitive to student-tutors, to student-writers, and to faculty. Tutors need to learn that *experienced, effective conversational partners for writers regularly inhabit the role of "expert outsider,"* and tutors need to learn the skills necessary for inhabiting that role. The dual emphasis of the term *expert outsider* embodies, we hope, the paradoxical nature of tutoring expertise. Tutors draw on knowledge of writing processes and genres, as well as the affective, institutional, and ideological contexts for writing, to inform their conversations with writers; much of this expert knowledge is reflected in the threshold concepts articulated in this book and has been detailed in this chapter. However, because tutors cannot possibly hope to be content experts for every writer and draft they encounter, they can instead capitalize on lack of content knowledge to position the writer as bringing a different type of knowledge and the tutor as an interested, rhetorically savvy audience wanting to better understand that knowledge. This "outsider" positioning, when combined with expertise in writing, can help writers better engage the social and rhetorical dimensions of their writing and learning. Helping tutors accept and learn to work within this role of expert outsider is a big part of our work—and a threshold concept worthy of further inquiry within the writing center profession.

Responding in part to the "generalist versus specialist tutor" debates that appear in the writing center scholarship (Hubbuch 1988; Kiedaisch and Dinitz 1993; see Dinitz and Harrington 2014 for an important exploration of the limits of outsider knowledge), the expert-outsider construct foregrounds the relationship between the expert knowledge embodied in the five threshold concepts of writing and the day-to-day manifestations of expertise enacted by writing center tutors working in disciplines far outside the field of writing studies. Based on our observations, as well as our readings of writing center scholarship and the threshold concepts literature, we believe tutors who inhabit the role of expert outsider regularly see with and through the five threshold concepts of writing. But frankly, many tutors are reluctant to relinquish the authority and security of a more teacherly role. We also believe the obstacles to helping tutors become expert outsiders—to helping them effectively deploy their knowledge of the threshold concepts of writing while understanding the strengths and limitations of their lack of content knowledge—are both individual and institutional.

Individually, we know—both from our own anecdotal observations and from the recurring insistence of the threshold concepts literature—that although threshold concepts can be "transformative" and "irreversible" for writers, they are also "liminal" (Meyer and Land 2006a). Learning to see through and with *any* threshold concept is not simply a matter of flipping a light switch from off to on; rather, it is a cognitively (and sometimes emotionally) complex emergent understanding (Meyer and Land 2006b). We see this in the writing center: tutors begin their work with different understandings of the threshold concepts of writing and of the expert-outsider role; they embrace and resist the various concepts throughout their professional development, and their progress is neither linear nor inevitable.

Institutionally, tutors face an additional challenge as they work to understand the nature of their own tutoring expertise. The type of expertise embodied in writing center tutors—an expertise that rests in large part on knowledge of the social and rhetorical dimensions of constructing knowledge through writing—profoundly challenges traditional disciplinary notions of expertise. As Cheryl Geisler (1994) argues, the educational system in the United States is designed in a way that effectively foregrounds the knowledge domain while masking the rhetorical domain of expertise; the rhetorical domains of knowledge construction often become visible only during advanced undergraduate or graduate studies. And even then the rhetorical domains are often so naturalized that many practitioners never recognize that their expertise with writing products and processes is grounded within specific disciplinary or professional traditions. The expert-outsider model posits that tutors can help writers create knowledge in their disciplines and can work with writers who are more advanced and knowledgeable, in part because tutors understand the rhetorical domain of knowledge construction in ways other writers often do not. However, that claim is only persuasive for individuals who already recognize the rhetorical dimensions of expertise. Absent that recognition, the expert knowledge of writing center tutors seems not just flexible and tacit, but arbitrary and invisible. Learning to embrace this expert-outsider role is often, quite understandably, a difficult process—but it is also, we argue, part of what can make working as a tutor or a writing fellow such a powerful, even transformative, educational experience.

CONCLUSION

We conclude this chapter by looking forward, inviting writing center scholars and others to conduct research that explores in greater detail the implications of these threshold concepts of writing and tutoring. Potential research questions include the following: Are writing center tutors in fact better equipped for their work if they see with and through the threshold concepts of writing? What are the practical advantages and limitations of introducing the threshold concepts framework into tutor education? We anticipate, for instance, that this line of research would engage (and extend existing research on) important, complex issues surrounding power dynamics in conferences, consultations, and tutor education.

In addition to the threshold concepts of writing, are there other threshold concepts of tutoring that can be identified? And returning to the threshold concept of tutoring we propose in this chapter, what is the precise nature of expert-outsider knowledge? Based on preliminary findings (Hughes 2012; Nowacek 2013), we believe genre knowledge is a key component. What else might we learn about expert-outsider knowledge through fine-grained, empirical analyses of tutoring in a range of centers? Finally, we wonder whether the threshold concept of the expert outsider may have resonance beyond the writing center. After all, it is not only writing center tutors and writing fellows who regularly work outside their areas of established expertise. Writing instructors in other institutional contexts—teaching assistants, contingent faculty, faculty members from across the curriculum teaching in first-year seminar programs—are often asked to coach student-writers composing on topics unfamiliar to them. We have argued throughout this chapter that the threshold concepts of writing inform writing center practice; it may also be the case that threshold concepts of tutoring made visible in the writing center—like the view of expertise embodied in the expert outsider—can, in turn, illuminate approaches to coaching writers and writing instructors across the university.

References

Bruffee, Kenneth A. 1984. "Collaborative Learning and the 'Conversation of Mankind.'" *College English* 46 (7): 635–52. http://dx.doi.org/10.2307/376924.

Condon, Frankie. 2007. "Beyond the Known: Writing Centers and the Work of Anti-Racism." *Writing Center Journal* 27 (2): 19–38.

Denny, Harry. 2010. *Facing the Center: Toward an Identity Politics of One-to-One Mentoring.* Logan: Utah State University Press.

Dinitz, Sue, and Susanmarie Harrington. 2014. "The Role of Disciplinary Expertise in Shaping Writing Tutorials." *Writing Center Journal* 33 (2): 73–98.

Ede, Lisa. 1989. "Writing as a Social Process: A Theoretical Foundation for Writing Centers?" *Writing Center Journal* 9 (2): 3–13.

Geisler, Cheryl. 1994. "Literacy and Expertise in the Academy." *Language and Learning Across the Disciplines* 1 (1):35–57.

Geller, Anne Ellen, Michele Eodice, Frankie Condon, Meg Carroll, and Elizabeth H. Boquet. 2007. *The Everyday Writing Center: A Community of Practice.* Logan: Utah State University Press.

Greenfield, Laura, and Karen Rowan, eds. 2012. *Writing Centers and the New Racism: A Call for Sustainable Dialogue and Change.* Logan: Utah State University Press.

Grimm, Nancy Maloney. 1999. *Good Intentions: Writing Center Work for Postmodern Times.* Portsmouth, NH: Heinemann-Boynton/Cook.

Grimm, Nancy M. 2012. "Retheorizing Writing Center Work to Transform a System of Advantage Based on Race." In *Writing Centers and the New Racism: A Call for Sustainable Dialogue and Change,* edited by Laura Greenfield and Karen Rowan, 75–100. Logan: Utah State University Press.

Grutsch McKinney, Jackie. 2013. *Peripheral Visions for Writing Centers.* Logan: Utah State University Press.

Hall, Emily, and Bradley Hughes. 2011. "Preparing Faculty, Professionalizing Fellows: Keys to Success with Undergraduate Writing Fellows in WAC." *WAC Journal* 22. http://wac.colostate.edu/journal/vol22/hall.pdf.

Harris, Muriel. 1995. "Talking in the Middle: Why Writers Need Writing Tutors." *College English* 57 (1): 27–42. http://dx.doi.org/10.2307/378348.

Haviland, Carol Peterson, Sherry Green, Barbara Kime Shields, and M. Todd Harper. 1999. "Neither Missionaries Nor Colonists Nor Handmaidens: What Writing Tutors Can Teach WAC Faculty about Inquiry." In *Writing Centers and Writing Across the Curriculum Programs: Building Interdisciplinary Partnerships,* edited by Robert W. Barnett and Jacob S. Blumner, 45–57. Westport, CT: Greenwood.

Hobson, Eric H. 1992. "Maintaining Our Balance: Walking the Tightrope of Competing Epistemologies." *Writing Center Journal* 13 (1): 65–75.

Hubbuch, Susan M. 1988. "A Tutor Needs to Know the Subject Matter to Help a Student with a Paper: ___ agree___disagree___not sure." *Writing Center Journal* 8 (2): 23–30.

Hughes, Bradley, Paula Gillespie, and Harvey Kail. 2010. "What They Take with Them: Findings from the Peer Writing Tutor Alumni Research Project." *Writing Center Journal* 30 (2): 12–46.

Hughes, Bradley. 2012. "Focusing on Transfer in Writing Center Tutor Education." Paper presented at the International Writing Across the Curriculum Conference, Savannah, GA, June 7–9.

Jablonski, Jeffrey. 2006. *Academic Writing Consulting and WAC: Methods and Models for Guiding Cross-Curricular Literacy Work.* Cresskill, NJ: Hampton.

Kiedaisch, Jean, and Sue Dinitz. 1993. "Look Back and Say 'So What': The Limitations of the Generalist Tutor." *Writing Center Journal* 14 (1): 63–74.

Lunsford, Andrea A. 1991. "Collaboration, Control, and the Idea of a Writing Center." *Writing Center Journal* 12 (1): 3–10.

Malenczyk, Rita. 2013. "'I Thought I'd Put That in to Amuse You': Tutor Reports as Organizational Narrative." *Writing Center Journal* 33 (1): 74–95.

Meyer, Jan H. F., and Ray Land. 2006a. "Threshold Concepts and Troublesome Knowledge: An Introduction." In *Overcoming Barriers to Student Understanding: Threshold Concepts and Troublesome Knowledge*, edited by Jan H. F. Meyer and Ray Land, 3–18. London: Routledge.

Meyer, Jan H. F., and Ray Land. 2006b. "Threshold Concepts and Troublesome Knowledge: Issues of Liminality." In *Overcoming Barriers to Student Understanding: Threshold Concepts and Troublesome Knowledge*, edited by Jan H. F. Meyer and Ray Land, 19–32. London: Routledge.

North, Stephen. 1984. "The Idea of a Writing Center." *College English* 46 (5): 433–46. http://dx.doi.org/10.2307/377047.

Nowacek, Rebecca. 2011. *Agents of Integration: Understanding Transfer as a Rhetorical Act.* Carbondale: Southern Illinois University Press.

Nowacek, Rebecca. 2013. "Genre Knowledge and 'Transfer Talk' in the Writing Center: Findings from a Pilot Study." Paper presented at Critical Transitions: Elon Conference on Transfer, Elon, NC, June 25–26.

Villanueva, Victor. 2006. "Blind: Talking about the New Racism." *Writing Center Journal* 26 (1): 3–19.

Warnock, Tilly, and John Warnock. 1984. "Liberatory Writing Centers: Restoring Authority to Writers." In *Writing Centers: Theory and Administration*, edited by Gary A. Olson, 16–23. Urbana: National Council of Teachers of English.

12

EXTENDING THE INVITATION
Threshold Concepts, Professional Development, and Outreach

Linda Adler-Kassner and John Majewski

In one of only a handful of studies examining the role that threshold concepts might play in faculty members' professional development, Jan H. F. Meyer outlines a trajectory along which he believes faculty move through engagement with the idea. The trajectory includes four phases: (1) describing threshold concepts of their discipline; (2) using threshold concepts as an "interpretive framework" through which to consider teaching; (3) reflexively incorporating them into teaching practices; and (4) conducting research on teaching and understanding teaching as research (Meyer 2012, 11). Meyer's study echoes elements of other literature focusing on professional development, such as Middendorf and Pace's (2004) Decoding the Disciplines (DtD) process, which leads faculty through a seven-step process beginning with identification of "learning bottlenecks" (points where students get stuck in a course), which leads to an examination of expert knowledge related to the bottleneck, finally resulting in the design and assessment of pedagogical activities that address the sticking point (decodingthedisciplines.org). In the frameworks of both Meyer and Joan Middendorf and David Pace, teaching is intimately connected to creative application of expert knowledge in a manner similar to academic research. As Sarah Bunnell and Daniel Bernstein argue, the application of this knowledge (here represented in threshold concepts) to teaching is a "scholarly enterprise" that includes understanding teaching as an "active, inquiry-based process" and seeing teaching as a "public act contributing to 'community property'" that leads to "open dialogue about teaching questions and student work" (Bunnell and Bernstein 2012, 15).

This chapter builds on these existing models by examining how discussions about threshold concepts usefully facilitate faculty development and outreach. As in Meyer's model, the study we describe here suggests

DOI: 10.7330/9780874219906.c0012

that involving faculty in systematic discussions about threshold concepts in their discipline provides a welcome opportunity to reflexively consider the nature of their own expertise, as in the DtD process. While this consideration begins with definitions of a discipline's threshold concepts—what we can think of as a first layer of expertise—it quickly leads to a second layer, expertise associated with knowledge about how to learn and represent threshold concepts (such as how to select, interpret, and use evidence within the discipline). The argument here, then, is that discussions about threshold concepts are particularly productive starting points for professional development precisely because faculty are invested in their own disciplines. By asking faculty about "their own forms of evidence and ways of knowing" (Bunnell and Bernstein 2012, 17), discussions of threshold concepts can lead to considerations of the nature(s) of these levels of expertise and, ultimately, to professional development efforts to make threshold concepts more visible for students.

To illustrate, we begin this chapter by drawing on interviews with colleagues from our institution during which faculty described threshold concepts in their disciplines and considered how these were made visible to students enrolled in general education courses. The interviews show faculty members working through their own liminal stages of thinking associated with three concepts associated with teaching: (1) threshold concepts are a threshold concept; (2) my discipline is not the universe; and (3) successful student learning involves demonstrating particular ways of thinking and can be supported through deliberately sequenced learning opportunities. Faculty members' thinking around each of these concepts provides glimpses of how they articulate elements of professional expertise and shows how consideration of that expertise can open doorways for professional development that represents movement along the trajectory described by Meyer, the shifts in thinking outlined by Bunnell and Bernstein, and the stages of "decoding" described by Middendorf and Pace. To show what this thinking looks like in a more fully realized form, John then discusses changes he has made to one of his courses, History 17b, a large general education course, as a result of our collaborative (and ongoing) study of threshold concepts and the teaching of history—a study that has, in fact, served as professional development for both of us.

TC 1: THRESHOLD CONCEPTS ARE A THRESHOLD CONCEPT

Our interviews with colleagues across disciplines were intended to help them name what they knew and wanted to help students learn. However, our interviews quickly demonstrated that faculty are seldom presented with such opportunities to do this naming (a phenomenon we experienced in compiling the entries in part 1 of this collection in our own discipline, as well). This lack of opportunity demonstrates the value of conversations that start from a position of inquiry *about* threshold concepts for professional development since these reflect faculty members' "own forms of evidence and ways of knowing" (Bunnell and Bernstein 2012, 17). Our experience echoed that of threshold concepts researchers Naomi Irvine and Patrick Carmichael, who found that the "'concept of threshold concepts'" both started and focused discussions about these critical ideas and also led faculty to a "self-conscious consideration of disciplinary distinctiveness" (Irvine and Carmichael 2009, 113). If we can help our colleagues name their fields' threshold concepts, it becomes possible to then create opportunities for professional development that will assist them in planning courses, curricula, and assignments that move students to and through those concepts.

For disciplinary experts like the faculty we interviewed, the realization that there *are* threshold concepts critical for understanding and practicing their discipline was itself a threshold concept. In these instances, the recognition was sometimes troublesome, certainly transformative, and potentially irreversible. Faculty began to see their discipline as what Jean Lave and Etienne Wenger describe as a "community of practice," a group sharing common language, rituals, and experiences and (importantly) approaches to learning that move members along a continuum with these practices from novice to expert (Wenger 2008). As Lave and Wenger note, the more expertise members in a community of practice have, the less visible practices associated with that community become. Instead, these practices seem like commonplaces that "everyone knows." Once they recognized that their disciplines had threshold concepts, faculty also quickly saw that these were related to content, but perhaps even more to ways of thinking, attitudes, and orientations toward learning that were distinct from other disciplines in important ways.

The nature of threshold concepts as a threshold concept can be seen across the range of our interviews. Historian Patricia Cohen, for instance, eagerly described what she considered to be key threshold concepts within her discipline. Cohen, whose specialty is eighteenth- and nineteenth-century American history, opened the conversation by saying that "[Threshold concepts is] a new concept to me!" Early in the interview, she named "contingency . . . [the idea] that when you study history, you do it from the viewpoint of the present and you know how things turned out at the end, but that they didn't need to turn out that way[, that] things could have been very different at many different moments in history," as a threshold concept. As the discussion continued, she returned to the idea of threshold concepts twice more. In both instances, the language she used pointed to thoughtful engagement with the idea of these concepts themselves and illustrated the ways in which that the idea of threshold concepts was, for her, a threshold. As she considered a question about the larger aim of general education courses, for instance, she actively thought aloud, asking and immediately answering her own question: "But the larger aim is to make them realize that . . . what is the larger aim? . . . That anyone's version of reality is kind of constructed and it's based on what you have to construct it out of, and historians are very conscious of what we have." A few moments later, discussing a women's history course she taught, Cohen again stopped herself to interject another concept, saying, "So I guess—ah! Here's one of the most troubling concepts in history." She then went on to name "periodization in narrative," which she linked to the conscious decision by historians to select (and deselect) both events within a narrative and frameworks within which narratives are constructed, as another key concept.

Lisa Jacobson, a twentieth-century American historian, also astutely identified threshold concepts in history, differentiating between these concepts in lower- and upper-division courses. At the lower division, she said, an important concept was that "history is about interpretation, about, you know, contested narratives . . . there are different ways of thinking through a historical problem, and historians debate. [Historians] read evidence in different ways or combine evidence in different ways or draw upon different kinds of evidence, so their answers are different, even to the same question." As students moved into more specialized courses, these concepts became more specific, such as the idea that "concepts like childhood and motherhood and fatherhood are not . . . timeless and universal, but they're culturally constructed, they're historically contingent, they vary by race, class, religion, ethnicity, and time. And that is a very basic concept that's so assimilated in a historian, it's kind of a common sense."

Both of these interview excerpts show the ways in which threshold concepts are a threshold concept for faculty, leading them to think about what they know and believe in ways they have not before. Engaging faculty in a process of discussion *about* threshold concepts illustrates the value of the idea for professional development, as it positions them to move from identifying those concepts to considering aspects of expertise associated with them (as in Middendorf and Pace's

Decoding the Disciplines model) and using threshold concepts as a framework through which to consider teaching (as in Meyer's use of threshold concepts for faculty development).

TC2: MY DISCIPLINE IS NOT THE UNIVERSE

Recognizing their own discipline's threshold concepts helps faculty members realize that their discipline's beliefs, knowledge, and conventions are not beliefs-in-general but quite context specific. Once faculty come to this realization, various professional development activities might next help them develop activities whereby students can begin to understand the concepts within that discipline and then perhaps differences from one discipline to another. This is what Baillie, Bowden, and Meyer (2012, 6) refer to as "experience of variation" (rather than varied experience) and is discussed more fully in Heidi Estrem's chapter in this volume.

The perception that "my discipline *is* the universe" is perpetuated throughout the very structure of the academy. While there are certainly areas of interdisciplinary overlap, all faculty are grounded in what Gary Poole refers to as an "academic home" where "knowing the rules as well as the genre reinforces discipline-based thinking" (Poole 2009, 50). The idea that these are not universal (i.e., my rules are not everyone's) sometimes comes as a surprise. This is especially true in regard to writing because faculty members sometimes regard writing as a universal skill applicable in all contexts rather than a series of particular disciplinary conventions (see concept 2.3, "Writing Is a Way of Enacting Disciplinarity" and 3.4, "Disciplinary and Professional Identities Are Constructed Through Writing"). Faculty members who complain that that they are frustrated with student writing but are unwilling to reallocate "content" time to writing instruction have not yet recognized that what they might consider a form of "universally" good writing is quite specific to their disciplines and thus inextricably linked to content.

Engaging faculty members in discussions about threshold concepts has the somewhat surprising result of helping faculty realize the role that threshold concepts play in giving shape to the boundaries of their disciplinary communities. They also begin to identify and, ideally, make explicit these threshold concepts for nonexperts—in other words, students—and to consider differences in threshold concepts (and other practices) shared in other (disciplinary) communities—or at least to consider that their practices are not, in fact, universal. Faculty begin to

see disciplinary threshold concepts not as a given but as a way of thinking "affected by a number of individual, social, and contextual issues"
(Meyer 2012; see also Meyer and Land 2005 and Entwhistle 2008).
Without integrating this threshold concept into their understandings of
teaching, instructors maintain a rigid conceptualization of what it means
to teach and learn (a conceptualization typically involving transmis-
sion and unmediated uptake of information from teacher to student).
Unless faculty members develop a more flexible understanding of the
process of teaching and learning, they quickly become frustrated when
this sender-receiver/transmission-reception model does not play out as
they expect it to.[1]

Threshold concepts help give faculty a more sophisticated and subtle understanding of why students sometimes struggle with fundamental disciplinary skills. Faculty begin to understand their disciplines as
distinctive—and not immediately intuitive—ways of thinking about the
world. As he discussed "slow reading," a threshold concept he considered central to English studies, early-modern scholar Jim Kearney came
to the recognition that his view of close reading was not the view held
by faculty in other disciplines. "Everyone," he said, "wants their students
to read well and read closely and read carefully . . . [but] I think it's
interesting we use the term *close reading* both to mean a certain kind of
practice of reading and also a practice of writing. We ask students to *do* a
close reading . . . to *do* a reading—which is a kind of performance, which
I think is different than other disciplines in the humanities. . . . It does
seem like this idea that one would sort of perform an interpretation of a
text is . . . different than you might get elsewhere." Recognitions such as
these, facilitated through direct discussions of threshold concepts, can
provide opportunities for faculty to identify what *is* distinct in their disciplines. These, in turn, might lead to professional development workshops that help faculty do more explicit teaching toward the goals of
their course and discipline—hypothetically, in this case, to help teach
students engage in a particular kind of close reading and to clarify for
students how this close reading might be similar to or different from
what they have done elsewhere.

Lisa Jacobson (History) also said thinking through the lens of
threshold concepts led her to understand that the ways of thinking she
expected students to use were distinctive. Reflecting on techniques for
conducting oral history interviews, she said she realized that conducting a good interview "in some ways . . . just boils down to curiosity. Is
this person curious if they're, you know . . ." Curiosity, she then said, "is
very hard to teach. You either have it or you don't . . . [but] after I read

the [chapter on] threshold concepts, I thought, well maybe it's not just curiosity, it's that they need to, it's this undefined way of thinking historically that automatically pops up certain questions in people's mind." She continued, elaborating on characteristics and dispositions she associated with this "way of thinking historically":

> It's not just this abstract amorphous curiosity, there is more to it. It's whether you've absorbed this way of thinking, and I think that's the best way to sort of approach threshold concepts in history. It is about assimilating a particular way of thinking. Also, another way of putting it is a way of wondering . . . about why did it happen this way, what were the consequences of this and that? It's a way of wondering about how to contextualize [events and phenomena]. And so, you know, . . . teaching students the importance of context, the richness of context, the multiple layers of context that can be informing a particular set of actions or decisions or events or whatever, that's really, really important.

Jacobson moves in this excerpt from thinking about a "way of thinking" to thinking about *teaching* a way of thinking represents yet another opportunity for professional development made possible through engagement with threshold concepts. Jacobsen has named the practice; she is also beginning to consider what aspects of context it is important to teach students to apply in their history courses.

Beth DePalma Digeser, who specializes in Roman history, also described how situating texts and events within a context was a *particular* way of reading and interpreting specific to history. "I would say if you're functioning purely historically, you're not about making value judgments about the people you're engaged with. There's a sense of the past being interesting for its own sake. What would make me different from a classicist? . . . [A] classicist is going to be more interested in genre and a particular kind of text and a language, and I'm going to be more interested about the nexus of connections that produced that text. . . . A sociologist might study the past to figure out—they might be more interested in using the past for present concerns, or case studies to develop a particular kind of theory. I might use that theory, but I probably wouldn't develop that theory."

Themistogenes (a pseudonym), who specializes in ancient history, considered these differences in relation to writing in the discipline. Expectations for writing, he said, were "like . . . tacit knowledge—we all assume that you know what it is to write a history paper, right?" But as he reflected, he realized there were similarities and differences to writing he imagined in other disciplines, though admitted he didn't "know enough about other disciplines to say specifically. I assume," he said, "that every discipline asks people to read textual material and to think about it and interpret it and then use that information to help assemble some sort of analysis. And I think in that sense we're similar—we're similar to other disciplines." But, for ancient history,

> you often have to argue very obliquely or indirectly from a piece of evidence that doesn't necessarily say exactly what you want, but which if you . . . read it carefully can tell you about the absence of something. . . . That kind of reading of evidence can be very specific to ancient history, because we have so little of it. . . . So that is maybe a very ancient history-specific thing—having to read carefully to see not just what information your evidence tells you but what it doesn't tell you and what you might be able to infer from that.

While the identification and explicit discussions of distinct disciplinary practices (sometimes in contrast to other disciplinary perspectives) may seem commonsensical to writing studies scholars, it is critical to remember that writing researchers see those distinctions through—and because of—their own disciplinary lenses. The point we wish to emphasize here, then, is the value of the threshold concepts framework for engaging faculty to reflect on their practices (in a manner that may be intuitive for writing studies faculty) as yet another opportunity for professional development that becomes more accessible through this framework. By prompting faculty to reflect on the unique practices of their own disciplines, a threshold concepts framework encourages faculty to adopt a more cosmopolitan understanding of the many forms of thinking and writing within the university.

TC3: SUCCESSFUL STUDENT LEARNING INVOLVES DEMONSTRATING PARTICULAR WAYS OF THINKING WITHIN THE DISCIPLINE AND CAN BE SUPPORTED THROUGH DELIBERATELY SEQUENCED LEARNING OPPORTUNITIES

Some faculty approach their courses with the belief that the primary goal of teaching is to convey disciplinary content. Our interviews attest to how, once they begin thinking about threshold concepts, faculty find it is the application of *practices* associated with disciplinary content that is critical. They realize, in essence, that they are not conveying information but teaching a particular way of thinking supported by content. This realization reflects the position articulated by Carolin Kreber, that learning within disciplines involves both "looking at" and "looking through or with" (Kreber 2009, 10–11). It can provide particularly exciting professional development opportunities related to writing. It can also provide particularly exciting professional development opportunities related to many of the threshold concepts introduced in part 1 of this book (e.g., 1.1, "Writing Is a Knowledge-Making Activity; 2.0, "Writing Speaks to Situations and Contexts through Recognizable Forms"; and 3.4, "Disciplinary and Professional Identities are Constructed Through Writing").

Faculty invoked a number of actions and verbs to refer to these concepts: "to do a close reading" (Kearney/English); to "engage" actively listening to music (Derek Katz/musicology); to understand "history . . . [as] about a process" (Themistogenes/history); "conceiving . . . receiving, perceiving [and] coconstruct[ing]" history (Randy Bergstrom/history). "If you're given a document," said historian Elizabeth DePalma Digeser, "you want to ask questions about it. Who's it by? Should I believe it? Why is it being written? What does it want me to do? How do I find out more about this subject? What do I want to know about this subject? How do I set out most effectively what I think about this subject?"

These ways of thinking, faculty quickly realized, could (and, in some cases, were) supported through sequenced learning opportunities. This step—which is central in the Decoding the Disciplines process outlined by Middendorf and Pace, is included in Bunnell and Bernstein's idea of making teaching "public," and is reflected in Meyer's trajectory as faculty reflexively use threshold concepts to design classes and assignments—represents an exciting possibility for professional development because it has the potential to affect classroom practice.

Elizabeth (E.) Hackendorn Cook (English), for instance, described an activity (designed by a former TA, William Hall) incorporated into her classes to illustrate "slow reading" using "differently colored words [to] try to build visual connections among words through color coding . . . so that students have a sense of the . . . the rich ways in which writers build connections among concepts and terms that don't just have to do just with what the words mean." Cook also described "an exercise in which [students] can choose to imitate the voice and literary genre of one of the people they've read during the term and then write an essay about that. So there would be an example of a . . . writing practice that . . . ask[s] them to think about . . . features of a text that don't necessarily have to do with ostensible content."

Describing her large early American history course, Cohen (History) discussed the ways in which she altered writing assignments to involve students more actively in threshold concepts associated with "thinking historically," as well as with the challenges associated with this kind of thinking in large lecture courses.

> I'm trying to give them opportunities to figure out that behind the scenes is different, [so] I ha[ve] them do assignments based on large databases on the web where instead of me handing them ten runaway slave ads and say, 'Write me a documents-based analysis of these things,' I say, 'Here are four thousand ads and I want you to cruise around in this. . . . Just spend an hour just reading these, just seeing where they take you. And see if thoughts occur to you. And then pick . . . no more than five . . . to write a five-page paper about. . . . Having to search for them themselves was something [students] were really at first uncomfortable with, and then a little frightened by, and I said this is what historians do. We generate hypotheses, we go to the archives where we think we'll find things, and we sift through a whole lot of stuff that never sees the light of day. You know, there's a lot left on the cutting-room floor when you're done.

Stefania Tutino, a historian specializing in early modern Europe, also described the ways she scaffolded learning opportunities for students to participate in what she defined as two threshold concepts in history: (1) the meaning of concepts changes over time, and (2) reading primary sources requires constant movement between texts and contexts. Tutino, who was born and raised in Italy and educated in Italy and England, described carefully observing both her expectations and students' experiences with these concepts as she designed her general education courses. "Sure," she said, "I know the content. But I've got to write and read in a language that is not mine. How does that work? Has it changed my way of thinking? Does it make me pay more attention?" Tutino then reflexively extended this analysis to her teaching. Describing her large (three-hundred-plus person) lecture course, she said,

> Every time I lecture I have a primary source that I print out and I distribute it in lecture. So the last twenty to thirty minutes of lecture is spent with me going in the aisle and asking students, 'Okay, let's just read this paragraph. Let's just read this phrase.' And so they really get a sense of what does it mean. And most of them, when they paraphrase the phrase they just read, they don't get it right. So [I say], "Okay. Let's go back. Let's read. Why? What does this word actually mean?"

The intent, she said, is to distinguish this type of reading from students' reading practices in normal life:

> When you skim things you see through the page [and] that gives you access to certain information. That means you have a lot of information and you quickly have to sort out what you need and what you don't. When you read as a historian . . . the beauty of reading in a different way is that

you have tiny little information that you extract as much content out of it as possible.

THRESHOLD CONCEPTS AND THE TRANSFORMATION OF HISTORY 17B

The liminal moments highlighted in these faculty interviews show that thoughtful reflection on threshold concepts has the potential to change the way faculty think about their teaching. This kind of openness to change provides an ideal point from which to engage in professional development. A key question, though, is how can an introduction to threshold concepts change actual teaching practice? We have one case study to add to existing examinations of these questions (such as those described within Land, Meyer, and Smith 2008; Meyer, Land, and Baillie 2010). John's History 17b, a survey of US history from 1820 to 1920, was revised in 2013 to reflect his interest in threshold concepts. John's experiences reflect a final stage in the trajectory described by Meyer and the Decoding the Disciplines process outlined by Middendorf and Pace, in which faculty reflexively incorporate analysis of threshold concepts or aspects of expertise associated with thinking into their teaching practices and view that incorporation (with its attendant changes to teaching practices) as a site of inquiry.

John has taught History 17b—which typically enrolls 400 to 450 students—since 1995. Older iterations of the course, to be sure, reflected many of the threshold concepts mentioned in the faculty interviews. In earlier versions, for example, the course was entitled Contested Visions of American Liberty, immediately denoting the possibility of alternative interpretations and viewpoints in the construction of historical narratives. The syllabus's introductory paragraph made clear that that history, as defined in the course, did not consist of "one damned fact after another" but rather of "complex issues that still confront us today" that students would understand through the interpretation of "original documents from our time period." Lectures were often explicitly framed as questions, such as "Why did northerners oppose Slavery?" and "Did the slaves free themselves?" The assignments consisted of two papers (five to six pages) and an all-essay final exam that required students to take a side on an analytical question. The course's two writing assignments provided students opportunity to tackle open-ended questions and also offered opportunities to develop the kind of analytical stance required on the final exam. One assignment, for instance, asked students to "analyze the relationship between Jacksonian democracy and racism. As America became more democratic for white men, why did racism become more entrenched?" Given that they had to incorporate a variety of primary and secondary documents into their answer, students could practice approaching this open-ended question in much the way a historian might. Weekly discussion sections reinforced that point: students were required to come to the section ready to discuss and debate their own particular interpretations of the material.

The problem with older versions of History 17b like this one, though, was that historical thinking and other threshold concepts tended to be implicit rather than explicit. The syllabus, assignments, and sections demonstrated this kind of thinking without defining its various elements, the actions and activities packed into the term. While questions framed many of the lectures, content was usually king. The issue of why some questions (such as the one about racism in the Jacksonian period) were significant to historians today was never directly addressed. How history differed from other disciplines—especially sociology, economics, and political science, which are also intimately tied to the past—was completely absent.

As part of our initial research on what was incorporated in good historical thinking and how that was fostered in the course, John realized that he and his TAs instinctively focused on course themes rather than on disciplinary concepts (Adler-Kassner, Majewski, and Koshnick 2012). Like most college courses, then, History 17b was on an island all its own with its instructor, teaching assistants, and students isolated from the rest of the general education curriculum and even from most other history courses. From the perspective of writing, there were additional challenges. Good writing was taken as a universal given—good writing in 17b was equated with good writing in general. The result was that a course that stressed how context was essential for understanding texts in the past failed to teach students the particular context of their own thinking and writing within the course. Historical thinking, it was assumed, was the only possible way to approach the material, rather than being seen and explicitly incorporated into the course as an approach embedded within a particular community of scholars.

In 2013, John revised the course to reflect to disciplinary threshold concepts. To make these concepts more explicit, the title was changed to An Introduction to Historical Thinking: Contested Versions of American Liberty, 1820–1920. The syllabus still told students that history was not "one damned fact after another" but also predicted (perhaps optimistically), "You will begin to think like a historian—and understand how historical thinking differs from other disciplines on campus." To that end, five historical thinking mini-lectures were integrated into the course, each aimed at teaching a particular threshold concept, whether it involved defining history as a series of significant and competing narratives (lecture 1) or stressing the importance of historical empathy (part of lecture 9 on how enslaved African Americans responded to the domestic slave trade).

In addition, John incorporated lectures and opportunities for interaction that made the practices associated with historical thinking explicit. More emphasis was put on teaching skills specific to a history course, such as reading primary sources or connecting historical evidence to arguments. To illustrate the way historians read and the importance of identifying context, for instance, students viewed a video of a think-aloud exercise in which John struggled to interpret a primary source document from ancient Rome. In a similar fashion, students were instructed in lecture on specific ways historians craft arguments, especially how to approach an analytical thesis and how to directly link evidence to argument. The necessity of having a meaningful argument was repeatedly emphasized—to write history, students could not just summarize facts but had to interpret facts in ways that made them significant. To do so, they had to write analytical narratives that flowed chronologically but still made an overall argument. The course thus explicitly reminded students that their analytical narratives were particular to the threshold concepts of history and reinforced these concepts through lecture and hands-on activity. They were writing in a particular context that would develop a different set of skills than would courses in other disciplines.

Susannah McGowan, a PhD student in education who studied John's work integrating threshold concepts in History 17b, gathered data from student surveys and interviews to learn more about how these changes affected students' learning about historical thinking and, accordingly, their writing practices. Her findings indicate that some students found the historical thinking portion of the course helpful in moving students toward the threshold concepts of history (just as John's experience working with the approach to and syllabus and assignments for 17b reflect his movement to and through threshold concepts of teaching outlined in this chapter). Even a limited degree of helpfulness is a good sign, if only because the course revisions were incomplete. The assignments, for example, remained similar to older versions of 17b, which resulted in a lack of connection between the historical thinking portion of the course and student writing. Additional revisions will correct this problem—students, for example, will be assigned a short paper in which they reflect on the differences between writing a history paper and writing a paper in another discipline. But McGowan's research also points to additional practices John will incorporate into 17b to continue scaffolding students' learning. For instance, her data reveal that not only were assignments disconnected from historical thinking, so, too, was instruction of the teaching assistants, who did not fully understand threshold concepts and the desire to incorporate them fully into the course. The incompleteness of the revisions suggests that instructors (and, by extension, the courses they design) can move toward thresholds without fully crossing them, just as students can.

The experience of 17b has also enabled John to raise an additional question about teaching related to the threshold concepts framework, one that seems particularly generative for professional development as faculty members start to think about connections between their courses and others: how much can we reasonably expect a single course to accomplish in moving students toward disciplinary thresholds? As students to move back and forth across disciplinary thresholds, they need repeated exposure and practice. This question, in turn, has led us together to ask questions about the larger structures in which our general education work is situated. If a threshold concepts framework is productive for faculty and students in helping them understand the role these concepts play within communities of practice, as our interviews have suggested it is for faculty (and additional research has suggested it is for students; see Adler-Kassner, Majewski, and Koshnick 2012), we also understand that a single course is unlikely to elicit the transformative impact that is the ultimate goal. Teaching threshold concepts might thus be highly networked—the payoff of repeated exposure in a series of courses will be far greater than the payoff for a single course. The problem is that many general education programs (including the one on our campus)—and even some majors—are designed around types of knowledge and not types of thinking. History 17b, for example, fulfills the UC-wide American Institutions requirement, which can be met through any number of courses in multiple disciplines. It also can be used as credit toward Area D, social science, a distribution requirement within the UCSB's general education program. The course is also required of political science and sociology majors. It is not clear if these departments value courses such as 17b for the contextual information they convey or because it is believed that students need contextual background information seen as important by political scientists and sociologists.

As John's course revision illustrates, engaging faculty in discussions of threshold concepts can lead to both significant revisions of courses and, in our case, broadened perspectives on learning within academic programs, whether general education or within majors. The implications of the research that has emerged from our discussions with faculty and John's work on History 17b, for instance, is that general education should be a way of giving students practice in decoding threshold concepts, an idea that Heidi Estrem's chapter in this volume explores in more detail. Having a series of courses take a threshold concepts approach on any given campus is a tall order, but keep in mind that from the standpoint of writing and transfer, these courses do not have to be in the same discipline. A variety of courses in different disciplines—each stressing its own particular ways of thinking—would give students repeated practice in figuring out threshold concepts. They would learn to decode disciplines and understand how a variety of communities of practice operate. The idea that disciplines are communities of practice with their own threshold concepts is, after all, a threshold concept of learning and teaching. Having students pass that particular threshold is ultimately a more realistic (and in some ways a more desirable) goal than a transformative experience in any single discipline. This suggests that in a threshold concepts approach, evaluating writing within general education on the level of individual courses is not optimal.

CONCLUSION: THRESHOLD CONCEPTS AS A WAY OF STARTING DIALOGUE ON WRITING AND TEACHING

John's experience of using threshold concepts as both a way of revising teaching and as an area of research is, thus far, atypical on our campus. The interviews suggest, however, that the threshold concepts can engage faculty in discussions about their disciplines that become a gateway for additional professional development activity intended to improve students' opportunities to access expertise. This speaks to the analytical potential of the threshold concepts framework, which offers compelling ways to think about why students struggle with supposedly basic disciplinary questions. Faculty we interviewed found threshold concepts interesting because the framework gets at the heart of scholarly identity. Interviewees thoughtfully articulated the questions, ideas, and methods that define their discipline and the ways their discipline differs from others. Our experience suggests that simply asking about threshold concepts leads instructors to think about their teaching (including how they teach writing) in new and interesting ways. Outside of John's History 17b, we do not know if these interviews generated changes in classroom practice, but they certainly made faculty more thoughtful about their teaching. That, in itself, is an important accomplishment.

The interviews also suggest that one reason faculty responded so well to threshold concepts is that the framework is liberating for instructors who fear that students just don't get it—or that students are unlikely to get it within the context of a single course. The threshold concepts framework encourages instructors to be somewhat humble about the limits of what students can achieve in any one learning experience. Once reminded that their course and discipline is not the universe, an instructor in history, for example, must confront the fact that they themselves have not mastered many disciplinary threshold concepts of subjects that they have been exposed to. Most history professors, one presumes, have not crossed key disciplinary threshold concepts of chemistry, calculus, and cell biology. How can they reasonably expect their GE students to cross all the threshold concepts in history courses? Threshold concepts, in some way, help experts see what they have thought of as "natural" as something that is often difficult. As Jacobson (History), explained, "When you're in the discipline, it's so natural that you sometimes forget. You've totally assimilated it . . . so you can't identify it anymore." Digeser (History) reported that even as an undergraduate, she could not master Hobbes as a theoretical political philosopher—she could only view Hobbes as "a man of the seventeenth century and he thought this way because of what was going on." She noted that "my students have the flip problem . . . they don't see things as embedded in a context, they don't see that someone could absorb, that someone could be influenced by, things going on around them that they're not necessarily even engaging with directly." In reminding instructors of their own expertise—and of their own limits relative to other disciplines—threshold concepts encourage a more empathetic view of the student experience that helps foster more effective teaching.

Note

1. This is not to elide the research in composition (i.e., Thaiss and Zawacki 2006; Carter 2007) that also points to important ways to identify areas of overlap among and between disciplines; however, the first step toward a reconceptualized notion of areas of overlap and divergence between and among disciplines begins with the recognition that disciplines indeed do *have* distinctive ways of seeing.

References

Adler-Kassner, Linda, John Majewski, and Damian Koshnick. 2012. "The Value of Troublesome Knowledge: Threshold Concepts in Writing and History." *Composition Forum* 26.

Baillie, Caroline, John A. Bowden, and Jan H. F. Meyer. 2012. "Threshold Capabilities: Threshold Concepts and Knowledge Variability Linked Through Variation Theory." *Journal of Higher Education and Educational Planning.* 65 (2): 227-46. http://eric.ed.gov/?id=EJ998868.

Bunnell, Sarah, and Daniel Bernstein. 2012. "Overcoming Some Threshold Concepts in Scholarly Teaching." *Journal of Faculty Development* 26 (3): 14–8.

Carter, Michael. 2007. "Ways of Knowing, Doing, and Writing in the Disciplines." *College Composition and Communication.* 58 (3): 385–418.

Entwhistle, Noel. 2008. "Threshold Concepts and Transformative Ways of Thinking within Research into Higher Education." In *Threshold Concepts within the Disciplines*, edited by Ray Land, Jan H. F. Meyer, and Jan Smith, 21–36. Rotterdam, Netherlands: Sense.

Irvine, Naomi, and Patrick Carmichael. 2009. "Threshold Concepts: A Point of Focus for Practitioner Research." *Active Learning in Higher Education* 10 (2): 103–19. http://dx.doi.org/10.1177/1469787409104785.

Kreber, Carolin. 2009. "Supporting Student Learning in the Context of Diversity, Complexity, and Uncertainty." In *The University and Its Disciplines: Teaching and Learning Beyond Disciplinary Boundaries*, edited by Carolin Kreber, 3–18. New York: Routledge.

Land, Ray, Jan H. F. Meyer, and Jan Smith. 2008. *Threshold Concepts within the Disciplines.* Rotterdam, Netherlands: Sense.

Meyer, Jan H. F. 2012. "Variation in Student Learning as a Threshold Concept." *Journal of Faculty Development* 26 (3): 9–13.

Meyer, Jan H. F., and Ray Land. 2005. "Threshold Concepts and Troublesome Knowledge (2): Epistemological Considerations and a Conceptual Framework for Teaching and Learning." *Higher Education* 49 (3): 373–88. http://dx.doi.org/10.1007/s10734-004-6779-5.

Meyer, Jan H. F., Ray Land, and Caroline Baillie, eds. 2010. *Threshold Concepts and Transformational Learning.* Rotterdam, Netherlands: Sense.

Middendorf, Joan, and David Pace. 2004. "Decoding the Disciplines: A Model for Helping Students Learn Disciplinary Ways of Thinking." *New Directions for Teaching and Learning* 8 (98): 1–12. http://dx.doi.org/10.1002/tl.142.

Nowacek, Rebecca. 2011. *Agents of Integration: Understanding Transfer as a Rhetorical Act.* Carbondale: Southern Illinois University Press.

Poole, Gary. 2009. "Academic Disciplines: Homes or Barricades?" In *The University and Its Disciplines: Teaching and Learning Beyond Disciplinary Boundaries*, edited by Carolin Kreber, 50–57. New York: Routledge.

Thaiss, Chris, and Terry Myers Zawacki. 2006. *Engaged Writers and Dynamic Disciplines: Research on the Academic Writing Life.* Portsmouth, NH: Boynton/Cook.

Wenger, Etienne. 2008. *Communities of Practice.* Cambridge: Cambridge University Press.

13

CROSSING THRESHOLDS
What's to Know about Writing across the Curriculum

Chris M. Anson

The time [in the weeklong workshop] spent on articulating goals for assignments and sequencing them, breaking down larger projects, using low-stakes writing to strengthen learning, facilitating peer response, and discussing rubrics has helped me see how I can better support students' writing, experience success in the class, and generate excitement about the content.

—Faculty member, art history.

Faculty in disciplines across the curriculum—civil engineering, musicology, plant genetics—daily put to use extensive knowledge about writing. Whether they're working on the next article for the *Journal of Behavioral Science*, typing advisory comments on a student's thesis, designing a syllabus, or contributing to a committee report, they are, in the best sense of the word, *writers*. And although most writing-across-the-curriculum (WAC)[1] experts can share anecdotes about faculty who self-deprecatingly call into question their own writing ability, any glance at their routines will show that within their fields of specialization, they usually do just fine.

When brought to the surface, these faculty members' knowledge about writing sometimes provides them with strategies for mentoring novices in their classrooms, especially at the higher reaches of the curriculum. A nanotechnology researcher, for example, knows how to structure a good poster presentation for a conference and will guide a student to learn the conventions of this genre. However, for most faculty, concepts that inhabit the world of writing studies and its pedagogy may be distant memories fading at the edges of their own early undergraduate education in composition—if there was even much there to remember (Jarratt et al. 2009).

DOI: 10.7330/9780874219906.c0013

One role of WAC leaders is to (re)introduce threshold writing concepts through the terministic screen of pedagogy: What can teachers do in their content courses to help students scaffold their communication abilities to higher levels of sophistication? How can teachers use writing to help students understand complex material and develop skills of critical inquiry in specialized fields? Such writing concepts are imbricated with disciplinary knowledge taught and learned in a specific course (see Adler-Kassner and Majewski, this volume). But first and foremost, threshold concepts about writing reflect a kind of metaknowledge that brings together fundamental principles of discipline-based communication with principles of writing instruction and support.

This chapter explores the function of threshold concepts in writing across the curriculum. Complicating this exploration is the relationship between expert knowledge about writing—what faculty learn through repeated practice and slow enculturation into their fields—and expertise in the teaching or support of writing development, which is neither intuitive nor routinely introduced to most teachers in the disciplines. These two kinds of knowledge clearly overlap, but neither is sufficient alone to achieve hoped-for communication outcomes for student learning.

THRESHOLD CONCEPTS IN WAC: FACULTY DEVELOPMENT

All threshold writing concepts are as relevant in courses and departments across the university as they are in centralized composition courses like first-year writing. However, faculty teaching in both discipline-based general education courses and courses in the major generally don't think of themselves as teachers of writing. They confess that they lack what they see as specialized knowledge to teach writing—grammar and rhetorical analysis—and they worry about loss of content coverage if they spend too much time on writing (Lea and Street 1998). As a result, WAC leaders face special constraints that both limit and order the way they work threshold concepts into their outreach to these faculty colleagues.

Overarching principles in the WAC literature abound, such as those presented by Elaine Maimon at a conference and summarized by David Russell (1997b): that writing is a complex process related to thinking; that writing helps students make connections; that WAC leads to other reforms in pedagogy, curriculum, and administration; and so on. But among all such principles, six appear so often in both the scholarly and instructional literature on WAC, and in WAC outreach, that they have risen to the level of threshold concepts, historically guiding the movement and activities within it. In operational terms, these concepts inform the movement by

- defining writing as a disciplinary activity;
- reconceptualizing the social and rhetorical nature of writing;
- distinguishing between writing to learn and writing to communicate;
- establishing shared goals and responsibilities for improvement;
- understanding the situated nature of writing and the problem of transfer; and
- viewing student writing developmentally.

Each of these six concepts represents both a domain of inquiry and a domain of praxis, contributing to the formation and sustainability of the WAC movement, driving its scholarship, and helping to enrich the understandings and activities of faculty across dozens of disciplines.

Writing in a Discipline Reflects the Ways that Knowledge is Produced There (see 2.3, "Writing Is a Way of Enacting Disciplinarity," and 1.5, "Writing Mediates Activity").

This is perhaps the most axiomatic threshold concept in the WAC movement. In the field of writing studies, this concept articulates the relationship between the production and nature of writing within a discipline and its epistemologies, or ways of "making knowledge" (Carter 2007). Charles Bazerman's early and influential study comparing articles in three academic disciplines reveals how texts "serve as dynamic mediating mechanisms, . . . bring[ing] together worlds of reality, mind, tradition, and society in complex and varying configurations" (Bazerman 1981, 379). Playing an almost anthropological role, qualitative researchers and text analysts have explored and described writing across disciplinary contexts, revealing myriad differences in styles, structures, persona, lexis, and other conventions and their socially or organizationally based sources (Paretti 2008). At first these conventions were assumed to be sedimented and normative, but genre theorists soon showed how features of texts evolve over time within their (often unstable) communities of practice (Miller 1984; Russell 1997a; Swales 1990).

To write successfully in their own fields, faculty across the curriculum must have what Beaufort describes as five kinds of knowledge: *writing process knowledge, subject matter knowledge, rhetorical knowledge,* and *genre knowledge,* as well as *knowledge of the discourse community* in which these other forms must be deployed (Beaufort 2007, 17). For example, chemical engineering faculty working on industry-based projects must know how to engage in processes of collaborative writing and document cycling. They need the rhetorical knowledge to shape reports for different audiences and purposes within a company (varying from highly specialized researchers to less specialized marketing teams). They need to know the conventions of specific genres such as *phase reports, object-condition reports,* or *crits* (Anson et al. 2012). And they must represent high-level disciplinary content in ways that match the expectations of their discourse communities.

Leaders of most WAC programs face an epistemological challenge as they work in various disciplines: how much of faculty members' extensive discourse knowledge resides at a level of behavioral consciousness and how much is buried in the tacit domain, like spoken language, informing the production of text somewhere below the surface of constant awareness? Using qualitative methods, including unique data-collection tools such as discourse-based interviews (Odell, Goswami, and Herrington 1983) or composing-aloud protocols (Becker 2006), writing researchers can bring to the surface aspects of this complex, interconnected tacit knowledge. But without such prompting, many faculty in academic disciplines don't routinely reflect on what they do to perform effectively: they "know how" but don't always "know that" (Ryle 1949). This observation may explain the common assumption across the curriculum that writing well is something students should have learned to do early on, and that those skills ought to be deployed in every writing situation without regard for disciplinary variation or convention. Students are challenged to acquire these forms of knowledge to write effectively (Haswell 1991; Herrington and Curtis, 2000; McCarthy, 1987; Sternglass 1997), but their teachers often express dismay with what they turn in. Their disappointment comes from a mismatch between their expectations of students' abilities—grounded in these forms of knowledge—and students' unfamiliarity with the genres and conventions of what they are writing, together with their only partially formed knowledge of the content they're writing about (Hilgers, Hussey, and Stitt-Bergh 1999). For many WAC specialists, therefore, helping faculty members embrace this threshold concept is central to faculty development and curricular transformation.

Writing Is a Social and Rhetorical Activity
(see 1.0, "Writing Is a Social and Rhetorical Activity")

Professionals know tacitly that when they write, they are usually participating in a socially rich activity system designed to convey and negotiate meaning. However, the constant demands for assessment in the educational context often cause them to decontextualize students' writing, or to create a more rhetorically closed context for it. The writing becomes a test of acquired knowledge (as in an essay exam) or writing ability. The interaction, such as it is, involves an expert making evaluative decisions about what a novice has learned.

Although such evaluation can't be ignored in an institution designed to certify learning, WAC leaders take great pains to help faculty imagine more authentic kinds of writing situations and audiences. This threshold concept has its roots in some of the earliest work on WAC (e.g., Britton et al. 1975). As Kevin Roozen puts it (see 1.0, "Writing Is a Social and Rhetorical Activity"), understanding the rhetorical aspects of writing "is essential if writers are to make informed, productive decisions about which genres to employ, which languages to act with, [and] which texts to reference." The resulting mixed and blended contexts, where external or professional audiences and rhetorical situations seep into the more conventional, assessment-driven ones inside academia, create hybrid genres in what Deanna Dannels and I have called "conditional rhetorical space" (Anson and Dannels 2004). In these spaces, students must navigate complex sets of expectations, writing simultaneously "through" a teacher to an imagined or sometimes real external audience, yet "to" the teacher as evaluator of their success in reaching that audience. In addition, scholarship in WAC has repeatedly pointed to the processes of students' identity formation and enculturation into their disciplines as they move into the higher reaches of their majors and begin anticipating their work in professional communities of practice (e.g., Cox et al. 2010; Gee 2000; Poe, Lerner, and Craig 2010). As Roz Ivanic (1998, 32) has put it, "Writing is an act of identity in which people align themselves with socio-culturally shaped possibilities for self-hood." Analyzing these complexities complicates the work of WAC leaders as they consult with faculty, but the resulting understanding of the relationship between the goals of professional communication and those that entail learning and assessment can be especially illuminating (see Bizzell 1985).

Writing Can Be a Tool for Learning or Communicating

A third crucial threshold concept for WAC initiatives concerns the somewhat oversimplified but instructive distinction between writing to learn and learning to write (or communicate), or what Susan McLeod (1987) calls the "cognitive" and "rhetorical" approaches to classroom writing. The former orientation emphasizes the relationship between writing and the formation and integration of thought (Emig 1977). Writing in coursework helps students to grapple with complex ideas, test out their understanding, and incorporate new knowledge into old. Assignments are often informal or low stakes, taking the form of reflective journals, dialogues with other students, or blog entries. Writing for *Sociology Teacher*, for example, Frances Coker and Allen Scarboro contrast the conventional approach to writing in which "most sociologists have seen the value of students' writing primarily in the documentation of learning" through "the finished product, the post hoc proof" (Coker and Scarboro 1990, 218) with an approach that emphasizes writing as input. Writing becomes "a critical process of thinking and learning," not all of it read and evaluated by teachers but shared with other students or used only for the writer's own edification and reflection. Similarly, in a *History Teacher* article, Barrie Beyer (1980, 167-68)) differentiates this "input-based" approach from the more conventional use of writing as a means to assess acquired knowledge or ability:

> We can use writing as a method for teaching and learning in history rather than simply as an evaluative device. . . . Writing is thinking. The effort employs such analytical skills as inference making, classifying, separating relevant from irrelevant data, and identifying part-whole relationships. It also involves skills of synthesis and evaluation. . . . When students engage in writing they are thinking.

In this approach, the teacher typically downplays the quality of the writing, including its style and correctness, in favor of encouraging exploration, tentativeness, and eventual understanding. This constructivist orientation first influenced the composition curriculum in the late 1960s but began developing in content-area courses in the 1980s, as reflected in a shift in the focus of teaching-related articles in various discipline-based pedagogical journals (Anson 2010; Anson and Lyles 2011).

In contrast, the rhetorical or learning-to-write perspective focuses on the production of final, well-written texts designed to be read by audiences that demand clarity, persuasiveness, readability, correctness, and adherence to the conventions of writing in their shared communities of practice. The goal shifts from the discovery or exploration of ideas to their convincing presentation, emphasizing the "contextual and social constraints of writing" and seeing the "discourse community as crucial to the understanding of both the writing process and the conventions of the finished products" (McLeod 1987, 20). For this reason, the formal characteristics of the text call out for attention; the stakes get higher, and teachers now play the role of a judge rather than a coach, reaching verdicts about what students have learned.

These two views of writing are not mutually exclusive. Many courses that emphasize writing in content areas mix and blend learning-based assignments with more formal, higher-stakes projects, or allow the former to inform and iteratively contribute to the latter. Some WAC programs, such as the one at the University of St. Thomas in St. Paul, Minnesota, allow options for faculty to focus entire courses predominantly on writing to learn, and other courses to pay more attention to the development of higher-stakes, discipline-based projects in writing-intensive and writing-in-the-disciplines options (Engebretsen 2011).

The distinction expressed in this threshold concept can also structure the scaffolding of faculty-development efforts. In many WAC programs, leaders strategically begin with a strong focus on writing to learn rather than the production of formal, discipline-based writing. This focus is designed to reduce apprehensions that come from faculty perceptions of their role and authority (ability to "teach" writing), or the time it will take them to evaluate formal texts, or the way formal writing could cut into the necessary coverage of content. Instead, lower-stakes, learning-based writing activities reinforce the main interests of faculty: to help students to acquire discipline-based knowledge and the intellectual skills that produce and interpret it. Realigning teachers' priorities with an emphasis on writing to learn allows for an eventual transition from ways that lower-stakes assignments can help students develop ideas, and the words to express them, toward the development of more formal projects. When intentionally interwoven with the learning goals of the course, writing no longer intrudes on coverage but becomes a way to ensure it.

Improvement of Writing Is a Shared Responsibility

The entire WAC movement is founded on a belief that teachers of all subjects share responsibility for supporting the development of advanced student literacies. This threshold concept takes a prominent place on the home pages of dozens of WAC program websites, such as the University of Minnesota's (2013): "Because writing is instrumental to learning, it follows that writing instruction is the shared responsibility of content experts in all academic disciplines."

Yet, partly for reasons discussed earlier, many faculty associate the teaching of writing with belletristic pursuits or with the study of grammar, rhetoric, and general composition, areas outside their own purview as experts in specific subjects. From this perspective, it's easy to blame those who are assumed to teach literacy (English departments and composition programs) for not preparing students adequately, as if that preparation can be accomplished in sixteen weeks of first-year writing instruction or by the end of the senior year of high school.

The threshold WAC concept of shared responsibility focused initially on writing across the liberal arts (Connelly and Irving 1976) but soon spread into other disciplines. Today, dozens of writing-intensive and other WAC programs in universities large and small stand as testament to the gains that have been made in accepting this threshold concept and acting on it. But misunderstanding continues, and a lack of knowledge about the history of writing instruction and its increasing distance from subjects not associated with rhetoric, English, grammar, and literature doesn't help (Russell 1992). As a result, faculty are often incredulous when I point to the high level of activity around writing in mathematics and quantitative disciplines (see Bahls 2012). Writing may still be associated with certain groups of people and certain academic interests. For their part, students may also bring their own misguided beliefs about writing into a WAC course, as Sullivan and Kedrowicz (2012) found in a study of engineering students' resistance to communication instruction based on identity construction and gender roles.

The values associated with "community" also complicate the concept of shared responsibility. Community implies unity, shared practices, shared goals and audiences and genres; yet the academic community at large consists of "an aggregate of discourse communities" in which "the conventions (and beyond them the assumptions and methodologies) of the various disciplines are characterized more by their differences than their similarities" (Russell 1990, 54). An apparent contradiction can result in which one threshold concept—that Writing in a Discipline Reflects the Ways that Knowledge Is Produced There—wrestles with another that focuses on uniting disparate fields, courses, and teachers with a common goal. For this reason, unpacking the threshold concept of shared responsibility for writing means threading delicately between the goals of general education and those of professional and disciplinary preparation. The general goals of improved writing ability and better preparation to meet new demands of writing must be understood as part of a shared enterprise even as practices and conventions differ. As assessments of WAC programs become more commonplace, however, we will learn more about the effects of this cross-disciplinary infusion in students' writing abilities, self-concepts as writers, and ability to produce specific forms of discourse within specific communities of practice (see Hilgers et al. 1995).

Writing in All Contexts Involves Situated Learning, Challenging the "Transfer"
of Ability (see 2.0, "Writing Speaks to Situations through Recognizable Forms")

Considerable new work is emerging on the concept of transfer of discursive knowledge and ability as writers move from one context to the next (Frazier 2010; Lettner-Rust 2010; Nowacek 2011; Wardle 2013; Yancey, Robertson, and Taczak 2014). The greater the difference between two contexts, the greater the challenge for the writer to deploy existing higher-level skills (such as knowing how to structure a text, what style to use, how to represent one's persona, which lexical items are most appropriate, what stance or perspective should be taken toward the subject, etc.). Recognizing this principle helps faculty to realize that no amount of prior knowledge from a generalized composition course will help students know how to cope with new genres that, as Elizabeth Wardle describes them, "are context-specific and complex and cannot be easily or meaningfully mimicked outside their naturally occurring rhetorical situations and exigencies" (Wardle 2009, 767).

Although very few scholars believe such transfer or adaptation requires little or no effort, their beliefs about transfer typically fall somewhere along a continuum from strong to weak versions of the negative-transfer hypothesis. Weaker versions claim that writers do carry certain abilities and understandings with them as they move across communities of practice, helping them adapt to new writing situations, albeit not without some challenge (e.g., Carter 1990). In this view, students with high degrees of metaconsciousness, strategies for figuring out how writing works in their new settings, and exposure to threshold writing concepts, will perform better than those without such training. Stronger versions of the negative-transfer hypothesis argue that writers will always struggle and fail to write effectively in an unfamiliar setting until they can experience steady enculturation into its community, exposure to its forms of discourse, plentiful practice, permissible trial and error, and helpful, individual mentoring.

In both the weaker and stronger versions of this hypothesis, the threshold concept of situated learning provides a way for faculty to understand the need to support students' writing experiences in every course, especially courses that involve unfamiliar genres and methods of discourse production. The assign-collect-grade regimen gives way to activities that can help students interpret task constraints, practice intellectual processes required in the task, create working drafts, receive response, and learn to revise effectively based on that response or other criteria for success. These processes of support are especially important in the context of individual teachers' idiosyncratic variations on stock academic genres or creative, unique assignments not part of the academic canon of student writing. The clearer the nature of the task, the more explicit the criteria for success, and the more supportive the activities leading up to a final text, the stronger the students' feelings about their learning and engagement in the course (Anderson et al. forthcoming). Helping faculty to understand the need for such guidance is therefore a central goal of most WAC programs.

Writing Is Highly Developmental
(see 3.3, "Writing Is Informed by Prior Experience")

Among those abilities deemed important by virtually all academics and business leaders, learning to write effectively requires slow, steady development over many years of (diverse) practice. Unlike many learned processes, it continues to develop across the span of people's lives. For this reason, another common threshold concept in faculty workshops and seminars refocuses attention away from the writing itself and toward the development of the writer's knowledge, ability, and expertise at a particular learning or career stage. Stephen North's oft-cited line from his article "The Idea of a Writing Center" has become its own threshold concept: "The axiom . . . is that we aim to make better writers, not necessarily— or immediately—better texts" (North 1984, 441). Focusing on writers' experiences, their diverse learning styles, their manifold prior experiences both good and bad, both instructive and wrong, moves teachers beyond thinking of writing as something that can be taught and absorbed in static and invariant ways. Instead, forms of active learning characterize much of the work with writing: small-group discussions as students are formulating ideas; peer and teacher responses on drafts in progress; discussion of interestingly problematic, anonymous samples of previous students' papers; practice understanding and applying evaluative criteria; and sharing final products with others. This threshold concept also helps faculty to begin interpreting more richly the diverse voices and communicative styles of their students, especially those for whom English is not a first language or who bring culturally significant dialect variations or alternative rhetorical traditions to their writing (see Anson 2012; Inoue and Poe 2012). Such understandings break down simplistic models of writing as a normative set of skills learned uniformly across broad swaths of the population and rebuild those models around concepts in which writing development and ability are tightly wound with identity, self-efficacy, and the psychology of the self.

Some conditions in education, such as large lecture courses or reward systems that place high value on research and publication, present obstacles to this threshold concept, reinforcing an ideology of learning in which most of the responsibility falls on students to perform well rather than on teachers to support them. Whether through faculty development, departmental or individual consulting, or shared writing assessment activities, many WAC programs try to reveal the complexities of student writing and the difficulties students experience learning to write across different courses and curricula. Faculty unable to do much to help individual students can still be shown ways to provide support through more detailed information about assignments, online peer-review opportunities, or class visits by campus writing center staff to call attention to their services, and some WAC programs have created other innovative ways to help faculty, such as embedding undergraduate writing fellows into specific courses (Hall and Hughes 2012).

Understanding these six threshold concepts can represent an important step for faculty to think in principled ways about incorporating writing into their courses, regardless of discipline. Of course, the hard work begins in implementation, where many other related threshold concepts from allied movements such as the scholarship of teaching and learning, problem-based and inquiry models of education, and critical thinking initiatives can play a role as well.

THRESHOLD CONCEPTS IN WAC: CURRICULAR DEVELOPMENT

In many academic departments, lack of opportunities for faculty to share their teaching conspires with their instructional autonomy to create a fragmented assortment of courses, undisciplined in their idiosyncrasies and uncoordinated as an educational experience for students (Biggs 2003). History majors taking a course in western civilization may write papers that demonstrate their understanding of key events—a kind of objective synthesis—and then are asked in their next course to show how history is socially constructed by trying to reconcile two or more different primary accounts of an event. The second teacher assumes that students bring into her course an enactable understanding of threshold writing concepts relating to the social construction of history and sees no need to provide support for this knowledge. Dismayed by the students' puerile, objective accounts of historical information, she concludes that they can't write and wonders what went wrong earlier in the curriculum.

Developing symmetry among threshold concepts for writing beyond specific courses requires a collective interest in reaching common understandings about the nature and role of writing across a department or field. Ideally, that understanding can begin with the negotiation and eventual agreement of a common vocabulary or terminology emerging uniquely from disciplinary ways of knowing but overlapping with broader rhetorical concepts (see Anson and Dannels 2009). Terms for academic genres, for example, can vary in their meaning dramatically across different courses even within the same department. Among the most notorious is the *research paper*. At the most general level, we might expect that all cases of this writing assignment involve *research*, yet the kinds of research (secondary, primary, observational, clinical, etc.) and the conventions for rendering it into a *paper* vary wildly in different academic settings. Similarly, terms for intellectual processes essential for writing effective papers, such as *analysis*, are tossed casually into assignments without sensitivity that these terms can mean utterly different things in different disciplines, baffling students when they try to apply a previously learned analytical method in a new, unfamiliar content area requiring a new, unfamiliar genre of writing.

Such conversations aren't meant to stifle the creative impulses of individual teachers or silence those who don't follow the consensus. Instead, they're meant to bring together the different values, dispositions, assumptions, and strategies of faculty and then find ways to recognize and label their different contributions and what they value in student writing (Broad 2003). I once consulted with several faculty who taught the same heat-transfer experiment in their own versions of a required engineering course. The length of the lab report samples they sent me varied by course section. When we met, I asked about this discrepancy. Two teachers felt that the lab report had to be extremely concise, a tightly wound synthesis of the key experimental methods and findings. Three others allowed for more extensive explanations, a requirement that "tested students' deeper knowledge of what they were observing." Neither group wanted to change their guidelines and grading rubrics. In this case, agreeing on different characterizations of the genre of the lab report provides the department (and students) with a common understanding, such as the difference between a concise lab report and an elaborated lab report. Students moving from one course to another and encountering the same agreed-upon labels for genres can more easily tap into their prior knowledge and writing experience even as the course material increases in sophistication.

This principle extends easily to broader discussions of genre labels. Investigations of writing assignments across the disciplines (e.g., Bridgeman and Carlson 1984; Eblen 1983; Harris and Hult 1985) have used faculty surveys to categorize assignments by well-known genres, such as the research paper, the article summary, or the reflective journal. Although such surveys may be useful in the aggregate, they miss important ways each of these generalized genres is instantiated within specific classrooms. More sophisticated analyses based on aims, audiences, and rhetorical features help (Melzer 2003), but because these surveys are conducted beyond the contexts where the assignments are given life, they still lack explanatory adequacy and may not be of much use within majors and departments. When faculty gather to discuss what they mean by the labels they give their assignments, however, similarities and differences in instructional goals for writing become clear. The focus soon embraces goals beyond the learning of specific *kinds* of writing (as discussed earlier), and these goals may be realized in entirely idiosyncratic but appropriate classroom-based genres.

Like discussion of nomenclature and other aspects of writing in a department, deeper explorations of threshold writing concepts can help to achieve consistency, curricular symmetry, and shared goals. Experiments with departmental models of WAC at some universities have encouraged groups of faculty and administrators to carefully articulate their entire curriculum based on writing and communication goals (Carter 2003). Some departments examine ways writing serves the interest of outcomes for majors, creating grids with courses along one axis and individual goals along another. Each course is then weighted for the intensity of its coverage of certain principles, methods, genres, and processes, which allows redesign based on areas of weakness. Infusing threshold WAC concepts into such discussions allows for more sophisticated analysis and change—for example, as faculty consider various developmental trajectories for student writing and scaffold them across the major.

A FINAL CAUTION: WHEN NOT TO CROSS THE THRESHOLD

The optimism reflected in this chapter should not drown out the voice of caution about using threshold concepts in WAC advocacy. As WAC experts have noted for decades, working on writing with faculty in various disciplines requires great sensitivity to existing (mis)conceptions of the nature of writing and the roles and purposes associated with its cross-disciplinary development. Barbara Walvoord warns writing experts not to adopt a mindless "training" approach or an evangelical "conversion" approach, or to assume a "Right Way" of supporting writing (Walvoord 1992, 11). The many competing interests of academic departments in the university hierarchy create, as David Russell puts it, "a cultural, economic, or political stake in the expansion (or restriction) of advanced forms of literacy" (Russell 1990, 66).

When threshold concepts are reduced from verbs to nouns, from their fully articulated, active form (along with plentiful explanation) to buzzwords and catch phrases, many faculty will balk, and resistance can follow. During some campus visits, my hosts have counseled me never to use a specific word among the faculty, such as *outcomes* or *rubric* or even *WAC*, usually because some earlier curricular disaster or failed innovation poisoned the entire campus to whatever the term meant at the time. Although it is less likely, certain threshold concepts introduced too glibly can trigger false assumptions, resistance, or confusion among faculty. An example familiar to most WAC leaders takes the problematically reduced form of advice not to focus first (or even at all) on the surface features of students' writing: "students' grammatical mistakes are not as important as what they are trying to say" or even "don't focus on grammar." Unpacking this assertion means delving into the relationship between form and meaning, the effects of certain pedagogies on students' self-efficacy and further writing behaviors, the relationship among writing assignments and learning goals, students' linguistic backgrounds, and a host of other complicated issues.

It is only in the careful, considered exploration of such concepts that meaningful change can begin.

Note

1. For simplicity, all cross-disciplinary faculty-development programs supporting student communication (writing in the disciplines, communication across the disciplines, etc.) will be subsumed under the term *writing across the curriculum*.

References

Anderson, Paul, Chris M. Anson, Robert Gonyea, and Charles Paine. forthcoming. "The Contributions of Writing to Learning and Intellectual Development: Results from a Large-Scale National Study." *Research in the Teaching of English*.

Anson, Chris M. 2010. "The Intradisciplinary Influence of Composition on Writing Across the Curriculum, 1967–1986." *WAC Journal* 21:5–20.

Anson, Chris M. 2012. "Black Holes: Writing Across the Curriculum and the Gravitational Invisibility of Race." In *Race and Writing Assessment*, edited by Asao B. Inoue and Mya Poe, 15–28. New York: Peter Lang.

Anson, Chris M., and Deanna P. Dannels. 2004. "Writing and Speaking in Conditional Rhetorical Space." In *Classroom Space(s) and Writing Instruction*, edited by Ed Nagelhout and Carol Rutz, 55–70. Cresskill, NJ: Hampton.

Anson, Chris M., and Deanna P. Dannels. 2009. "Profiling Programs: Formative Uses of Assisted Descriptions in the Assessment of Communication Across the Curriculum." *Across the Disciplines* 6. http://wac.colostate.edu/atd/assessment/anson_dannels.cfm.

Anson, Chris M., Deanna Dannels, Pamela Flash, and Amy L. Housley Gaffney. 2012. "Big Rubrics and Weird Genres: The Futility of Using Generic Assessment Tools across Diverse Instructional Contexts." *Journal of Writing Assessment* 5 (1). http://journalofwritingassessment.org/archives.php?issue=1.

Anson, Chris M., and Karla Lyles. 2011. "The Intradisciplinary Influence of Composition on Writing Across the Curriculum, Part Two: 1986–2006." *WAC Journal* 22:7–19.

Bahls, Patrick. 2012. *Student Writing in the Quantitative Disciplines: A Guide for College Faculty*. San Francisco: Jossey-Bass.

Bazerman, Charles. 1981. "What Written Knowledge Does: Three Examples of Academic Discourse." *Philosophy of the Social Sciences* 11 (3): 361–87. http://dx.doi.org/10.1177/004839318101100305.

Beaufort, Anne. 2007. *College Writing and Beyond: A New Framework for University Writing Instruction*. Logan: Utah State University Press.

Becker, Ann. 2006. "A Review of Writing Model Research Based on Cognitive Processes." In *Revision: History, Theory, and Practice*, edited by Alice Horning and Anne Becker, 25–49. West Lafayette, IN: Parlor.

Beyer, Barry K. 1980. "Using Writing to Learn in History." *History Teacher* 13 (2): 167–78. http://dx.doi.org/10.2307/491918.

Biggs, John B. 2003. *Teaching for Quality Learning at University*. 2nd ed. Buckingham, UK: Open University Press/Society for Research into Higher Education.

Bizzell, Pat, and Bruce Herzberg. 1985. "Writing across the Curriculum Textbooks: A Bibliographic Essay." *Rhetoric Review* 3 (2): 202–17. http://dx.doi.org/10.1080/07350198509359094.

Bridgeman, Brent, and Sybil B. Carlson. 1984. "Survey of Academic Writing Tasks." *Written Communication* 1 (2): 247–80. http://dx.doi.org/10.1177/0741088384001002004.

Britton, James N., Tony Burgess, Nancy Martin, Andrew McLeod, and Harold Rosen. 1975. *The Development of Writing Abilities (11–18)*. London: MacMillan Educational.

Broad, Bob. 2003. *What We Really Value: Beyond Rubrics in Teaching and Assessing Writing*. Logan: Utah State University Press.

Carter, Michael. 1990. "The Idea of Expertise: An Exploration of Cognitive and Social Dimensions of Writing." *College Composition and Communication* 41 (3): 265–86. http://dx.doi.org/10.2307/357655.

Carter, Michael. 2003. "A Process for Establishing Outcomes-Based Assessment Plans for Writing and Speaking in the Disciplines." *Language and Learning Across the Disciplines* 6 (1): 4–29.

Carter, Michael. 2007. "Ways of Knowing, Doing, and Writing in the Disciplines." *College Composition and Communication* 58 (3): 385–418.

Coker, Frances H., and Allen Scarboro. 1990. "Writing to Learn in Upper-Division Sociology Courses: Two Case Studies." *Teaching Sociology* 18 (2): 218–22. http://dx.doi.org/10.2307/1318494.

Connelly, Peter J., and Donald C. Irving. 1976. "Composition in the Liberal Arts: A Shared Responsibility." *College English* 37 (7): 668–70. http://dx.doi.org/10.2307/376468.

Cox, Michelle, Jay Jordan, Christina Ortmeier-Hooper, and Gwen Gray Schwartz, eds. 2010. *Reinventing Identities in Second Language Writing*. Urbana, IL: National Council of Teachers of English.

Eblen, Charlene. 1983. "Writing Across the Curriculum: A Survey of University Faculty's Views and Classroom Practices." *Research in the Teaching of English* 17 (4): 343–48.

Emig, Janet. 1977. "Writing as a Mode of Learning." *College Composition and Communication* 28 (2): 122–28. http://dx.doi.org/10.2307/356095.

Engebretsen, Kelly. 2011. "Writing Across the Curriculum Program Receives High Marks From Top Educator in the Field." Newsroom, University of St. Thomas, Oct 18. http://www.stthomas.edu/news/writing-across-curriculum/.

Frazier, Dan. 2010. "First Steps Beyond First Year: Coaching Transfer After FYC." *WPA: Writing Program Administration* 33 (3): 34–57.

Gee, James Paul. 2000. "Identity as an Analytic Lens for Research in Education." *Review of Research in Education* 25: 99–125.

Hall, Emily, and Bradley Hughes. 2012. "Preparing Faculty, Professionalizing Fellows: Keys to Success with Undergraduate Writing Fellows in WAC." *WAC Journal* 22: 21–40.

Harris, Jeanette, and Christine Hult. 1985. "Using a Survey of Writing Assignments to Make Informed Curricular Decisions." *WPA: Writing Program Administration* 8 (3): 7–14.

Haswell, Richard H. 1991. *Gaining Ground in College Writing: Tales of Development and Interpretation.* Dallas: Southern Methodist University Press.

Herrington, Anne J., and Marcia Curtis. 2000. *Persons in Process: Four Stories of Writing and Personal Development in College.* Urbana, IL: National Council of Teachers of English.

Hilgers, Thomas L., Ann Shea Bayer, Monica Stitt-Bergh, and Megumi Taniguchi. 1995. "Doing More Than 'Thinning Out the Herd': How Eighty-Two College Seniors Perceived Writing-Intensive Classes." *Research in the Teaching of English* 29 (1): 59–87.

Hilgers, Thomas L., Edna Lardizabal Hussey, and Monica Stitt-Bergh. 1999. "'As You're Writing, You Have These Epiphanies': What College Students Say about Writing and Learning in their Majors." *Written Communication* 16 (3): 317–53. http://dx.doi.org/10.1177/0741088399016003003.

Inoue, Asao B., and Mya Poe, eds. 2012. *Race and Writing Assessment.* New York: Peter Lang.

Ivanic, Roz. 1998. *Writing and Identity: The Discoursal Construction of Identity in Academic Writing.* Philadelphia: John Benjamins.

Jarratt, Susan C., Katherine Mack, Alexandra Sartor, and Shevaun E. Watson. 2009. "Pedagogical Memory: Writing, Mapping, Translating." *WPA: Writing Program Administration* 33 (1–2): 46–73.

Lea, Mary R., and Brian V. Street. 1998. "Student Writing in Higher Education: An Academic Literacies Approach." *Studies in Higher Education* 23 (2): 157–72. http://dx.doi.org/10.1080/03075079812331380364.

Lettner-Rust, Heather. 2010. *Questions of Transfer: Writers' Perspectives on Familiar/Unfamiliar Writing Tasks in a Capstone Writing Course.* PhD diss., Old Dominion University, Norfolk, VA.

McCarthy, Lucille P. 1987. "A Stranger in Strange Lands: A College Student Writing across the Curriculum." *Research in the Teaching of English* 21 (3): 233–65.

McLeod, Susan. 1987. "Defining Writing Across the Curriculum." *WPA: Writing Program Administration* 17 (1–2): 19–24.

Melzer, Dan. 2003. "Assignments Across the Curriculum: A Survey of College Writing." *Language and Learning Across the Disciplines* 6 (1): 86–110.

Miller, Carolyn R. 1984. "Genre as Social Action." *Quarterly Journal of Speech* 70 (2): 151–67. http://dx.doi.org/10.1080/00335638409383686.

North, Stephen M. 1984. "The Idea of a Writing Center." *College English* 46 (5): 433–46. http://dx.doi.org/10.2307/377047.

Nowacek, Rebecca S. 2011. *Agents of Integration: Understanding Transfer as a Rhetorical Act.* Carbondale: Southern Illinois University Press.

Odell, Lee, Dixie Goswami, and Anne Herrington. 1983. "The Discourse-Based Interview: A Procedure for Exploring the Tacit Knowledge of Writers in Nonacademic Settings." In *Research on Writing: Principles and Methods,* edited by Peter Mosenthal, Lynne Tamor, and Sean A. Walmsley, 220–36. New York: Longman.

Paretti, Marie. 2008. "Teaching Communication in a Capstone Design: The Role of the Instructor in Situated Learning." *Journal of Engineering Education* 97 (4): 491–503.

http://dx.doi.org/10.1002/j.2168-9830.2008.tb00995.x.

Poe, Mya, Neal Lerner, and Jennifer Craig. 2010. *Learning to Communicate in Science and Engineering: Case Studies from MIT.* Cambridge, MA: MIT Press.

Russell, David R. 1990. "Writing across the Curriculum in a Historical Perspective: Toward a Social Interpretation." *College English* 52 (1): 52–73. http://dx.doi.org/10.2307/377412.

Russell, David R. 1992. "American Origins of the Writing-across-the-Curriculum Movement." In *Landmark Essays on Writing Across the Curriculum,* edited by Charles Bazerman and David R. Russell, 3–22. Davis, CA: Hermagoras.

Russell, David R. 1997a. "Rethinking Genre in School and Society: An Activity Theory Analysis." *Written Communication* 14 (4): 504–54. http://dx.doi.org/10.1177/0741088397014004004.

Russell, David R. 1997b. "Writing To Learn To Do: WAC, WAW, WAW—Wow!" *Language and Learning Across the Disciplines* 2 (2): 3–8.

Ryle, Gilbert. 1949. *The Concept of Mind.* Chicago: University of Chicago Press.

Sternglass, Marilyn S. 1997. *Time to Know Them: A Longitudinal Study of Writing and Learning at the College Level.* Mahwah, NJ: Erlbaum.

Sullivan, Katie R., and April A. Kedrowicz. 2012. "Gendered Tensions: Engineering Student's Resistance to Communication Instruction." *Equality, Diversity and Inclusion: An International Journal* 31 (7): 596–611.

Swales, John. 1990. *Genre Analysis.* Cambridge: Cambridge University Press.

University of Minnesota. 2013. "WEC: Writing-Enriched Curriculum." http://wec.umn.edu/.

Wardle, Elizabeth. 2013. "What Is Transfer?" In *A Rhetoric for Writing Program Administrators,* edited by Rita Malenczyk, 143–55. Anderson, SC: Parlor.

Wardle, Elizabeth. 2009. "'Mutt Genres' and the Goal of FYC: Can We Help Students Write the Genres of the University?" *College Composition and Communication* 60 (4): 765–89.

Walvoord, Barbara. 1992. "Getting Started." In *Writing across the Curriculum: A Guide to Developing Programs,* edited by Susan H. McLeod and Margot Soven, 9–22. Newbury Park: Sage.

Yancey, Kathleen Blake, Liane Robertson, and Kara Taczak. 2014. *Writing across Contexts: Transfer, Composition, and Sites of Writing.* Logan: Utah State University Press.

ABOUT THE AUTHORS

LINDA ADLER-KASSNER is professor of writing studies and director of the writing program at the University of California, Santa Barbara, where she teaches undergraduate and graduate courses focusing on the study of and practice with writing in disciplinary and civic contexts. Her research focuses on strategies for making knowledge practices more visible for practitioners and learners within the university and publics beyond. This includes work on threshold concepts, remodeling general education, and helping writing instructors and program directors develop alliances and communicate with others. She is author, coauthor, or coeditor of nine books and many articles and book chapters. She is currently assistant chair of the Conference on College Composition and Communication.

ELIZABETH WARDLE is professor and chair of the Department of Writing and Rhetoric at the University of Central Florida, where she teaches courses such as Writing with Communities and Nonprofits, Rhetoric and Civic Engagement, First-Year Composition, and graduate seminars on composition theory and writing program administration. She is the coauthor of *Writing about Writing* as well as a variety of articles and book chapters on first-year composition, transfer, and genre theory.

CHRIS M. ANSON is Distinguished University Professor and director of the campus writing and speaking program at North Carolina State University, where he teaches graduate and undergraduate courses in language, composition, and literacy and works with faculty across the disciplines to reform undergraduate education in the areas of writing and speaking. He has published fifteen books and over one hundred articles and book chapters relating to writing and has spoken widely across the United States and in twenty-eight other countries. He is past chair of the Conference on College Composition and Communication. His full CV is at www.ansonica.net.

CHERYL E. BALL is editor of *Kairos: Rhetoric, Technology, and Pedagogy*. She has edited numerous special issues of digital writing studies journals and several book collections, including the award-winning *The New Work of Composing* (CCDP, 2012). She regularly publishes on digital scholarship, multimodal composition, editorial pedagogy, and academic professionalization in peer-reviewed and popular venues, including several textbooks on visual and multimodal rhetorics, such as *Writer/Designer: A Guide to Making Multimodal Projects* (with coauthors Kristin Arola and Jenny Sheppard) (Bedford, 2014). Her online portfolio is at http://ceball.com.

CHARLES BAZERMAN is professor of education at the University of California Santa Barbara, Steering Committee chair of the International Society for the Advancement of Writing Research, and recent chair of the Conference of College Composition and Communication. His books include *A Rhetoric of Literate Action*, *A Theory of Literate Action*, *The Languages of Edison's Light*, *Constructing Experience*, *Shaping Written Knowledge*, *The Informed Writer*, *The Handbook of Research on Writing*, *Traditions of Writing Research*, *Genre in a Changing World*, and *What Writing Does and How It Does It*.

COLLIN BROOKE is associate professor of rhetoric and writing at Syracuse University. He is the author of *Lingua Fracta: Towards a Rhetoric of New Media* (2009) and his work on rhetoric and technology has appeared in a broad range of journals and edited collections. He is the director of electronic resources for the Rhetoric Society of America and blogs at http://www.cgbrooke.net.

ALLISON CARR is assistant professor of rhetoric at Coe College in Cedar Rapids, Iowa, where she teaches classes in cultural studies, rhetoric of all kinds, and nonfiction writing, and where she also serves as director of the writing program. She received her PhD from the University of Cincinnati in 2014, writing a dissertation exploring the emotional content of failure in the writing classroom and advocating for pedagogies of writing that more openly and intentionally engage failure as a strategy for learning. Her work has appeared in *CCC, Composition Forum*, and *Computers and Composition Online*. She tweets about writing, language, baseball, food, and other matters @hors_doeuvre.

COLIN CHARLTON is associate professor of rhetoric, composition, and literacy studies at the University of Texas-Pan American, where he also directs first-year writing programs. That work has led him to design immersive and interactive classroom spaces for the writing program and to launch and coedit *Crosspol: A Journal of Transitions for High School and College Writers*. He has published on developmental reading and writing, writing program administration, and multimodality. Currently, he's working on a new kind of developmental textbook and a multimodal "coffee-table book" about the scenes of writing, learning, and teaching.

DOUG DOWNS is associate professor of writing studies and director of composition in the Department of English at Montana State University, where he also designed the department's writing major. He studies composition and research pedagogy through lenses of cultural and personal conceptions of writing, and his most recent research examines student reading practices in the current age of screen literacy. With Elizabeth Wardle, he authored *Writing about Writing*, an anthology of writing studies research that supports the writing-about-writing pedagogies the two first wrote about in their 2007 *CCC* article "Teaching about Writing, Righting Misconceptions: (Re)Envisioning FYC as Intro to Writing Studies."

DYLAN B. DRYER is associate professor of composition studies at the University of Maine. Since graduating from the University of Wisconsin-Milwaukee, he has been exploring the capacities for and consequences of genre uptake, a topic with implications for writing assessment, teacher training, identity formation, and the persistence of social institutions generally. His research articles, one of which won the 2013 CCCC Braddock Award, features usability studies, mixed-method qualitative investigations, and corpus analysis. He has just completed guest editing a special issue of *Composition Forum* on the past, present, and possible futures of rhetorical genre studies, available at http://compositionforum.com/issue/31/.

JOHN DUFFY is associate professor of English and the Francis O'Malley Director of The University Writing Program at the University of Notre Dame. He has published on the ethics of writing, the rhetoric of disability, and the historical development of literacy and rhetoric in cross-cultural contexts. He coedited the essay collection *Literacy, Economy, and Power*, and his book *Writing from These Roots* was awarded the 2009 Outstanding Book Award by the Conference on College Composition and Communication. Duffy is a recipient of a National Endowment for the Humanities Fellowship and teaches courses in rhetoric, writing, and literature.

HEIDI ESTREM is associate professor of English and director of the first-year writing program at Boise State University. Her research interests in first-year writing pedagogy, writing program administration, assessment, and instructor development and support have led to publications in *Writing Program Administration, Rhetoric Review, Composition Studies*, and several edited collections. She regularly teaches both first-year writing and a graduate seminar for new teaching assistants.

JEFFREY T. GRABILL is professor and chair of the Department of Writing, Rhetoric, and American Cultures at Michigan State University. He is also a senior researcher with WIDE Research (Writing in Digital Environments). As a researcher, Grabill studies how digital writing is associated with citizenship and learning. Grabill is also a cofounder of Drawbridge, an educational technology company. He has published two books on community literacy.

BILL HART-DAVIDSON is associate dean for graduate studies in the College of Arts & Letters and an associate professor of rhetoric & writing in the Department of Writing, Rhetoric, and American Cultures at Michigan State University. He is coeditor of *Rhetoric & the Digital Humanities*, published in 2014 by the University of Chicago Press. He is also a coinventor of Eli Review, a software service supporting teaching and learning in writing available at elireview.com.

BRADLEY HUGHES has been director of the writing center at the University of Wisconsin-Madison since 1984 and director of writing across the curriculum since 1990. Together with Harvey Kail and Paula Gillespie, he created the Peer Writing Tutor Alumni Research Project (writing.wisc.edu/pwtarp). He cochaired IWCA summer institutes in 2003, 2008, and 2009. Together with UW-Madison colleagues, he developed an authoring program for creating computer simulations to use in tutor education (Case Scenario Builder, writing.wisc.edu/cscr), and he has developed a collaborative blog about writing centers (writing.wisc.edu/blog).

ASAO B. INOUE is associate professor of rhetoric and composition in the Division of Interdisciplinary Arts and Sciences at the University of Washington, Tacoma, and is the director of university writing. He has published numerous articles on validity theory, program assessment, writing pedagogy, and, more recently, failure in writing. His coedited collection, *Race and Writing Assessment* (Peter Lang) won the 2014 CCCC Outstanding Book Award for an edited collection. He is currently finishing a manuscript on classroom writing assessment as ecology.

RAY LAND is professor of higher education at Durham University, having held similar positions at the Universities of Strathclyde, Coventry, and Edinburgh. He has been a higher education consultant for the OECD and was recently involved in European Commission higher education projects in Europe and Latin America. He has published widely in the field of educational research, including works on educational development, learning technology, and quality enhancement. He is best known for his theory (with Jan Meyer) of threshold concepts and troublesome knowledge. His latest book (with George Gordon) is *Enhancing Quality in Higher Education: International Perspectives* (Routledge 2013).

NEAL LERNER is associate professor of English and writing program director at Northeastern University in Boston, MA. His book *The Idea of a Writing Laboratory* won the 2011 NCTE David H. Russell Award for Distinguished Research in the Teaching of English. His is also the coauthor of *Learning to Communicate as a Scientist and Engineer: Case Studies from MIT*, winner of the 2012 CCCC Advancement of Knowledge Award, and of *The Longman Guide to Peer Tutoring*. He has published on the history, theory, administration, and practice of teaching writing in classrooms, laboratories, and writing centers.

ANDREA A.LUNSFORD is the Louise Hewlett Nixon Professor of English, Emerita, at Stanford University. The director of Stanford's program in writing and rhetoric from 2000 through 2011, she has designed and taught courses in writing history and theory, rhetoric, literacy studies, and women's writing and is the editor, author, or coauthor of twenty books, including *Essays on Classical Rhetoric and Modern Discourse; Singular Texts/Plural*

Authors; *Reclaiming Rhetorica; Everything's an Argument; The Everyday Writer; Writing Matters; The Sage Handbook of Rhetorical Studies; Writing Together;* and *Everyone's an Author.* A long-time member of the Bread Loaf School of English faculty, she is currently at work on *The Norton Anthology of Rhetoric and Writing.*

PAUL KEI MATSUDA is professor of English and director of second language writing at Arizona State University. Founding chair of the Symposium on Second Language Writing and editor of the Parlor Press Series on Second Language Writing, Paul has published extensively on issues related to language difference and its implications for writing, identity, and pedagogy and has received a number of awards for his work. In addition, he has given numerous lectures and workshops on language, writing, teaching, and learning at various institutions in various parts of the world and throughout the United States. http://pmatsuda.faculty.asu.edu

JOHN MAJEWSKI teaches in the history department at the University of California, Santa Barbara, a position he took after receiving his MA and PhD in American history from UCLA. He also holds an MSc in economic history from the London School of Economics and a BA in economics from University of Texas, Austin. His research interests have focused on the political economy of the US Civil War, as well as threshold concepts and the teaching of history. His latest book, entitled *Modernizing a Slave Economy: The Economic Vision of the Confederate Nation,* was published in 2009.

REBECCA S. NOWACEK is associate professor of English at Marquette University, where she directs the Norman H. Ott Memorial Writing Center. Rebecca's research focuses on transfer of learning and writing across the disciplines. Her publications include *Agents of Integration: Understanding Transfer as a Rhetorical Act, Literacy Economy and Power,* and *Citizenship Across the Curriculum;* her work has also appeared in *College Composition and Communication, College English,* and *Research in the Teaching of English.* Rebecca was a Carnegie Scholar with the Carnegie Foundation's CASTL program and the recipient of Marquette University's Robert and Mary Gettel Faculty Award for Teaching Excellence.

PEGGY O'NEILL, professor of writing, has served as director of composition and chair of the writing department at Loyola University Maryland. Her scholarship focuses on writing pedagogy, assessment, and program administration and has appeared in several journals as well as edited collections. She has coauthored two books, *A Guide to College Writing Assessment* (with Cindy Moore and Brian Huot) and *Reframing Writing Assessment to Improve Teaching and Learning* (with Linda Adler-Kassner) and has edited or coedited four books. She currently serves as coeditor of the *Journal of Writing Assessment.*

KEVIN ROOZEN is associate professor at the University of Central Florida. In addition to serving as the director of composition, Kevin teaches first-year composition as well as a range of undergraduate and graduate courses in rhetorical theory and practice, composition theory, and writing as social practice. Kevin's studies of literate activity focus on the interplay among multiple literate engagements and the implications those linkages and disconnects have for the extended development of literate persons and practices. His work has appeared in *College Composition and Communication, Research in the Teaching of English, Written Communication,* and in chapters for a number of edited collections.

LIANE ROBERTSON is assistant professor at William Paterson University of New Jersey. Her research focuses on writing transfer, especially curricular design for transfer, the role of threshold concepts in writing transfer, and the success and failure of transfer across writing contexts. Currently, she is involved in a multi-institutional study comparing the role of particular content in transfer across various sites of first-year composition instruction. Her recent work is featured in *Writing across Contexts: Transfer, Composition, and Sites of Writing* from Utah State Press, *Composition Forum,* and a number of forthcoming edited collections.

SHIRLEY ROSE is professor and director of writing programs in the Department of English of the College of Liberal Arts and Sciences at Arizona State University. She is a past president of the Council of Writing Program Administrators. She regularly teaches graduate courses in writing program administration and has published articles on writing pedagogy and on issues in archival research and practice. With Irwin Weiser, she has edited three collections on the intellectual work of writing program administration, including *The WPA as Researcher, The Writing Program Administrator as Theorist*, and *Going Public: What Writing Programs Learn from Engagement*. She became director of the WPA Consultant-Evaluator Service in July 2014.

DAVID R. RUSSELL is professor of English in the rhetoric and professional communication area at Iowa State University. He has published widely on writing in the disciplines and professions, international writing instruction, and computer-supported collaborative learning. All are theorized with cultural-historical activity theory and genre theory. His book, *Writing in the Academic Disciplines: A Curricular History*, examines the history of American writing instruction since 1870. He coedited a special issue of *Mind, Culture, and Activity* on writing research, *Writing Selves/Writing Societies: Research from Activity Perspectives*, and *Writing and Learning in Cross-National Perspective: Transitions from Secondary to Higher Education*. He edits the *Journal of Business and Technical Communication*.

J. BLAKE SCOTT is professor and associate chair of writing and rhetoric at the University of Central Florida. The author of *Risky Rhetoric* and coeditor of *Critical Power Tools* and the *Megarhetorics of Global Development*, Blake studies the rhetorics of health and medicine and, more recently, the development of writing and rhetoric majors. His articles have been published in *CCC, College English, QJS, RSQ, Rhetoric Review, TCQ, JBTC*, and other places.

TONY SCOTT is associate professor in the writing program at Syracuse University, where he is also director of undergraduate studies. His scholarship includes *Dangerous Writing: Understanding the Political Economy of Composition* (Utah State UP, 2009) and the collection he coedited with Marc Bousquet and Leo Parascondola, *Tenured Bosses and Disposable Teachers: Writing Instruction in the Managed University* (Southern Illinois UP, 2004). In 2014, he won the Richard Braddock award for "Democracy, Struggle, and the Praxis of Assessment," an article he coauthored with Lil Brannon.

KARA TACZAK is part of the writing faculty at the University of Denver, where she teaches first-year writing courses and advises first-year students. Her research centers on the intersection of reflection and transfer of knowledge and practices. Taczak's current research project seeks to determine how reflective practices encourage and/or support the transfer of writing knowledge and practices from first-year writing courses to other academic writing sites. Taczak's publications have appeared in *Composition Forum, Teaching English in the Two-Year College*, and *Across the Disciples* as well as in a number of forthcoming edited collections. Her most recent, *Writing Across Contexts: Transfer, Composition, and Sites of Writing*, addresses how composers transfer knowledge and practices from one writing context to another.

HOWARD TINBERG, professor of English at Bristol Community College, Massachusetts, and former editor of the journal *Teaching English in the Two-Year College*, is the author of *Border Talk: Writing and Knowing in the Two-Year College* and *Writing with Consequence: What Writing Does in the Disciplines*. He is coauthor of *The Community College Writer: Exceeding Expectations* and *Teaching, Learning and the Holocaust: An Integrative Approach*. He is coeditor of *What is "College-Level" Writing?* and of *What is "College-Level" Writing? Vol 2*. In 2004, he was recognized as US Community Colleges Professor of the Year by the Carnegie Foundation and the American Council on Education (ACE).

Victor Villanueva is Regents' Professor, Edward R. Meyer Distinguished Professor, the director of the writing program at Washington State University, and the editor of the Conference on College Composition and Communications' *Studies in Writing and Rhetoric.* He is the author of the award-winning *Bootstraps: From an American Academic of Color,* the 1999 Rhetorician of the Year award, the 2008 Advancement of People of Color Leadership Award of the National Council of Teachers of English, and the CCCC 2009 Exemplar, among other awards and honors. All of his work has centered on the connections between language and racism.

Kathleen Blake Yancey is Kellogg W. Hunt Professor of English and Distinguished Research Professor at Florida State University. She has served as president of NCTE, chair of CCCC, and president of the Council of Writing Program Administrators. Editor of *College Composition and Communication,* she codirects the Inter/National Coalition for Electronic Portfolio Research. Author/ coauthor of over ninety articles and chapters and author/coeditor of twelve scholarly books—including *Delivering College Composition: The Fifth Canon; Electronic Portfolios 2.0;* and *Writing across Contexts: Transfer, Composition, and Sites of Writing*—she is the recipient of the FSU Graduate Mentor Award, the WPA Best Book Award, and the Donald Murray Writing Prize.

INDEX

Page numbers that appear in bold indicate a table or illustration.

unconscious competence, 77
University Learning Outcomes (ULO), **94–96**
University of California, Santa Barbara. *See* History 17b, transformation of
University of Central Florida, Department of Writing and Rhetoric. *See* major in writing and rhetoric, University of Central Florida
University of Minnesota WAC program, 209
University of Wisconsin–Madison writing center, 179–180

validity and validation: consequential, 161–62; defined, 160; race and, 166; significance of, 158; as a threshold concept, 159
values and power, assessment linked to, 157–58
Vandenberg, Peter, 140–41
variation for composers and composing, 52–54
vertical writing strand, 100, 102
Visual and Material Rhetorics course, 130
Visual Rhetoric course, 144–45
Vygotsky, Lev, 49, 75

Walvoord, Barbara, 215
Wenger, Etienne, 65, 188
Wikipedia, 33, 146
Wood, Swarup, 91
words, meaning of (1.4), 23–25
working memory, 73, 74
"The Writer's Audience is Always a Fiction" (Ong), 20
Writing about Science and Technology course, 130

Writing Across Contexts: Transfer, Composition, and Sites of Writing (Yancey, Robertson, Taczak), xxi
writing across the curriculum (WAC): assessment of, 210; curricular development in, 213–15; developmental aspects, 212–13; disciplinary aspects, 205–6; faculty and, 203–4, 215–16; to learn, 207–9; mediation in, 205; role of, 207; shared responsibility in, 209–10; situated learning in, 211–12; social and rhetorical aspects, 206–7; threshold concepts in, 205–13; transfer in, 211–12
writing as a subject of study (metaconcept), 15–16
writing centers: conferences, 177–78; nature and purpose of, 172; outreach instruction, 180; threshold concepts in, 173. *See also* tutor-education programs
Writing for Social Change course, 126–27
writing in the disciplines, 176, 209. *See also* communication in the disciplines (CID) courses
writing studies: disciplinary boundaries, 2; as a discipline, xii; historical aspects, xxix–xxx; naming, 1; research on, 16; as a service discipline, 84. *See also* doctoral program in rhetoric and composition, Florida State University; major in writing and rhetoric, University of Central Florida; rhetoric and composition
writing to learn, 207–9

Yancey, Kathleen Blake, xxi
Yates, JoAnne, 40
Young, Richard, 111